Mad Blood Stirring

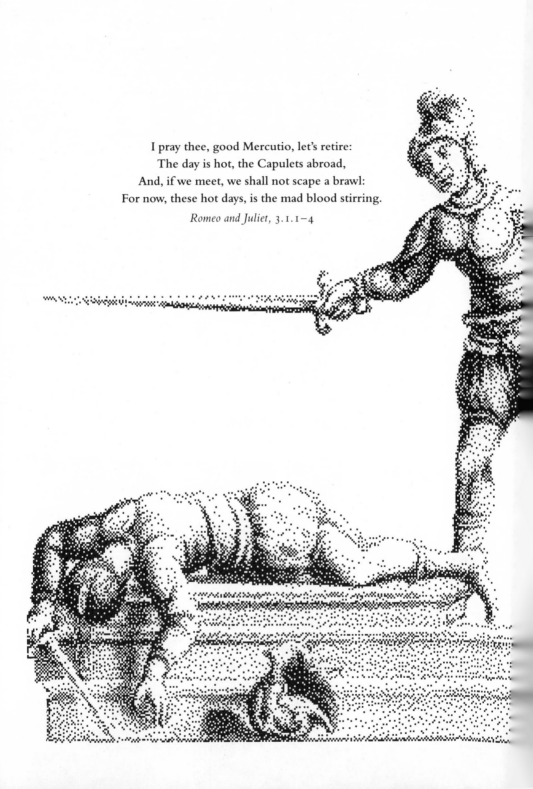

I pray thee, good Mercutio, let's retire:
The day is hot, the Capulets abroad,
And, if we meet, we shall not scape a brawl:
For now, these hot days, is the mad blood stirring.

Romeo and Juliet, 3.1.1−4

Mad Blood
STIRRING

Vendetta in Renaissance Italy

EDWARD MUIR

Reader's Edition

THE JOHNS HOPKINS UNIVERSITY PRESS
BALTIMORE AND LONDON

The original edition of this book was brought to publication with the generous assistance of the Gladys Krieble Delmas Foundation.

The Johns Hopkins University Press
2715 North Charles Street
Baltimore, Maryland 21218-4363
The Johns Hopkins Press Ltd., London

Library of Congress Cataloging-in-Publication Data will be found at the end of this book.
A catalog record for this book is available from the British Library.

ISBN 0-8018-5849-6 (pbk.)

To Linda

Contents

Illustrations

Author's Note to the Reader's Edition

This volume abridges a previously published edition of the same book, which bears a different subtitle, *Mad Blood Stirring: Vendetta and Factions in Friuli during the Renaissance* (Baltimore: Johns Hopkins University Press, 1993). In preparing the abridgment I have retained the original conception and argument of that volume but have eliminated the sections of technical historical analysis that were originally written for specialists, especially the sections dealing with the details of Friulan social history. Except for references to direct quotes, the extensive notes and bibliography of the original edition have also been dropped, which means that readers who wish to find the primary sources and to follow the scholarly debates should refer to the first edition.

Since the publication of the first edition of *Mad Blood Stirring*, an important new study of the same events has appeared, Furio Bianco's *1511, La "crudel zobia grassa": Rivolte contadine e faide nobiliari in Friuli tra '400 e '500* (Pordenone, 1995), a book properly honored with the Risit d'Aur Prize for 1996. Professor Bianco, who teaches in the Department of History at the University of Trieste, and I began our projects at about the same time without knowledge of each other, but now that we have discovered our common interest in the remarkable Friulan peasant rebellion and noble vendetta of 1511 we have engaged in an on-going discussion. I wish to offer my gratitude to Professor Bianco for his hospitality in inviting me to discuss my work at the Circolo Culturale "Menocchio" in Montereale Valcellina, the hometown of the heretic Friulan miller made famous by Carlo Ginzburg, and in Trieste. In preparing this abridgment, I have refrained from engaging in a commentary on Bianco's work but would like to acknowledge that we agree far more often than we disagree.

A NOTE ON NAMES AND DATES

In the documents consulted for this study, names, particularly given names, can appear in four different forms: in Friulan, Venetian, Tuscan, and Latin. For example, the name *John* might appear as Giuan, Zuan, Giovanni, or Johannes with many variant spellings of each version. There is no easy way to standardize names, especially since the nineteenth-century solution of relentless Tuscanization is offensive to history, the ear, and current Friulan sensibilities. Following fifteenth- and sixteenth-century usage, I have favored the Venetian forms but have made no attempt to impose them universally and have merely tried to be consistent in the rendering of the name of each individual. The reader will thus discover both Alvise and Luigi, Nicolò and Niccolò, and other variants.

All dates in the text have been given in the new style.

Dramatis Personae

The following list includes persons who participated in the events of the Cruel Carnival of Udine in 1511.

Legend:
m = murdered
s = property sacked or looted
b = house or castle burned

STRUMIERI

Leaders

DELLA TORRE, Alvise, m, s, b (married to Tadea Strassoldo); his brother, Isidoro, m, s, b; their nephew, Nicolò, m (married to Giacoma Brazzacco)

Followers

AMASEO, Gregorio (originally a Zambarlano but in opposition to Antonio Savorgnan on Giovedì Grasso; he was not, however, a victim of violence)
ARCANO, Giovanni and Nicolò, s
ARCOLONIANO, Antonio, m; his brothers, Francesco, m (married to Cas-

sandra Della Torre, first cousin of Alvise) and Troilo, s; Daniele; Dario; Martino, s attempted; Pietro, s attempted

ATTIMIS, Guariento; Odorico

BERTOLINO, Bertolino; his brother, Battista, m, s

BOCCASTORTA, Andrea, m

BRAZZACCO (BRAZZÀ), Antonio, s; his son, Corado; Antonio's brother, Nicolò, s; their sister, Giacoma (married to Nicolò Della Torre)

CANDIDO, Giovanni, s (brother-in-law of Giovanni Enrico Spilimbergo); his cousin, Giovanni Battista, s; Francesco (wounded before Giovedì Grasso, later murdered Nicolò Savorgnan); Aloisa (married to Giacomo Spilimbergo)

CASTELLO, Giacomo, s, b; Pietro Urbano, s; Giovanni Battista, s; Doimo, s

CAPORIACCO (CAVORIACO), Giovanni Giacomo (later murdered Nicolò Savorgnan); Giovanni Nicolò; Nicolò Maria, m on January 1, 1511

CERGNEU (CERGNEO), Francesco, s (married to Antonia Frattina; their son-in-law was Troiano Guarienti)

COLLOREDO, Albertino, s; his sons, Leandro, Nicolò (later murdered Nicolò Savorgnan and Giovanni Monticolo), Girolamo, and Gregorio (both later murdered Antonio Savorgnan, Girolamo murdered Francesco Janis di Tolmezzo); Odorico; from a different branch, Teseo, m, s; from yet another branch, Federico, m, s

? COLOMBATTI, Francesco (gave refuge to Teseo Colloredo, Nicolò Della Torre, and Giovanni Leonardo Frattina, but it is questionable whether this act makes him a Strumiero)

CUCCAGNA, whole clan, individual names unknown

FRATTINA, Frattinate; Giovanni Leonardo, m, s; his brother, Polidoro, m?, s; Giovanni Leonardo and Polidoro's sisters, Angela (married to Apollonio Gorghi) and Antonia (married to Francesco Cergneu)

GORGHI (GORGO), Apollonio, m (married to Angela Frattina); Troilo, s; Antonio di Francesco

GUARIENTI (PERCOTO, PIRCUT, PORTO), Francesco; his son, Troiano, s (son-in-law of Francesco Cergneu); Troiano's son-in-law, Giovanni Francesco (surname unknown); Jaca, s; Guareto, s; Gotardo

GUBERTINO, Leonardo, s; Agostino (canon of Cividale)

MELS (MELSO, METZ), a branch of the Colloredo, individual names unknown MONFALCONE, Sebastiano, s; his son, Felice

MONTORIO, Francesco (probably a *bravo* of Giovanni Candido)

MOZENINI (MAZAVINO), Francesco, s; his brother, Hironimo, s

PARTISTAGNO (PARTENSTEIN), Agostino, s (married to Tranquilla Della

Torre; their son-in-law was Francesco Pavona); their sons, Alessandro, Ercole, Francesco, Girolamo; Agostino's brothers, Francesco, Alvise, and Isidoro

PASSERINO, Pietro

PAVONA, Francesco, s attempted (son-in-law of Agostino Partistagno); his son, Bernardino; Gerolamo

PERS (PERSO, PARSO), Antonio; Bernardino; Gerolamo (son-in-law of Soldoniero Soldonieri)

POLCENICO, Francesco; Giacomo Antonio

PORCÌA (PORCIGLIE, PURCIGLIE, PURZIGLIE), Bartolomeo; Federico; Giulio; Prosdocimo

PRAMPERO (PRAMPERGO), Andrea

SBRUGLI, the whole clan, individual names unknown

SOLDONIERI, Soldoniero, m, s; his daughter, Lucrezia (married to Gerolamo Pers)

SPILIMBERGO, Alberto; Barnaba; Giacomo (cousin of Alvise Della Torre); Girolamo; Troilus; Nicolò; Giovanni Enrico (brother-in-law of Giovanni Candido, later murdered Antonio Savorgnan); Urbano, m

STRASSOLDO, Ettore (married to Smirelda Della Torre); Tadea (married to Alvise Della Torre); Giovanni (exempted from Antonio Savorgnan's blanket condemnation of the clan)

? SUSANNA, Beltrame (canon of Aquileia who helped Giovanni Candido escape); his brother, Marco; Cristoforo

? TERZAGO, Antonio, s; Nicolò, s

TINGO, Nicolò

TOMASI DI MONFALCONE (MONTEFALCONE), Sebastiano, s; his son, Felice

VALENTINIS (VALENTINO), Enrico; Giovanni Guberto; Martino, s attempted

VALVASONE, Bertoldo, s; Modesto, s; Valenzio, s; Francesco (married to Tadea di Raimondo Della Torre, a first cousin of Alvise Della Torre)

VEGIA, Andrea

ZOPPOLA, Battista; Giovanni Giorgio (later murdered Antonio Savorgnan)

? ZUANE, Soldoniero, m

ZUCCO, Giovanni

ZAMBARLANI

Leaders

SAVORGNAN DELLA TORRE DEL ZUINO, Antonio (later murdered); his illegitimate son, Nicolò, called Il Cheribino (later murdered); Antonio's nephews, Francesco and Bernardino; Antonio's illegitimate brother, Pietro, called Il Cargenello; Antonio's sister, Lisabetta (mother of Luigi da Porto); Antonio's "familiars and dogs of the house," Bernardino da Narni, Matana, Zuanetto di Pietro del Pizol called Piccolo, Smergon, Guglielmo di Marco Floriti da Venzone called Tempesta, Giovanni di Leonardo Marangone di Capriglie called Vergon, Viso, Il Ferrarese, and Giovanni Pietro Fosca

SAVORGNAN DEL MONTE D'OSOPPO, Girolamo (not directly involved in the Giovedì Grasso events)

Followers

ARLATTO, Girolamo
ARRIGONI, Simone di Francesco di Antonio Parto
BRUGNO DA GEMONA, Bartolomeo (son-in-law of Mario Frattina)
CAINER, Nicolò (artisan and *decano* of a *borgo* of Udine)
CARNEVAL, Uccello
CORBELLO, Pietro (citizen of Udine)
? CORTONA, Francesco
DELLA ROVERE, Battista
DURISSINO, Pietro
FAGAGNA, Giovanni (artisan)
FILITINO, Alessandro (doctor)
FONTANABUONA, Rizzardo
JANIS DI TOLMEZZO, Francesco (doctor, supposedly responsible for a number of Giovedì Grasso deaths, later murdered by Girolamo Colloredo)
JUSTO, Pietro
LANCILLOTTO (notary)
LODRON, Antonio (count)
LUCADELLO, Giovanni
MELS (METZ), Girolamo (not one of the consorts of Colloredo–Mels but the son-in-law of a notary from Udine)
MONTICOLO, Giovanni (later murdered by Nicolò Colloredo); his brother, Nicolò (chancellor of Udine)
? MORIPOTE, Federico
PORTO, Luigi (Alvise) da (nephew of Antonio Savorgnan)
POZZO, Vincenzo
PROSDOCIMO, Raimondo
ROSSO, Giacomo
SBROIAVACCA, Ascanio (doctor); Girolamo
SCRAIBER, Odorico (doctor); Simone (executed by Council of Ten)
SPILIMBERGO, Alvise (condemned by Council of Ten); Tomaso (married to Beatrice de' Freschi de Cucagna)
SUSANNA, Odorico

Torso, Battista; Giovanni Francesco
Valvasone, Ippolito
Varmo, Asquinio; Federico
Vitturi, Antonio (retainer of Giovanni Vitturi and condemned by Council of Ten)
Zanni da cortona, Nicolò

Introduction

Men do injury through either fear or hate.

Machiavelli, *The Prince*, chap. 7

Such injury produces fear; fear seeks for defense;
for defense partisans are obtained;
from partisans rise parties in states;
from parties their ruin.

Machiavelli, *Discourses on the First Decade of
Titus Livius*, book 1, chap. 7

Late on the cold gray morning of February 27, 1511, more than a thousand militiamen, who had been searching since dawn for a raiding party of German mercenaries, stumbled back through the gates of Udine. It was the first day of carnival. The men were tired, hungry, angry. They began to drink. Through the mysterious alchemy of crowd behavior, the men ignited a conflagration, looting and burning the urban palaces of more than a score of the great lords of Friuli who were rumored to be in league with the enemy. A huge crowd of Udinesi and peasants in town for the holiday joined in, and during three days of rioting they killed between twenty-five and fifty nobles and their retainers.

As news of the wild carnival in Udine spread, peasants near and far assaulted the rural castles of the same feudal lords, all of whom were also the avowed enemies of the enormously popular militia captain, the nobleman Antonio Savorgnan, whose retainers played a suspiciously conspicuous role in the carnival violence. In a few weeks the most extensive and most damaging popular revolt in Renaissance Italy had run its course, an event that contemporaries understood both as a peasant rebellion and as the bloody backwash from a tidal wave of vendetta violence among the nobles who dominated the affairs of the region.

This book is about that event, its antecedents, and its consequences. The tale begins with the civil wars that plagued Friuli before the republic of Venice conquered the region in 1420, and it ends in 1568 when Venice finally imposed a formal peace on the vendetta clans. Although local historians have long considered the Cruel Carnival of Udine as one of the signal moments in the region's history, in the wider sphere of Italian and European concerns it has been recognized, if at all, as a minor episode in the War of the League of Cambrai, which was itself but one of several collisions at the turn of the sixteenth century among the various Italian states, France, Spain, and the Holy Roman Empire.

Nothing that happened in Friuli in the winter of 1511 altered the course of affairs in Europe or even in the republic of Venice. The significance of the Cruel Carnival lies elsewhere: in what it can reveal about the nature of vendetta conflict, the role of factions in politics, and the characteristics of a peasant revolt. The Friulan case provides a vivid look at how the hierarchic structures of noble-led factions interacted with the more egalitarian institutions of the communities and how high culture communicated with and responded to popular beliefs and practices. The Cruel Carnival provides a window on the many interconnections, the *bricolage*, among social groups in a decidedly backward society, and it also shows how fragile were the tinkering attempts at group cohesion and how social ties that reached beyond family and community could be easily broken by the miscalculations of local leaders and by intervention from outside.

Most notable is how the pressures generated by wider European events made local structures extremely vulnerable. The Italian wars of the early sixteenth century, which brought the modern European powers into their first epic clash, created a terrible and lasting fissure in the traditional patterns of living and mores in the towns and villages of Friuli. Although there has long been a tendency to minimize the violence of Renaissance warfare and to treat it as a minor sideshow to the grander achievements in the arts, humanism, and political thought, these wars hurt, and they hurt badly.

In Friuli the system of patronage embodied in two mutually antagonist factions collapsed in the years after the Cambrai wars, leaving the citizens of the region in a state of collective anomie. After the demise of the factions, through which peasant and artisan commoners had built bonds of clientage with the great feudal lords, the classes separated in various ways. Villagers achieved a modest form of representation with the institution of a peasant parliament, and nobles escaped into a fantasy world of aristocratic exclusivity, epitomized by their emulation of courtly manners. By the 1560s the traditions of vendetta, which had once bonded Friulans from all social levels in a common culture of revenge killing, dissolved as aristocrats took up dueling to settle old grievances and to counter new insults.

The persistent structures of pre-1511 Friuli subsumed an ecology of scarcity, a politics of foreign domination, and a society of intertwining patronage networks. Primarily a region defined by geographic and cultural isolation, Friuli lacked water and capitalists, which meant that it remained one of the most backwardly agrarian and feudal areas in northern Italy. The republic of Venice repeatedly fought the Holy Roman Empire for the suzerainty of the region not so much because the Venetians were lured by its potential riches as because they wanted to keep its strategic mountain passes out of the hands of the enemy.

Between the dominant city and the subordinate region, the center and periphery, lay a gap unbridged by common institutions, values, or even language. Failing in its promise to deliver equal justice and military security, Venice relied on interlocking patronage connections between members of its own patriciate and influential Friulan aristocrats, a situation that made the government hostage to private interests. When the gossamer institutions failed, patrons delivered. Given the inefficacy of both local and Venetian institutions of justice, vendetta remained the principal means for the resolution of conflicts, and factions provided the most cohesive form of collective solidarity.

Because contemporaries understood these various conflicts as aspects of vendetta, they used the terminology of revenge to explain what was happening in their society. The language of vendetta employed metaphors of blood, hot blood stirred, red blood spilled, common blood of kinship shared, and blue blood exalted. Or to raise the questions encoded in these metaphors, how should a man exhibit anger, how should he react to an insult or injury to himself, how should he respond to the injury or death of a kinsman, and how should he behave toward a person of a different rank?

To respect the diversity of answers to these questions and to keep from prejudging the nature of vendetta, I have started with Renaissance rather than modern definitions of vendetta. The usual modern distinction between *vendetta*, seen as a finite conflict between individuals, and *feud*, an interminable one between groups, obscures the manifold Renaissance uses of the word *vendetta*. As the paramount means of expressing anger among males, vendetta involved individuals and groups, produced short spasms of violence and enmities lasting centuries, and created ambiguous or conflicting obligations that contemporaries struggled to resolve.

Although Friulans from all social levels fought vendettas, the ones that overshadowed the affairs of the region were those among the castellans, those clans (*consorti*) that held the jurisdictional rights to castles and affiliated villages, producing a situation in which the very persons most responsible for the local administration of public justice were usually the same persons who presided over private vendettas. The Friulan castellan clan should be understood more as a dynamic process than as a fixed structure because it frequently incorporated friends and clients into what presented itself as a group of blood kin, and each clan survived through continuous negotiations with other clans, subordinates, and Venetian magistrates.

The clansmen formed alliances through marriages, but every new alliance between two clans excluded others and created the potential for new enemies. In addition, the personal retainers and familiars of the castellans often fought to preserve the honor they vicariously shared with their patrons. These élites and their men constituted the vendetta nuclei around which other social groups rotated. In conducting their affairs the castellans calculated social advantage, political connections, and economic interests but avoided the appearance of weakness even when they put off or failed to retaliate against an insult or injury. They made their own choices for their own reasons. Nevertheless, participants in vendettas followed certain patterns, especially in how they performed acts of violence. Killers murdered in public places, usually admitted the deed, normally exempted women and young boys, and maximized the amount of blood shed frequently by dismembering the victim or feeding him to animals.

The dominant way in which Friulans solidified and represented interclan alliances and enmities was through membership in a faction. Many social conflicts that had little to do on the surface with preserving aristocratic honor found an outlet in factional strife, including disputes over property, feudal dues, taxes, access to markets, appointments to public jobs, and the control of civic councils. Such conflicts resist definition in conventional terms because the vertical hierarchies supposedly embodied by the factions camouflaged many anomalies and complexities. For example, membership in the factions was so transitory that their composition can usually be discerned only at moments of confrontation when participants revealed allegiances by attacking members of the other side. One knows the factions by discovering who killed whom.

Despite the factions' amorphousness they provided shadow institutions that often substituted for the formal institutions of government at all levels, rendering necessary public services but at the same time frustrating the law and defying outside control. Within each faction protection, influence, jobs, loans, and ideas were exchanged. The factions also became the trusted executors of justice through managing vendettas. They provided more coherence and strength than any alternative form of organization or certainly any public institution above the level of the community.

The communities, themselves, which took the form of rural villages (*ville*) and urban neighborhoods (*borghi*), remained vital if beleaguered sources of support, particularly for the peasants and artisans. Although most were internally divided and dominated by client brokers for the great aristocratic clans, the communities survived as the only source of cooperation besides the factions. Many communities sustained a continuous but largely futile campaign for legal redress, and after the 1470s the establishment of local militia companies enhanced the capabilities of the male citizens for collective action.

Thus, clan, faction, and community provided the three social anchors for the inhabitants of a tempestuous region. Between 1499 and 1511 a conjuncture of forces frayed these traditional safety lines. A decline in agricultural prices precipitated an economic crisis, which was aggravated by the landlords' monopolizing access to village and urban markets and increasing the fiscal demands on their tenants. Foreign invasions sharpened the sense of insecurity and forced a series of violent rural protests against the escalation of war imposts. During these critical years the paternalistic leadership of Antonio Savorgnan, head of one of the factions, offered villagers an alternative to the traditional loyalties of feudal obligation so that the accumulated grievances of the peasants found expression in 1511 in outrage against the hereditary enemies of the Savorgnan. In the collective murder and pillage the body imagery of carnival merged with the rituals of vendetta killing to create a striking vocabulary of violent protest.

In the aftermath of 1511 Friulans from various social levels struggled to find meaning in the apocalyptic violence they had inflicted on themselves, and in retracing their struggles one can uncover contemporary mentalities. Whatever the antecedent structures and precipitating causes of the 1511 carnage, events followed the inherent dialectic of violence, a pattern of stimulus and response which derived its forms of representation from the cultural precepts about how to express certain emotions.

In Friuli, as in many other places, brief moments of spontaneous violence produced awful, unanticipated consequences that haunted survivors for generations. When sufficiently endangered or provoked, a man's mad blood stirred, producing an irresistible flare of choler or anger, that emotion biologically induced by what we would call the fight response. Renaissance society greatly valued the fight over the flight response; whereas fighting always produced risks, a failure to resist perceived antagonisms guaranteed shame, a social calamity perhaps more disastrous than any other for a man's relations with his fellows, as shameful for him as impurity for a woman. Whatever the encouragements of Christian morality, a man best avoided shame and preserved honor by answering anger with anger, insult with insult, injury with injury, death with death.

Although the expression of anger was widely viewed at the time as a natural phenomenon beyond individual control, it was, in fact, permeated by cultural influences. In the course of the fifteenth and sixteenth centuries many experienced an emotional education, revealing that their blood boiled not so much for natural as for learned reasons. Anger thus had a history that altered how the emotion manifested itself, how legal authorities treated it, how thinkers understood it. In Friuli the critical changes took place after 1511, and by the middle sixteenth century one of the great transformations in the history of emotions, which had taken hold in the social hothouse of the Renaissance courts, appeared among some Friulan aristocrats, a transformation from externalizing anger and projecting it onto other persons or even animals to internalizing it by adopting the self-control of good manners.

The Friulan search for the meaning of 1511 and the allure of the new aristocratic values for successive generations open windows on the shared assumptions—the *mentalités*—about violent behavior. One reaction to violence shows the processes of collective scapegoating in the search to find someone or some group to blame for the hard blows of fortune. The scapegoating process internalized within the community the causes for problems that had foreign or inexplicable origins. The opposite reaction externalized the sources of violence, projecting the anger of humans onto God or other supernatural beings by attributing deaths to the divine vendetta, to the necessary apocalyptic scourges of human sins, or to the rampages of the spectral armies of the dead.

A third common reaction was to arrange events into a story, what might be called a *revenge narrative*, which sustained vendetta obligations and provided revengers with a model for behavior. The narratives were given the form of legends continuously retold over generations on winter nights around the *fogolar*. In Friuli the *fogolar*, the large freestanding hearth surrounded by benches on three sides and located in an alcove attached to the kitchen of the great castles and even of modest rustic houses, provided the locus for social communication, much as did the piazza in the parts of Italy more urbanized and blessed with a climate hospitable to outdoor life. The intimate, private character of the *fogolar*, restricted to family, friends, servants, clients, and guests, undoubtedly contributed to the extreme cultural isolation and linguistic stratification of Friuli, the endemic distrust of strangers, the weakness of communal and public institutions, and the preservation of vendetta obligations.

During the sixteenth century revenge narratives often came to be written down, usually only in private family papers, occasionally in chronicles and histories, although eventually in highly crafted polemical broadsides and pamphlets. Found in several different genres, revenge narratives commented on vendettas and often structured the accounts to evoke certain emotions in listeners and readers, much as did medieval Icelandic sagas and the tales that convicts composed in Renaissance France to obtain a royal pardon for their crimes. Closely linked to cultural fashions, the narratives often evolved to suit prevailing notions of the vendetta. Moreover, these stories encouraged mimesis in hearers and readers, providing the crucial means by which individuals, especially males, formed their identities in imitation of heroic predecessors and in opposition to hereditary enemies. The narratives also embedded individual Friulans in a story, with a defined beginning, a clear plot, identifiable characters, a consistency of setting, and an anticipated end that implied expectations about their roles in life. It is thus no accident that the most popular story about vendetta in Western literature, the tragedy of *Romeo and Juliet*, found its primary source in the writings of a participant in the vendetta in Friuli, Luigi da Porto, author of a novella about revenge and love set in Verona.

The richest source for understanding the mentalities of vendetta comes not so much from what was said about the violence as from looking at the actual forms of killing. Three common and traditional practices specified how to kill humans and animals properly, thus justifying and explaining the act: vendetta established the necessary conditions for the socially acceptable murder of another human being; carnival provided a festive and ludic context for the butchery of domestic animals, especially of pigs; and hunting rituals made possible the slaughter of wild animals. These cultural seeds for the killing of humans and animals cross-fertilized one another, in particular making the butchery of animals the model for the killing of men.

Traditional Friulan vendetta practices derived their legitimacy from the accepted relationships between humans and animals, and changes in those relationships signaled changes in the legitimate forms of violence. Hunting created a hierarchic relationship between hunters and their animal prey, which was represented in the butchering of game and dividing it among the hunters. Vendetta borrowed and inverted the hierarchic practices of the hunt to transform human victims into shameful animals and to permit human killers to imitate hunting dogs, who went wild in the rabid desire for blood. Through the mimetic process of modeling vendetta killing on hunting, killers exempted themselves from the normal responsibilities of civilized mankind.

In the decades after the 1511 catastrophe, the Friulan factions began to lose their cohesion, and in turn the traditional mentality of vendetta waned, dissolving the link between the hunting band and the vendetta gang, between stalking game and ambushing men. In place of the old mentality that had been sustained by implicit rules of behavior and had been shared by all Friulans, some aristocrats adopted a new ideology that mandated highly regulated forms of behavior governed by explicit rules and which separated nobles from commoners. The new manners were disseminated by a spate of fashionable books and by Friulans exiled to the North Italian courts in which they had to conform to receive princely patronage.

Three important developments followed. First, the obsession with the collective honor of families and clans faded as concerns arose about preserving individual honor, which depended less on ancient lineage than on good manners. Second, the men who inherited family and personal obligations to avenge past injuries abandoned vendetta fighting for the duel, which regulated conflict according to precise rules and which disavowed revenge as a proper motive for a duel. Third, levels of interpersonal violence among the old vendetta clans declined precipitously in Friuli, making it possible for the Venetians to impose a permanent peace on the old combatants. The bestial cruelties of vendetta died on the domesticated fields of honor.

In writing a history of obscure events in a peripheral region of a failed state, I have tried to reexamine some of the themes of Renaissance historiography from the outside. Instead of the usual absorption with the institutions and culture of the large city-states, this book ponders the extrainstitutional, marginally literate, rural, feudal, and provincial, what might be called the other side of Renaissance Italy, the things the intellectuals and their patrons in the cities tried to forget or surmount. Whatever their rhetorical affectations, Petrarch and Machiavelli were not just conversing with dead ancients but arguing against social practices that surrounded them and which they found repulsive. Vendetta violence and factional conflict threatened the daily lives of far more people than could recite Latin orations or admire Botticelli, and the success in making safer the lives of those unnamed multitudes must be recognized. That success, however, came at the cost of the repression of individual emotions and the amassing of even more deadly powers in the hands of the state.

As is so often the case in history, apparent progress is fraught with irony, even tragedy. Here I shall attempt to cross back over a deep chasm to a lost time before good manners and the authoritarian state inhibited the expression of anger and made revenge an ugly word. Only by striving to understand the alien behavior of a remote time and place can one hope to understand whence we have come and how much of the past still lives unrecognized within us.

Mad Blood Stirring

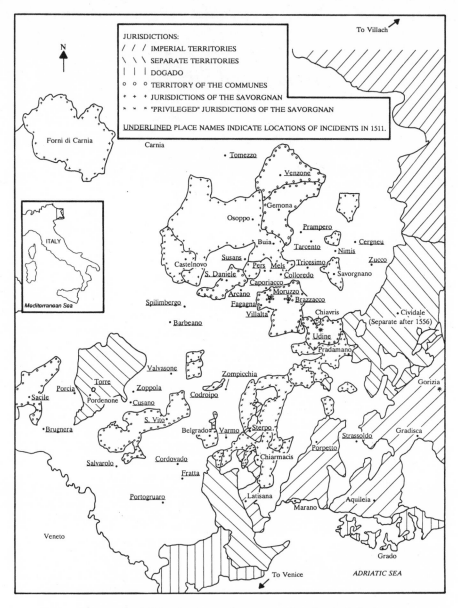

JURISDICTIONS:
/ / / IMPERIAL TERRITORIES
\ \ \ SEPARATE TERRITORIES
| | | DOGADO
o o o TERRITORY OF THE COMMUNES
+ + + JURISDICTIONS OF THE SAVORGNAN
× × × "PRIVILEGED" JURISDICTIONS OF THE SAVORGNAN

UNDERLINED PLACE NAMES INDICATE LOCATIONS OF INCIDENTS IN 1511.

To Villach

Forni di Carnia

ITALY

Mediterranean Sea

Carnia

Tomezzo

Venzone

Gemona

Osoppo

Prampero

Buia   Cergneu
        Tarcento   Nimis
Susans   Zucco
Castelnovo   Pers Mels Tricesimo
      S. Daniele   Colloredo Savorgnano
            Caporiacco
Spilimbergo   Arcano Moruzzo
         Fagagna Brazzacco
      Villalta   Chiavris
· Barbeano   Cividale
                Udine   (Separate after 1556)
              Pradamano

Valvasone
         Zompicchia   Gorizia
Torre   Zoppola   *
Porcia   Codroipo
Sacile Pordenone · Cusano
                S. Vito   Strassoldo Gradisca
         Belgrado Varmo Sterpo
· Brugnera   Porpetto
            Chiarmacis
Salvarolo Cordovado
         Fratta   Latisana
                                Aquileia
Portogruaro   Marano

Veneto

                              Grado

                To Venice   ADRIATIC SEA

Map of Friuli in the sixteenth century, showing jurisdictions.

Prologue

Dead men don't fight back.

Francesco Janis di Tolmezzo

Gregorio Amaseo, our principal guide to the Cruel Carnival of Udine, held an ambiguous position in his society. A notorious affair with a nun and his exceedingly modest abilities at Latin composition in the humanist mode had stymied his career as a school master, and his family's ancient patrons, the great Savorgnan clan, had abandoned him. To make matters worse, in the winter of 1511 the social fabric of his homeland began to unravel, and he held the Savorgnan responsible. Gregorio witnessed and later wrote the history of that strange unraveling, a bitter account that forms one of the most curious documents of strife and mayhem in Renaissance Italy.

Amaseo's account achieves much of its interest from the richness of its detail, its many tragic little episodes, concrete evocation of place, careful chronology, plethora of names, reports of what was said, and references to sources of information. He pushes his anti-heroic narrative through a series of edited scenes that flow from one to another with the quickening tempo of a tarantella, capturing the sickening horror of the slaughter but also constantly and tiresomely beating on the theme that that Judas, that Mohammed, that traitor, that Antonio Savorgnan, had orchestrated everything.

On the morning of Giovedì Grasso, the Thursday of carnival week, the "dogs of the house" of Savorgnan attacked young Nicolò Della Torre, son of the head of a rival clan, while he was attempting to paint the diamond blazon of his house on a well in the Savorgnan neighborhood. This little scuffle among aristocrats and their retainers (called dogs), a common enough event in Friuli, sparked something far more momentous. Nicolò quickly found himself surrounded by a crowd of artisan and peasant militiamen, many of whom had just returned from a long morning of fruitless searching for German mercenaries rumored to be in the area. The rumors also suggested that the Della Torre had rebelled against the Venetian overlords and planned to open the gates of the city to the enemy. The crowd, in Amaseo's words,

> suddenly began to yell "to arms, to arms"; at the place where the skirmish had already begun, the heads of the aforementioned peasants and plebs, who did not wait for anything else because of their desire for loot, shouted, "sack, sack, ruin the rebels"; they madly raced from everywhere and assaulted the Della Torre house with steel and fire, ringing at that point the tocsin bell in the castle to give notice to all their partisans, who rushed to the total destruction of their adversaries.[1]

The crowd rapidly grew into the thousands, surrounded the Della Torre palace, and subjected the aristocratic partisans who had found refuge there to a punishing siege:

> I, Gregorio Amaseo, a bona fide doctor, went first on that morning to the cathedral to mass with the Most Illustrious Luogotenente and then came back to the piazza with his party. Having earlier seen Savorgnan enraged . . . , I saw after dinner at the ringing of the tocsin all the armed squads march toward the houses of the Savorgnan and the Della Torre and heard from the windows of my house noises as if they were fighting. I first thought there must be a disturbance like the previous year . . . . Then seeing the flame and smoke that rose above the houses I determined to do everything possible to stop such an outrage, remembering that several times in the past the same sort of thing was remedied by my father.

Therefore, I left the house followed by Messer Girolamo, my brother, went toward the cathedral where I saw the first assault by the people and the firing of falconets, and it seemed to me the people were excited with the greatest rage, and much had already taken place. I was stirred even more by the desire to separate them as much as was possible. So I entered the courtyard of Savorgnan, who had just returned from the luogotenente's castle, and seeing him so rabid, smoking with anger, I suddenly remembered having heard from my father that Messer Nicolò Savorgnan, father of this Antonio, said many many times to my father because they were very close that he was grieved by Antonio, saying that the said Antonio had a bestial temper and was very dangerous so that Nicolò worried there would be a day when Antonio would cause some great trouble to the ruin of his house. Because of that memory I did not have the boldness to confront him, as I had first planned, especially seeing several of his close associates who did not admonish him. From that I at once thought he had dined with the Devil and asked two or three times several persons especially Doctors Francesco Janis di Tolmezzo and Girolamo Mels where the luogotenente was. Tolmezzo answered me, "What do I have to do with the luogotenente?" and said to my brother, "Messer Gregorio would do well not to be rash; he is looking for bad luck." Nonetheless by my insisting to know, Tolmezzo finally indicated that the luogotenente was somewhere around the church of San Francesco.

Gregorio left, searched about, and finally found the luogotenente, the Venetian authority in charge of maintaining order, who was accompanied by only five or six men because he had no others to call upon. Gregorio remembered saying to him:

What is Your Magnificence doing here? Can't you see what ruin there will be in this place today if you don't stop them? For the love of God don't hang around here; we'll go to Antonio Savorgnan's house, and you order them to put down the weapons and put out this fire; let's go, let's go, don't let Your Magnificence doubt this city, because we are all good partisans of Saint Mark.

They went to Savorgnan's palace where they found the Venetian treasurer, Antonio Badoer, surrounded by about fifty armed men, who supposedly shouted a long-winded profession of loyalty, "All for one cheer, Mark, Mark; we don't want any other lords in this land than the rectors of Saint Mark." Amaseo continued a story that focused rather much on himself:

> Antonio Savorgnan ran down into the courtyard without a hat on his head as if bewitched, threatening me with words similar to these, "Messer Gregorio, Messer Gregorio, you would do well not to rush into matters that don't concern you; if you aren't smart, I'll have you killed." He shouted so that more than a hundred armed men and many others who were around there heard. Responding to that, likewise in a loud voice, I ardently said to him, "Messer Antonio, what I do, I do for your own good; you don't have any idea what the Most Illustrious Signoria intends to do; don't think that it would ever forgive you for such a thing. I am not one of your new friends; our families' friendship is an old one of more than a hundred years standing. I believe I can counsel you better about your welfare than two hundred of the best of these men who will soon go back home." Continuously imploring him to put out the above-mentioned fire, I said to them all, "You have done plenty, don't go ahead, it is enough to have shown your enemies that you could destroy them; save them now, because if you do you will regain the greatest crown of glory ever achieved by a man of your house."

Gregorio continued to plead despite Antonio's implacable anger. The luogotenente ordered Antonio in reverence of Saint Mark to cease the attack, put out the fire, lay down arms, and send away the brigades. To all this Antonio replied, "I can't do anything more, do it yourselves, do it yourselves, it's not my fault." He turned to some aides, "armored from head to foot," made certain signs, and said in a low voice that they knew their tasks: "go, go, do it, do it."

> After the first argument and seeing nothing could be worked out with him, the luogotenente returned to the street, and as I, Gregorio, remember it, he began, while grabbing hold of

their shoulders, to command under penalty of the gallows and by decree of the Council of Ten that everyone put down their arms and leave and not threaten any person because the Most Illustrious Signoria recognized them all as good and most faithful sons. He was assisted by the treasurer. Several of the heads of the mob of peasants, armed populace, and the executioners of Iscariot responded to them boastfully that the Strumieri were neither good nor faithful but all rebels and consequently the Zambarlani wanted to punish them in their own way. They called in great haste, "to the ruin, to the ruin, to the sack of the rebels." Nevertheless, many others began to withdraw in order to obey, largely because a trumpeter in Savorgnan livery played a call to retreat, an act to which he was forced by the rector, who threatened him with the gallows, although the trumpeter immediately retired to the courtyard of the Savorgnan.

However, by the instigation of many, those who had left returned to the Della Torre palace where most had remained, so that right away they stormed the doors and unloosed the falconets, at every charge shooting guns, crossbows, and bows. Seeing that, the luogotenente entered the house of Savorgnan another time, imploring him with greatest insistence that he make those companies leave and quiet the uproar, excusing him and discharging him of responsibility, as before, because the luogotenente thought Savorgnan did not want such a thing to happen; but on the contrary Savorgnan right away urged them on with glances and gestures and speaking in the ear to this person and that so they went from bad to worse. Seeing from this that he could not accomplish anything, the rector had, by my recollection, the trumpeter Ludovico come, sound the trumpet, and announce the edicts and proclamations in a loud voice. Incited by some of the leaders, among others by Giovanni Monticolo, all the rabble loudly yelled that the trumpeter could not be heard, so that despite these proclamations they did not give up their evil deeds; instead those far away interpreted the call as an order to rout out the rebels. After that incident Savorgnan went out into the street to make sure that notwithstanding the edict his men were proceeding according to the order given. The

luogotenente implored him anew to stop them, and I heard
Savorgnan twice say with great rage, "I am so angry that I
am beside myself, and I don't know myself what I'm doing,"
after which it seemed of little use, so that I, Amaseo, did
not remind them again of their own welfare, but because I
had been threatened first by him and then by several others,
especially by Vincenzo Pozzo and Ascanio Sbroiavacca, who
had weapons handy to kill me, I left off saying anything
else to them just as already had the treasurer, threatened
with the same fate by Uccello Carneval, Pietro Justo, and
Pietro Durissino, who among others burned with rabid fury.
And at last the luogotenente, moreover, saw that neither
edicts nor entreaties were any use; rather they provoked more
evil deeds; while the traitor returned home, the luogotenente
followed him and brusquely accosted him telling him in the
following way, "Messer Antonio, one must have plenty of guts
to take the artillery of the Council of Ten; this was an intolerable presumption. I order you under penalty of the displeasure of the Signoria and of the gallows and by decree of
the Most High Council of Ten that you have all the artillery
and munitions immediately returned from where you took
them." He replied, "I don't know anything about it, you're
mistaken."

Having already been there from [about 2:00 to 4:00 p.m.]
and having continuously argued and supposing there was nothing more to do than had already been done, the luogotenente
mounted his horse and rode back to the castle with his officers . . . , and Amaseo with his brother returned home by
the shortest way, thinking to have done the best for the universal welfare, although nothing would be of any use to prevent Savorgnan and his accomplices from doing the worst
possible, to which the awful constellation of that day largely
inclined him.

As artillery balls began to pound down the main door of the
Della Torre palace, the company of nobles who had defended it
fled through the garden or across the roofs to nearby houses. The
treasures of the Della Torre were grabbed up by looters whom
Amaseo described as "a number of most wicked peasants, the ma-

jority banished for thefts and assassinations, inasmuch as they have brought in the scum off the balls of the villages, castles, and towns of the Patria." The poor, however, would remember this scum differently as heroes and patriots, as the true revengers of the people, and more than four centuries later would still dance in their honor every year on Giovedì Grasso.

Pillage turned to slaughter. One after another, aristocratic members of the castellan clans allied to the Della Torre were dragged from their hiding places, trampled, stoned, dismembered, and left as food for market dogs and wild pigs. Antonio offered a few noble refugees his protection but exacted a heavy price by shamefully forcing them to their knees to beg for their lives.

Others died at Antonio's explicit orders. After discovering their hiding place, Antonio promised his protection to three young nobles, Giovanni Leonardo Frattina, Teseo Colloredo, and Nicolò Della Torre, the last having managed to escape from the scuffle that had started the conflagration earlier in the day, but

about two hours after sunset Savorgnan returned with a large number of executioners and had the three come out; seeing the swarm of armed men, these three were instantly forewarned of their deaths, and because of this Giovanni Leonardo took off, was caught at the Hay Barn Square, was stopped by a blow from the halberd of Giovanni Pietro Fosca, and fell to the ground, unhappily cut to pieces by numerous blows. The other two, while walking down the street not far from Colombatto's house, were most cruelly quartered like cattle by . . . Vergon and others who, raising yells and screams to heaven, bloodied the whole street and scattered about bits of flesh, brains, and hair. Among these assassins was later said to have been one Giovanni di Leonardo Marangone di Capriglie, who on that night, drunk with wine and stuffed with stolen chickens, boasted of having hacked up Della Torre with a butcher's cleaver; his face covered with blood and the rings of the dead on his fingers, the fiend took the lighted torches from Giovanni Bianchino and said, "Kill! Kill those that still move!" At this word Vincenzo Pozzo, who had already been condemned to death in Venice for rebellion, like a rabid dog tortured [the survivors] with his weapons.

After two days of carnival frenzy, the allies of Antonio Savorgnan gathered to evaluate their success. One of his most ardent partisans was Dr. Francesco Janis di Tolmezzo, a man of deep legal learning, brother of the superintendent of the Carnia militia, reformer of the civic statutes of Udine, and distinguished member of the city council and the parliament of Friuli:

> With extreme elation rising up and down on his toes with his hands tucked in his belt and his hat pulled low over his dark face, averting his eyes and licking his lips, pompous and arrogant, Francesco Janis di Tolmezzo pronounced bombastically that never had a more notable thing been achieved by a man of the house of Savorgnan, although they had already killed a patriarch [a reference to the murder of John of Moravia in 1394] and had removed all the bad thorns that had been such a nuisance over the years. By means of this action they could control everything without any opposition to their wishes, adding that he had never slept that night and blabbing on about every detail of what had happened.

That from one of the citizens most responsible for public order. On Sunday the crowd celebrated the achievements of the previous days with a remarkable carnival masquerade.

> On that day, although all the rest of the city was mournful and sad, the sanguinary associates and followers of the most perfidious assassin had a great celebration, running from one diversion to another, dressed in the silk clothes and livery of the betrayed gentlemen, calling one another by the names of those whose clothes they wore. The piper Sebastiano Cornetto, dressed in the sumptuous velvets of the Della Torre, played to the people who were frolicking in the square, and not a year passed before he suffered punishment when he was vilely killed near Cormons. When the rapacious clods left for their villages in merry gangs, mocking and jeering the miserable nobility, they were dressed even as doctors and their women as ladies so that it appeared the world was upside down.

From Udine the merry gangs of peasants brought the Cruel Carnival to the countryside, and "the peasants of all the villages as far as Sacile took up arms against the castles to put them to sack and burn them, and where there was no resistance they entered into the castles to sack and burn them." [2]

As with the Udine uprising, the troubles in the countryside left a legacy of mawkish stories that the aristocratic victims told and retold to mythologize their losses. The most famous involved the escape through snow-covered fields of the children of Alvise Della Torre. Alvise and Nicolò Della Torre had left their wives, Tadea Strassoldo and Giacoma Brazzacco, at the clan's castle of Villalta where the peasants began to agitate within hours of the events in Udine. Tadea felt so threatened by the clamor that she sent her two eldest children, Raimondo and Girolamo, into the mud and snow to find refuge at Moruzzo. There they could hear the hub-bub from the assault on nearby Brazzacco and went on to Collo-redo di Monte Albano, where they were joined by their younger siblings, Giovanni and Ginevra, who were accompanied by two guards, a tutor, and an old family friend. From Colloredo the little band of refugees fled to Pers, then the elder two were taken to Gemona, where finally their adult cousin Giacomo Spilimbergo rescued them and with a guard of nine horsemen took them in the middle of the night to his castle. But the next morning, Spilim-bergo castle also came under attack, and Giacomo had to flee with his wards and wife to Brugnera, where they arrived in time to at-tend a carnival ball at which many of the wives of Giovedì Grasso victims, unaware that they were newly made widows, danced away the night. The beleaguered nobles finally found safety in Porde-none, but some fled as far as Venice. In the meantime, Villalta was sacked, and the rough-handed peasants tore a fourth Della Torre infant away from his wet nurse's breast. However, they spared the child and eventually turned him over to the care of his aunt. Other castellan families produced their own stories of danger and fear.

Gregorio maintained that Antonio Savorgnan coordinated even these far-flung disquiets. He supposedly sent agents out into the countryside to incite the peasants by telling them that the castellans had rebelled against Saint Mark and wanted to subject Friuli to the emperor, who would return the peasants to serfdom. Peasants had responded by attacking "like rabid dogs for they believed such things and also because of their desire for loot." On the left bank of the Tagliamento "the peasants were stirred up in a great number, armed as if for battle with artillery brought to overcome the fortresses; following them with carts came the endless numbers of their families who desired booty, and with a great outcry they thundered about the ruin of the nobles. To this end they had been inflamed by their Mohammed and his followers." [3]

These few scenes from Gregorio's angry and obviously partisan history, these few moments of confrontation in a vast wave of violence which permanently transformed Friulan society, raise numerous questions about what was going on during the Cruel Carnival. Who was rebelling against whom? Why were the Venetian authorities so inept? Why did a quarrel among a few feuding aristocrats set off such a major upheaval? How had the factions come to dominate so completely the loyalties of Friulan society? Who was in the crowd? What did they want? How much did the rioters act on their own, and how much were they merely pawns of Antonio Savorgnan as Gregorio suggests? What was the meaning of the macabre dismemberments and the feeding of corpses to animals? To answer these questions, the following chapters first take the story backward by more than a century when the Savorgnan and Della Torre vendetta began, Venice acquired Friuli, the factions formed. In searching for the answers to the little questions about this single event, a much vaster panorama unfolds, leading, I hope, to a keener sense of how vendetta operated in Renaissance Italy, how factions dominated its political life, and how contemporaries understood their own violence.

CHAPTER ONE

The Friulan Enigma

In 1420 after a long and vicious war, the republic of Venice conquered the Patria del Friuli, which had been an ecclesiastical principality ruled by the patriarch of Aquileia. The last patriarch with temporal powers, Ludwig of Teck (1412–39), went into exile in Germany, leaving his faction-ridden, mountain-ringed principality to be incorporated into the growing terraferma dominion of the maritime republic.

The dramatic character of the conquest notwithstanding, the Venetian absorption of the patria did not produce a radical intensification of Venetian involvement in Friuli or an alteration in the character of Friulan society and institutions. Friuli had long been a special concern of the Venetians. Since their earliest moves out of their protective lagoon, they had struggled against the patriarchs of Aquileia and had set up a rival patriarchal seat in Grado. Venetian merchants had had extensive economic interests in Friuli since the thirteenth century, and, after the murder of Patriarch John Sobieslaw of Moravia in 1394, the republic had sought to guarantee the selection of patriarchs friendly to its interests. The conquest merely replaced the patriarch with a Venetian administrator whose powers were no greater than those of his ecclesiastical predecessor.

Except for confiscating the temporal possessions of the patriarch, Venice left Friuli relatively untouched. Given the ambiguity of its legal claims to the patriarchate, Venice did not even assert full sovereignty over the region but merely asked the pope to accept the reality of its occupation and gave its governor the singularly tentative title of luogotenente (lieutenant). Friuli was just one of several mainland territories Venice acquired during the early fifteenth century as a defensive bulwark against its many rivals, but Venice had neither the personnel nor the bureaucracy to exploit intensively such a vast domain.

The handful of Venetian officials sent to administer Friuli after the conquest found an impoverished, mostly arid region, inhabited by people who spoke a strange language and practiced alien customs. Unlike the Italian-speaking, urbane citizens Venetian magistrates found in recently conquered Padua, Vicenza, and Verona, the Friulans were inscrutable and hostile, not so much because of a nostalgia for lost liberties, which they had never possessed, but because their long experience with war and civil strife had left them with a deep distrust of all strangers. Left with their own laws largely in place, the Friulans continued to suffer under a body of dysfunctional and conflicting feudal institutions which had made the region vulnerable to an economic giant such as Venice in the first place.

The Land Between

"In the time of which I write," Ippolito Nievo commented concerning late eighteenth-century Friuli, "matters remained as nature had made them and Attila had left them." Nature had fashioned Friuli as a vast stage set for a drama of recurrent civil strife which endured almost unchanged for centuries. The civil strife of fifteenth- and sixteenth-century Friuli was conditioned by geographical and ecological circumstances that compelled a heavy concentration of settlement within a confined area; placed a premium on access to scarce water resources; demanded a careful division of the available arable land and a constant supervision of streams, ponds, bogs, pastures, and woods; and required the occupation and fortification of strategic hills for defense against neighbors and recurrent invaders. During particularly intense periods of factional

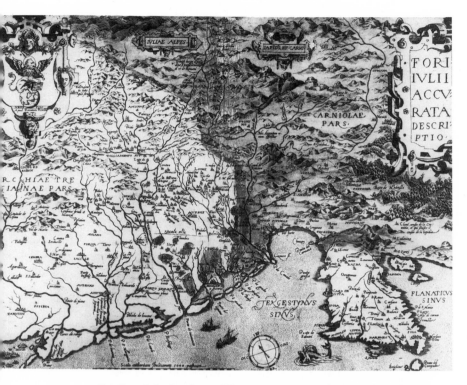

FIGURE 1. Friuli and the borders of Venetian territory (*shaded areas* show imperial lands), by Donato Bertellis (sixteenth century ?).

strife, Friuli approached the conditions of "total scarcity" Jacob Black-Michaud has posited as the necessary prerequisite for feuding, but the more common material precondition for conflict came from the habitually unequal distribution of scarce resources.[1]

Sixteenth-century writers who described the topography of Friuli frequently relied on theatrical metaphors to convey the showy way in which the Carnic and Julian Alps created a backdrop for the events played out in the cluster of castles and towns scattered at their feet. "So this patria . . . it seems to me should be described as a theater of endless mountains," began one anonymous local in a treatise addressed to the Venetian luogotenente, the Venetian governor of the region (Figure 1). Venetians who traveled there came home praising in Petrarchan fashion the spectacular scenery but lamenting the rude, endemic poverty of Friulan villages.[2]

In 1483 Marco Sanudo and two other patricians were elected
circuit judges (*auditori nuovi*) to tour the mainland hearing appeals
to sentences delivered by local judges. When Marco left on his
trip, which would last nearly six months, he brought along his sev-
enteen-year-old nephew Marin, who kept an account of what he
saw, a foretaste of his adult obsession with recording everything
that passed his way in his famously verbose diaries. Notwithstanding his youthful enthusiasm for things new, he could hardly miss
the sad ruin of many of the villages and the disease-ridden bodies
of the inhabitants. Aquileia, once a "most powerful and great city,"
shocked him particularly. Among its ruined walls and aqueducts
lived twenty-four canons, who officiated in the cathedral, preserving the liturgical functions of the much reduced and no longer
princely patriarch, and a handful of fishermen and their families,
most of whom suffered from the jaundice and lassitude of malaria.
Later in his career, however, Marin wrote a more formal description of Friuli which revealed more about his knowledge of the
ancient geographers than his ability to remember and trust in what
he had actually observed:

> In Europe under the Arctic pole at the extremity and in the
> tenth part of beautiful Italy, irrigated by pleasant rivers, deco-
> rated by opulent and rich cities, and furnished with proud
> castles, one sees spread out a pleasant and delightful plain . . . .
> It is enclosed on the northern and eastern sides by the valleys
> of very high mountains, on the southern by the Adriatic Sea
> and the western by the wide river of Livenza. The ancient
> cosmographers called it Carnia but now everyone knows it as
> the Patria del Friuli.[3]

As was the case with that of Marin Sanudo, other Renaissance
descriptions of the land and its people worked at odd cross-
purposes; some, especially those inspired by humanism, idealized
the country that had once been a prosperous Roman province and
was still so strikingly beautiful, whereas others, particularly those
with practical problems to solve, lamented the degraded condition of the peasants and their ruthless exploitation by the castellan
nobles. Luigi da Porto, the author of *Giulietta e Romeo*, wrote based
on his considerable experience. The castles and many of the towns
spread over the plain are pleasant, he said, but the "villages are

more for utility than for beauty," and he missed the palaces and gardens of his native Vicentino.[4]

With equal frankness the Venetian luogotenenti presented to the Senate at the end of their terms of office summary reports (*relazioni*) about conditions in Friuli, and these became a genre of lamentations. Girolamo Mocenigo wrote in 1574, "the peasants are all poor, and a few of them hang around the taverns and often make the women and children work the fields." The demands of Venetian wartime taxation, he added, were so onerous that they made life impossible for the peasants, many of whom abandoned their houses and emigrated. "The peasantry, principal nerve of public service in that patria," Tommaso Morosini continued in 1601, "finds itself because of a thousand adverse conditions in manifest ruin with little hope of improvement." Because of scarcities of virtually all goods as well as exactions from Venice, emigration had risen to such a point that the inhabitants had abandoned entire villages, weeds choked the fields, and aristocrats deserted their castles, leaving the few remaining peasants "in a thousand ways oppressed."

Just four years before the fall of the republic in 1797, Paolo Erizzo recapitulated the observation made by his predecessors over the previous four centuries, saying "the peasant lives vegetating like his sterile field, brutalized by ignorance and misery." These luogotenenti reported on a forsaken wasteland that contrasted with the euphoric floridity of the humanist descriptions. However, the sparsely inhabited, economically depressed region continued to attract the attention of Venice on the one hand and of the archdukes of Austria and the emperors on the other through its important commercial roads and its strategic position as the "great open door" to Italy.[5]

To guard this open door, numerous fortifications still appear on the tops of the thinly green hills and in a few locations across the lower soggy plain. Some of these are mere earthworks barely traceable among the brush; others are no more than a single ruined tower that seems to grow from the rock; some are pleasant country villas protected by entrenchments and a strong door; and still others are massive gray piles, proper castles complete with moat and drawbridges, battlements and ramparts, towers and keep. The governing rules of location for all of the fortifications were strategic

value, proximity to habitation, and access to water to make a moat.
The better sites had been occupied at least since the terrifying
Hungarian invasions that came with the fall of the Ottonian Empire. Girolamo Porcìa (1531–1601) distinguished forty-four modest castles, used primarily as noble residences; eleven large ones,
some of which served as garrisons; and thirteen walled towns,
which also had castles within them. In his time many scores more
of old fortifications were abandoned or in ruins. Palmanova, the
showpiece of Renaissance military architecture, was the only completely new location in the sixteenth century.

The fortifications testify to the insecurity of Friulan life, but the
threat as often as not came from within, from the castles' inhabitants, whose violent passions sometimes flamed forth. These lumps
of stone served the decaying power of the nobles who prized them
as signs of honor and who seldom risked closing their gates and
manning their towers against attackers more dangerous than their
own peasant tenants or their castellan neighbors. By the sixteenth
century only a handful of the castles retained any authentic military value, and most castellans quickly capitulated before they
would face a siege from a real army. The castellans formed a privileged military class that had lost its military functions and ability
but that still dominated the hill country around Udine. Members
of this class kept the vendettas alive, and their battles made the hill
region the locus of most violent conflicts. Thus, the geographic
concentration of feuding in the Friulan hills contrasts with the
typical Mediterranean pattern of mountain feuds.

To the north and east of the fortified hills appear the Carnic and
Julian Alps. The Venetians sought control of mountain passes for
both commercial advantages and military defense. Almost every
description of the Friuli dwells at length on the opportunities the
passes provided for the enemy—Turks, Hungarians, or Austrians—to bring troops, provisions, and artillery into the Veneto.
Since geographical studies were the stepchild of military science,
one expects such a preoccupation, but the recurrent invasions and
threats of invasion, particularly in the late fifteenth and early sixteenth centuries, created a monomaniacal concern with the condition of mountain roads and with provisions for fortifications
guarding access to Italy.

The excessive focus on passes led to some disastrous follies. Seldom were the Venetians able to ward off with mountain defenses a well-organized invasion—the famous victory of Cadore in 1508 was the exception—but they continued to delude themselves that mountain defenses could provide security on the cheap. Partly as a result of his observations of the manifold failures of Venetian policy during the War of the League of Cambrai, Machiavelli disparaged guarding passes, pointing out that the most one could accomplish was to prevent the enemy from crossing one pass rather than another. "If, then, you lose a pass which you have set out to hold and which your people and your army trust, almost every time such great terror seizes your people and the remainder of your soldiers that, without a chance to test their valor, you become a loser. Thus you lose all of your fortune with part of your forces."[6]

Any significant army invading from Austria had to use the Imperial Road through the Carnic Alps to bring in artillery, and when the strategy of guarding mountain passes failed, the defenders of Friuli fell back upon Osoppo. The rock of Osoppo is a place of many fables. Occupied before the Romans came, used by the Lombards to defend themselves against the Avars and by 364 revolutionaries against a long Austrian siege in 1848, garrisoned in the First World War and bombed in the Second, Osoppo has long been the keystone of Friulan and northeastern Italian defenses. In 1513 and 1514 after Marano and Gradisca had fallen to the Austrians, Venetian forces had abandoned Udine, and nearly all the castellans had gone over to the enemy, Girolamo Savorgnan and a few hundred men held out at Osoppo against the siege of the combined imperial armies and forced the enemy to abandon Friuli and return most of it to Venetian rule. Situated between the Imperial Road and the Tagliamento River a few miles below where the river breaks onto the plain, the moraine rises precipitously some 350 feet above the fields, providing a strategic position from which all movement to and from the mountains could be observed (Figure 2). Girolamo Savorgnan described it as he found it:

This mountain, located in such a convenient and opportune place, so strongly protected, and one can truly say built by Nature in the model of a marvelous fortress, has three faces: that which looks toward the East is 450 *passa* [765 meters] long, the other toward the North is 200 [340 meters], and on

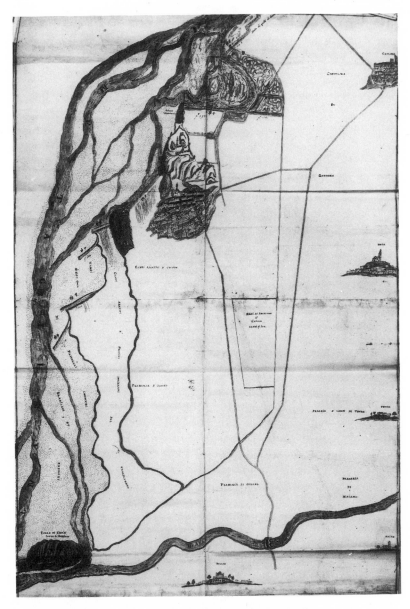

FIGURE 2. Osoppo and Buia, from a map dated July 30, 1714.

these two faces the living rock has been so cut and broken up that it is impossible to imagine it, let alone climb up it; the third face toward the West, on which Nature left for the convenience of the inhabitants a ridge for a cart road, is so well defended by various sentry posts and many towers of living rock that no architect could possibly want them in more opportune locations, and this third face covers 405 *passa* [688.5 meters]. This place from all that I have been able to find was held in great esteem by the ancients, a fact which is demonstrated to me by certain stones found with some most beautiful Roman epitaphs, some mosaic pavements, and two very large cisterns cut into the rock, made in the Roman fashion with an artificial wall and at great expense. There is still a most lovely pond, completely round, that is seventy *passa* [119 meters] across, for use of the animals, and there is still a large stand of trees so that we shall have plenty of water and fuel.[7]

With its extraordinary strategic value Osoppo gave its possessor military primacy in Friuli, a primacy as useful in times of peace as in war.

Osoppo was, significantly, a fief of the Savorgnan family. Accumulators of vast possessions, honorary members of the Venetian patriciate, veritable lords of Friuli, the Savorgnan held fast to Osoppo like hounds to prey. The family used this precious prize in their collection of fiefs to play for concessions from the Venetians. The Venetians, in turn, recognized that their continued dominion over Friuli was hostage to the lords of Osoppo and always had to tailor their rule to satisfy whichever member of the Savorgnan clan held the fortress.

Friulan topography, in sum, created a peculiar environment that, by cutting the landscape into radically distinct zones, forced most of the populace to inhabit a scattering of hills around Udine. From these ramparted mounds the castellans looked with vigilance toward their noble neighbors on the nearby rises, with severity down on the peasants living in squalid wooden huts below them, and with jealousy at privileged Udine and the ambitious Savorgnan. From the luogotenente's hilltop palace in Udine many of these castles could be watched and the immense alpine peaks observed and feared. This little land, dwarfed by mountains and gigantic enemies, the home of scrubby poverty and deceptive greenery, of ignorant arrogance and tattered chivalry, constituted a house divided against itself, ever at war within, and from without vulnerable to the ruses and assaults of greedy foreigners.

"The people are handsome," wrote Count Girolamo of Porcìa of his fellow Friulans, "especially the nobility, the women as much as the men. They possess good blood, are vigorous, but the people have an obstinate pride and are given to the vendetta; they are a coarse people and have quasi-barbarian customs, particularly those that a few let slip out. They have a difficult language, and to be understood they speak Italian." In the sixteenth century the population of the patria varied in cycles between 140,000 and 194,000 people, rising gradually and falling precipitously as in 1570 when more than 25,000 people died from famine. The whole region put together had about as many persons as lived in the city of Venice itself, which in 1553 hosted 153,397 inhabitants, a figure that placed it among the ten most populous cities in Europe. Among the terraferma subjects of La Serenissima, the number of residents in the patria was second only to the Bresciano, but the population was overwhelmingly rural, and urban structures were less well developed than in any other area in the Veneto. In 1548 Udine had a population of 14,597, making it the sixth largest terraferma city after Verona (52,109), Brescia (42,660), Padua (34,075), Vicenza (21,268), and Bergamo (17,707). Udine, however, was far larger than any other town in Friuli: Portogruaro had only 3,500 souls; Cividale, 2,903; Pordenone, 2,710; Gemona, 2,070; and Spilimbergo, 1,285.[8]

In the sixteenth century four linguistic strata can be identified among the general population. At the base were speakers of Friulan or Furlan, the language of the mass of uneducated peasants and artisans. Friulan survived as a language in opposition to those employed by the authorities, and nearly all examples of written Friulan from this period were by persons of limited literacy who used writing for practical and personal reasons. The monolingualism of most of the Friulans segregated them from outside influences. A peasant defendant before the tribunal of the Holy Office in 1649,

for example, asked the court to provide an interpreter because he could not understand the questions put to him by the inquisitor from Orvieto. At the more elevated social levels of the peasant-artisan group, some, who needed to work in a wider ambit and were at least marginally literate such as the heretic Menocchio studied by Carlo Ginzburg, also spoke Veneto when necessary. A third linguistic level consisted of those who habitually spoke Veneto. A tiny fourth group knew Tuscan and maybe Latin. In his 1484 rendering into the vernacular tongue of the *Constitutions of the Patria del Friuli*, humanist Pietro Capretto discussed the problems he faced in deciding which vernacular to choose. Tuscan, he wrote, was too obscure for the Friulan people, but Friulan itself presented problems: "Furlana is not universally spoken in all Friuli, and one can write it poorly and even worse pronounce it by reading." He finally chose the Trevisan form of Veneto, the *lingua franca* of the Venetian mainland.[9]

Friuli constituted a land between, both in the literal sense that it was a border region in which the Venetian republic and Holy Roman Empire met, and in a metaphoric one that its leaders were suspended between, on the one hand, a population whose rural poverty and linguistic isolation underlay a feudal and archaic culture and, on the other, a sophisticated, capitalist, imperialist city-republic that had become the paragon of Renaissance civic culture. Topography and culture also conspired to keep Friuli divided within itself. Residential location and class had dramatic correlates in speech, dividing some groups from one another so completely that there was little common ground for communication or mutual understanding. Despite centuries of independence under the patriarchs of Aquileia, Friuli was bound together by phantom institutional threads that were easily broken and, more substantially, by the webs of factional clientage.

Among all of the territories in the Venetian terraferma dominion, Friuli alone had been a feudal principality rather than a city-state prior to conquest. Elsewhere during the twelfth- and thirteenth-century heyday of the communes, cities such as Verona, Vicenza, and Padua had politically absorbed the surrounding rural *contado* and smaller towns in the vicinity. In Friuli towns were communal islands in a still feudal countryside, which had long been formally unified around its ecclesiastical prince, a titular unity recognized after the conquest by the official designation of the region as a patria. However, when the Venetians conquered Friuli, its unity, undermined by decades of civil war, had become a legal fiction.

To Venetian officials Friuli presented a special enigma, in part because the absence of a clear hierarchy of authority weakened Venetian rule. Although the Venetian luogotenente in Udine had general responsibility for all Friuli, he could not supervise other Venetian rectors in the region effectively because they too were patricians elected to their post. Because they reported directly to the College of the Senate and Council of Ten, they could easily outmaneuver or ignore the luogotenente's orders. In addition, procedural red tape often tied his hands because, as one luogotenente observed, when Venice conquered Friuli it only added new institutions without eliminating the old, making the new system even less effective than the patriarch's.

In the sixteenth century jurisdictional lines divided Friuli into 816 communities (ville): Venice governed 49 of these directly, the Holy Roman Empire controlled 29, the patriarch of Aquileia retained 10, and the luogotenente had appellant jurisdiction over the remaining 728. Subinfeudations parcelled out the luogotenente's territory into 60 or more subjurisdictions, each with its own privileges and powers. Feudal lords or their deputies held most of these subjurisdictions, prelates had some, and independent towns controlled quite a few. The many jurisdictions made justice a particularly rare commodity for peasants since when they appealed their cases, they usually came before their own lord, and they could seldom afford to go to Udine to plead before the luogotenente. In 1553 a former luogotenente, Francesco Sanudo, identified the many jurisdictions as the cause of all the strife of the patria: "with the many doctors of law and advocates clear matters are made obscure, and all esteem their own privileges too highly so that for every minor cause conflicts arise among them for which they then kill one another." [10]

Among all the various institutions, both Friulan and Venetian, only the parliament encompassed all of Friuli. Officially founded by the patriarch in 1269, the parliament assumed great prestige and authority, especially over financial affairs, and, until the arrival of the Venetians, constituted the most successful feudal assembly in

Italy. Under the Venetians, however, the parliament became primarily a forum for the castellan aristocrats whose worst excesses could be checked by Venice through the luogotenente's presence in parliamentary sessions, a development that made its activities mere routine and its prestige hollow. After 1446, the membership divided into two parties on most issues, one made up of the luogotenente, the Savorgnan family, and the representatives of Udine; and the other of most of the aristocrats and the delegates of a few communities, especially Cividale.

To ensure their loyalty after the conquest, Venice promised the members of the second estate that their "libertates, iura et consuetudines" would be respected. Although Venice honored these liberties, rights, and customs with legalistic formality and never challenged the castellans outright, the dominant city encouraged as much as possible Udine's claims against the castellans, a situation that left them prickly about the slightest infringement of their position. Udine threatened their privileges because it wanted to break the castellans' economic stranglehold on the city. The castellans regulated the flow of products from the country to the city through protectionist laws, tolls, judicial regulations, and the confiscation of goods. Conflict between the city and the lords intensified during the sixteenth century, particularly when inflation diluted the castellans' fixed incomes, forcing them to alienate some of their lands and to send younger sons away to seek their own fortunes in foreign courts.

During the Renaissance the great castles, such as those at Villalta, Colloredo, Spilimbergo, Valvasone, and Zoppola, flew red flags as signs of the personal inviolability of the inhabitants and housed the nobles, their retainers, and servants. The various nuclear families of the noble clans usually lived in a common residence on the premises. The clansmen were bound together by blood ties that could extend as far as first- and second-degree cousins. Occasionally affines or even unrelated persons who had bought their way in or taken possession upon the default of a loan subdivided the castle with proper members of the clan. The nobles who lived together in the same castle and exercised its jurisdictional rights called themselves castellans (*castellani*) or consorts (*consorti*). The consorts often established different apartments or even different houses within a castle complex for each nuclear family, and these

separate units could be alienated, sold, and willed away. The social
ideal was one of patrilocality and of solidarity among consorts, but
social ideals, especially in Friuli, often had little relationship to
reality.

A lord's control of his own lands depended heavily on the men
who actually handled the day-to-day management of his affairs.
One of the lord's familiars served as steward (*caniparius, canipario,
canevar*) who collected and registered rents (*censi*) from the peasants
on the appointed day of payment. In most cases, however, the
steward relied on a local peasant deputized to collect the rents and
to transport them to the lord's castle. Usually the village head (*decano, jurato, brico, meriga,* or *massaro*), the local collector served as
the linchpin in the whole manorial system. Lords and stewards
might cultivate personal ties with him especially in the villages in
which the consorts had jurisdictional rights, but the *decano* labored
in an ambiguous position inasmuch as he represented both the
lord to the village and the village to the lord. The Savorgnan carefully nurtured their relationship with such men, who could then
be relied upon to bring out the villagers in support of the lord in
his fights with his castellan enemies. Less effective proprietors than
the Savorgnan, however, might find the *decani* leading the peasants against them during one of the rural rebellions. Usually elected
for one- or two-year terms by the village assembly (*vicinia*), the
decano handled civil and criminal matters at the most basic level,
organized public works, and collected the *estimo*. In a few places
the lords had the right to appoint a *gastaldo* to exercise authority
more directly than was possible when the villagers chose their own
leader.

At the village level peasant families found themselves enmeshed
in several distinct and sometimes quite incompatible institutional
structures: the feudal jurisdiction, a contractual obligation to pay
rents to a lord who may or may not have been the judge of his
jurisdiction, the *vicinia* headed by a neighbor who was *decano*, a
pasture association, a fiscal unit for taxation, and a parish of the
church. Until the organization of the peasant militias at the end of
the fifteenth century and the creation of the peasants' parliament,
called the *contadinanza*, in the middle of the sixteenth, villages offered few consistent sources of solidarity beyond kin groups.

Although it was the only town in Friuli large enough to be

called a city, modest Udine retained a strongly rural orientation, enclosing large tracts of farm land within the outer circuit of its walls. Based on the observations from his visit in 1483, Marin Sanudo described the city as composed of three concentric circles defined by walls. Within the inner circle around a hill were the luogotenente's castle and two churches. The second circuit of walls enclosed the *citadella* of noble palaces, and the third protected the *borghi* inhabited by artisans and peasants.

Friulan and Udinese institutions failed to function very efficiently. They created an oppressive burden of vested interests in which every obscure office and every procedure were the privileged rights of someone; moreover, institutions worked against one another, furthering rather than resolving conflicts. As a result, noninstitutional relationships comprised the real life of the society.

The creation of influential relationships came partly from family background, wealth, status, and official position but also from more fleeting characteristics such as the strength of personality and talent, the ability to recognize and grasp opportunity, the judicious building of friendships and alliances, and the willingness to use force appropriately. Every Friulan lived within multiple, overlapping, sometimes competing networks, some cohesive enough to constitute groups, others loose connections among individuals. Vertical bonds between patrons and clients or fathers and sons coexisted with horizontal ones among friends, siblings, and neighbors. The small communities of Friuli defined themselves through these ties as much as through legal definitions of citizenship, but individuals within each community were also linked outside it to trading partners, debtors and creditors, clients and patrons, fellow militiamen, and factional comrades. In the villages each individual lived within several shifting, noncorporate associations, in what Giovanni Levi has called a system of continuous tensions. In moments of crisis, groups might temporarily form along class lines, but these could easily decompose and recompose into clientage groups or factions.

The family had a central position in the social webs entangling each individual. In Friuli the family cannot be reduced simply to the household, a fiscal unit useful for taxation and agricultural management, or consanguinity, so valued in the rhetoric of patriarchy. The family was both of these and a range of alliances created through intermarriage, patronage, and friendship as well. Individuals did not act within their social world in isolation but in continuous reference to the interests of the family knot. Even economic choices depended less on the legal or market forces that determined price than on the social implications of any given decision for relatives, allies, and clients. However, on many occasions in Friuli the family knot unraveled, forcing individuals to seek solidarity elsewhere. Such a system of tensions placed heavy burdens on the intermediaries among the networks, especially on those who mediated between artisan-peasant clients and aristocratic patrons—the local notables, those men of relatively substantial property, the *decani*, militia captains, and notaries.

Faced with extraordinary opportunities resulting from their brokerage of resources and protection of local rights and privileges, these men also subjected themselves to great dangers inasmuch as the disgrace or treason of a protector might be as disastrous for them as for him. Trapped into serving multiple masters, including their own townsmen, feudal lords, factional chiefs, and Venetian officials, the intermediaries sometimes acted as enforcers but more often as patrons with a constituency and interests of their own. The disruptions of vendetta violence and of war created special opportunities by occupying the powerful figures from outside the villages in other matters.

Vendetta

Venetians governed the mainland more through administrative habits forced on them by long-standing local practice than through a coherent policy and system. Each subject town had its own past glories, intense pride, corporate rights, and privileges. Each honored its own statutes, distinctively blended from Roman, common, canon, and Lombard law. To defend its local interests, each hired its own professional experts, usually trained in law at Padua. Venetian laws were dramatically different from those found in the terraferma cities because Venice incorporated few Lombard and Frankish principles in its statutes, Venetian jurists had ignored the reintroduction of Roman law during the twelfth and thirteenth centuries when it was associated with the extension of imperial rights, and Venetian merchants abhorred the influence of lawyers in their affairs. To dilute opposition to its initial conquest, Venice asked the subject towns to sign a formal pact in which they agreed to accept Venetian sovereignty in return for a guarantee that the Venetian signoria would respect local statutes. Where local laws interfered too gravely with Venetian prerogatives, as in Verona, Padua, Vicenza, Brescia, Bergamo, Udine, and the Patria del Friuli, the signoria formed an ad hoc board of local jurists who rendered local government more accessible to Venetian influence, but there was no wholesale reconciliation of differences in legal systems.

In Friuli the reformed statutes were translated and published in the Veneto vernacular as the *Constitutioni de la Patria de Friuli* (Udine, 1484), but they still embodied numerous contradictions which Venice failed to eliminate despite repeated Friulan complaints. The signoria gave the luogotenente of Friuli the self-contradictory charge to rule according to "their and our statutes, ordinances, and customs." [11]

The result of Venice's failure to create its own coherent system of rule was that its officials were hostage to the advice of local lawyers who mediated between Venice and the provincial oligarchs, a situation that had both technical and political consequences. Venetian jurists and appellate judges had little contact with their colleagues on the terraferma, reinforcing the disharmony between these two judicial worlds. The business of government became so inefficient that Venetian rulership appeared at best arbitrary and at worst grossly exploitative.

The absence of sufficient and competent police forces also hindered Venetian justice. The rectors relied on *sbirri* or *zaffi* in the towns and on *campagnoli* who patrolled, if one can so dignify the wanderings of licensed thugs, the rural districts. Usually recruited from among the ranks of criminals who were offered the jobs as alternatives to punishment, their proverbial brutishness and lack of discipline were hardly discouraged by a level of pay so low that robbery or extortion was necessary for survival. The people thoroughly feared and hated them. It was not unusual for a company of *sbirri* sent by the rector on a legitimate mission to be met by the sounding of the tocsin and armed opposition of hostile townsmen. Tommaso Garzoni described a *sbirro* as

truly malicious in every action, no matter what one is talking about, because to steal he becomes the friend of thieves, carries the torch to light the way for all their plunderings, keeps company with them, serves them as a spy. . . . Everyone is ashamed to deal with the cops, so marked are they by such an ugly and shameful character.[12]

The rectors, moreover, suffered from a chronic shortage of men willing to accept the dubious attractions of the profession and often had to rely on unemployed soldiers of fortune or, worst of all, on Croatian and Albanian shepherds recruited, often at the point of a sword, for the task. If these substitutes failed, as they often did, rectors accepted the voluntary collaboration of private persons who agreed to help, usually for pay but also for the cover such assignments provided for private vendettas. No matter how responsible a podestà, captain, or luogotenente was, no matter how benevolent his intentions or great his wisdom, he simply lacked the forces necessary to police his territory; and in the more feudal areas such as Friuli he could not compete with, let alone confront, local lords capable of assembling scores of mounted retainers.

The available methods for investigating crimes were equally inadequate. Three types of penal procedures could initiate a trial: a secret denunciation, an inquisition in which a judge proceeded *ex officio*, or a mixture of the two in which the judge relied for information on local functionaries such as village mayors, neighborhood chiefs in the cities, or surgeons who treated the wounded. The system thrived on rumor, innuendo, personal animosities, and public reputations with little sifting of evidence until the trial stage, if then. Even after a trial and sentencing Venetian procedures permitted if not encouraged violence and endemic criminality through the absence of enough prisons; a typical sentence for a crime of violence involved a fine and exile. Exiles became bandits who by the late sixteenth century were so numerous they formed private armies that turned Venetian law and order into a dead letter outside of the walled cities. As Gaetano Cozzi and his students characterize it, the Venetian judiciary was one of the most peculiar in Europe, providing a quick and severe punishment for any crime that threatened Venice's hegemony, but in most other cases the weakness or laziness of officials and a heavy reliance on provincial functionaries made it one of the most permissive systems anywhere. In addition, Venetian nobles who served as judges brought to their task a fathomless ignorance of the law and a defensive cunning that led them to subordinate legal principles to political expediency.

The only means the republic devised to achieve some measure of legal uniformity in its terraferma dominion was through judicial appeals. The advocates of the commune (*avvogadori di comun*) in theory defended proper procedures by intervening in cases appealed to the provincial rectors. However, the advocates frequently found themselves in conflict with the auditors (*auditori nuovi*), patrician circuit judges who were supposed to respond to the grievances of the terraferma population by hearing appeals from any court including those of the rectors. Their annual circuits gave provincials access to the highest levels of Venetian judicial authority because the auditors acted as agents of the *quarantia*, the major Venetian court of appeals. Although they had the potential to become quite powerful on the terraferma by reducing the competence of both the local courts and the Venetian rectors, the auditors were hampered by the superior efficiency of the local courts and by the contradictions of their mission. On the one hand, they were supposed to ensure that uniform principles applied through the entire appeals process, but on the other, the initial agreements between Venice and the conquered territories obliged them to adhere to the customs and statutes of the subject cities. However, because the auditors were never in one town for more than a few days, they could hardly master the local statutes in such a short time and were at the mercy of local attorneys and notaries for advice. Locals, moreover, could exploit the right of appeal as a means of evading the law and delaying judgments.

One of the most common kinds of conflict and certainly the most troublesome one Venetian magistrates faced in Friuli was vendetta. In the attempts to control vendetta through administrative decrees and criminal prosecutions, Venetians encountered a system of primitive law and a form of social organization governed by implicit rules that provided models for individual behavior, defined the membership in social groups, and, most importantly, regulated conflicts by promising retaliatory punishment for insults and aggression. Theoretically, official justice and vendetta justice were incompatible because, on the one hand, private vendettas impinged upon the most basic prerogatives of the state and, on the other, avengers who relied on the courts rather than their own valor could be seen as shameful cowards. However, in the real world of fifteenth- and early sixteenth-century Friuli the two forms of justice often worked hand in hand, the Venetians going easy on friendly families and relying on modest judicial punishments of exile, which permitted many vendettas to continue, and the Friulans manipulating and corrupting the courts when it was to their advantage to do so. For more than a century after the Venetian conquest, the two systems of law cohabited in an inconsistent yet symbiotic relationship.

Friuli shared in the Mediterranean-wide culture of feuding which has been studied by legions of anthropologists and historians. In such cultures persons assume that disputes of any sort will inevitably take the form of a feud or vendetta and that all calculations about power and honor are based on the status of ongoing vendettas. The pursuit of vendettas was inextricably linked to the Mediterranean ideal of masculinity, which David Gilmore has characterized as striving for "performative excellence." A man who is "good at being a man" follows a script that involves him in public displays of physical risk, which he meets with decision and useful action—that is, behavior directed toward a specific purpose, such as protecting vulnerable family members. The "good" man is neither a saint nor a bully but someone who employs aggressiveness to deter challenges and is above all loyal to his own. When he or someone close to him is hurt by another, either in word or deed, the good man seeks revenge by which he retaliates in an appropriate way, ideally matching the injury with an equal or slightly greater injury. By pulling off such performances well he acquires honor, that most precious and perishable of social attributes, and the reputation for being an honorable man helps him avoid further challenges. The performative aspect of masculine honor is embodied in the very word, *vendetta*, which implied a forceful demonstration of potency, and its Friulan variant, *svindic*, conveyed an especially strong message of anger.

The common law of Friuli retained many vestiges of Lombard principles, which recognized the Old German concept of *faida*, the requirement of revenge that fell on the closest blood relative of a victim, who in effect replaced the dead man in the household. Early Lombard edicts attempted to limit the effects of *faida* by confining it to a very narrow range of participants but recognized it as a popular custom. Although no longer a necessity as it had been among the ancient Germans, *faida* remained an important means of personal defense parallel to judicial combat and private pledges. Friulan law went far in prohibiting the behavioral legacy of *faida* but implicitly recognized that vendettas still served as a system of private justice, a legal situation that reflected a deep ambivalence about vendetta in Friulan society.

A vendetta need not have begun with assault or murder but only required a perceived insult. An affronted man becomes very dangerous, especially if his honor has been questioned by calumnies against his female relatives or his own lack of courage. Insults could be symbolic, physical, or verbal, and the laws promised heavy penalties for those who affronted another. In areas most influenced by Roman legal learning, the statutory rubrics distinguished between simple derision, which attributed to the offended person physical or moral defects or compared him with an animal, and more threatening imputations against his honor. The law demanded in the latter case that proof of the charge be forthcoming and provided heavy sentences for false accusations. Friulan codes were especially rich in statutory provisions against various kinds of ridicule. In Udine the scale of penalties enacted higher fines for taunts heard in the public streets, and threats spoken in the city square, communal council, or the courts received the heaviest punishments. Fines for verbal abuse (*rusticitates iniuriosae*) applied only to the aggressor and not to the person provoked even if he replied in kind. In cases in which it was unclear who started the confrontation the court divided the fine between the two. The statute listed the scornful words that should not be spoken and provided penalties for knocking off someone's hat or jerking down his hood. It exacted special punishments for abuse committed by women and treated with unusual severity Tuscans domiciled in Udine who threatened their countrymen.

The authorities remained vigilant for verbal affronts and symbolic acts of calumny which publicly unbalanced the delicate relationships of the community. As a result, people had to be cautious about what was said to whom, and aggressive joking, in particular, required a sensitivity to the style of native discourse, to what Basil Bernstein calls "restricted codes," which are peculiar to all local and class relationships and which employ condensed symbols and metaphors that contrast with the elaborate linguistic codes of the learned. The more restricted the verbal codes of the community, the more likely creative forms of abuse and plays upon everyday imagery might be both valued and dangerous if taken too far. At the most extreme, insults could be understood as similar to curses, words spoken in such a way that they conveyed a malevolent power through their very utterance. Illiteracy and cultural isolation, thus, contributed to the hothouse atmosphere of Friuli, leaving the Friulans with a body of concrete images, usually about animals, which, when spoken in derision, left little room for the ambiguous interpretations that contemporary diplomats, for example, found so useful for avoiding confrontations.

The principal means available to Venetian magistrates and local Friulan judges for controlling vendetta was to sentence culprits to exile, an act that put them outside of the protection of the law and made them, as far as the law was concerned, members of "the living dead." In outlawing men for crimes of violence the government sought not only to rid itself of public nuisances but also to focus the wrath of the community on guilty scapegoats whose legal death would have a healing effect for the community as a whole.

Exile may be the oldest legal method for dealing with disturbances of the peace and for preserving the borders of society. Ancient Roman law distinguished between simple exile, the expulsion from the place where one normally lived; relegation, the obligation to remain in a defined place; and deportation, the forced removal across the sea. The outlaw might suffer the loss of his property, and others were prohibited from giving him water or fire, depriving him in effect of the benefits of membership in the human community. He would be denied access to all sacred sites and ceremonies because he was a source of pollution. If anything, Germanic custom was even more thorough in denying the humanity of a person banished for crime. His chief considered him dead, his wife became a widow, his children orphans, and his property was either destroyed or returned to the tribe. If he were caught and killed, his captors left the corpse in the wilds to be ravaged by animals. If he escaped, he became a *wargus* or werewolf who must be attacked and killed by anyone who found him; in fact in many medieval statutes the head of an outlaw brought the same reward as the head of a wolf. Banishment, thus, constituted legal, social, and very often literal death. The Edict of Theodoric of 507 combined Roman imperial and German tribal principles, creating the concept of banishment passed on by the Carolingian codes. In following these traditions, Friuli and Venice employed relegation, deportation, and (because most offenders were contumacious) simple exile as the normal penalties for almost all crimes of violence.

The connotations of the word *bandit* reveal the kind of life that awaited most banished persons. Up until about the middle of the fifteenth century, bandits in northern Italy often joined others who had suffered the same fate and formed armed companies to plot their return or to raid their enemies, robbing to survive. Bandits had traditionally been able to rely on the aid and comfort of foreign princes who used them to stir up trouble in the territory of their neighbors; but after the Peace of Lodi in 1454 resident ambassadors helped guarantee the prohibitions of the Italic League against supporting the exiles of a neighboring prince.

This salutary general development only marginally touched Friuli, in which imperial enclaves and the difficult terrain continued to provide a ready refuge. At no time during the fifteenth and sixteenth centuries, moreover, did Venice have the police forces necessary to catch culprits. By making proclamations and offering bounties Venice had to rely on subjects rather than officials to apprehend or kill delinquents, and the city seldom employed the army, even when it was at full strength and in the field, to capture fleeing criminals or to combat brigands. The authorities had little choice but to rely on the time-honored expedient of banishment as a means of controlling and punishing crimes, but the system created a vicious circle in which an exile had few incentives to keep from continuing his violence because he could do so without hindrance unless some private citizen determined to stop him.

The statutes of Venice and Udine devote a great deal of space to regulating banishment and to the treatment of bandits. Before the Venetian conquest, Friuli had a draconian version of the *interdictio aquae et ignis* according to which judges had a ditch dug around a culprit's house and private citizens could neither give him water and fire nor speak with him. After the conquest, Udine's revised statutes eliminated the *interdictio* and provided for two kinds of exile: ordinary banishment for life, in which the condemned suffered the effects of a civil death, and capital banishment, in which anyone could kill the exile without criminal penalty. But in one of the typical contradictions of Venetian rule, Venetian law failed to make the same distinctions as Udinese law, meaning that anyone banished from Venetian territories could, in many cases, be legally assassinated. The question thus became which laws should apply to Friulan cases; there was never a consistent answer. Moreover, Venetian authorities had the flexibility to apply the law as they wished, offering bounties on the heads of exiles according to political considerations.

The Venetian provisions that allowed the killing of declared bandits and those who helped them caused enormous problems that reveal the dilemmas produced by the system. For a few years Venice experimented with a rule that allowed an exiled person to escape his ban by bringing in the head of another exile, but this provoked so much crime it had to be revoked. The Council found itself repeating a cycle of expanding the right to assassinate exiles and then revoking it a few years later as the number of assaults and murders increased. The privilege of some Friulan castellans, such as the lords of Spilimbergo, to offer refuge to outlaws especially troubled the Venetian rectors who recurrently tried to circumscribe the practice, but the council did not definitively abrogate the entitlement until 1581. In the most atrocious cases a banned person lost his property; but in Friuli, where brothers jointly held most private property, carrying out this provision against one member of a fraternal consortium might prove difficult and encourage relatives to assist the exile.

An exiled person was banished beyond a fifteen-mile perimeter around the territory; but unless specifically stated otherwise, the ban only applied to the territory of the jurisdiction in which the crime had been committed. The multiple jurisdictions in Friuli produced a nightmare, especially because many jurisdictions were not even fifteen miles across. Moreover, a loophole in the law which was not corrected until 1541 permitted persons banished from a terraferma jurisdiction to find refuge in Venice itself, a rather pleasant prospect for many rural ruffians. As if these complications did not inhibit enforcement enough, rectors issued many safe conducts to those banished from other jurisdictions, a practice that may have been lucrative enough for the rectors but made a mockery of justice.

The numerous anomalies in the Venetian provisions against vendetta permitted even a modestly clever outlaw considerable freedom of movement and action. A law of 1504, for example, stipulated that persons banished *ad inquirendum* (awaiting judgment), presumably because they were contumacious, had up to sixteen months after the term of office of the rector who banished them ended to present themselves to the court or face banishment for life. By 1524, however, numerous criminals had complained that because they had been away when banished, they had not known about their own exile and had not returned in time to defend themselves against false accusations. The Senate, therefore, revoked the 1504 law. It soon became evident, however, that the very persons whose complaints had led to the revocation had in fact conspired with other exiles to take advantage of the opportunity to return to commit crimes in Venetian territories. The 1504 statute had to be reinstituted.

Another trick was to apply to several different Venetian councils for a pardon, to appeal rejections of pardons several times, and to use a pardon, once granted, to exact revenge on old enemies. Only in 1565 did the Council of Ten reserve for itself the right to issue pardons from sentences of exile.

Despite the ancient traditions behind the scapegoating of outlaws, the process largely failed in Friuli. Exiled persons very often remained members of society, even when absent, and sentences of exile seldom turned communities against culprits. Exiling failed for several reasons. First, although exiles might be legal nonpersons, their sentences merely put them in trouble with the distant and vague Venetians; and if outlaws had strong local support, they were relatively safe. Second, many of the castellans who administered the lower levels of justice were themselves participants in feuds. As a result outlaw proclamations often lacked legitimacy and were unenforceable in the villages and castles in which more informal social pressures governed behavior. Third, Venetian law was not very intimidating, especially compared with the dangers that came from ignoring a personal affront. Notwithstanding the many disjunctures in Friulan kinship patterns, the internal clan ruptures among brothers and cousins, and the dereliction of allied families in defending their friends, vendetta constituted the real law and often the only justice. Through vendetta the fictive dead men of exile and literal dead men of combat could fight back.

FACTIONS

Several castellan lineages, which were akin to clans in the Scottish fashion, dominated the vendettas and formed the core group of the factions. However, members of the castellan clans also had a tendency to fight among themselves, undermining the strength of lineages as a pervasive source of stability, a tendency that makes them less cohesive, for example, than the *parentele* of Liguria, which provided a language and structure for all political and economic relationships.

The castellan clans of Friuli might best be understood as the manifestations of a dynamic process that can be traced through marriage choices, which reveal the changing identities of the clans. Given the apparent fragility of clan solidarity, the factions became the most potent organizations for regulating local conflicts, protecting the vulnerable and weak, and providing a source of collective identity. These factions consisted of a variety of persons allied to but not usually related by blood or marriage to a dominant family, and in Friuli the membership of the two dominant factions coalesced primarily along class lines, divisions that also expressed community tensions.

For more than two centuries the Savorgnan and Della Torre clans fought an on-again, off-again vendetta that recurrently expanded into factional warfare. The followers of the Savorgnan called themselves the Zambarlani, those of the Della Torre the Strumieri. The pervasive, dominating extralegal influence of the Savorgnan and challenges to that influence stimulated the formation of the factions and created the central political fact of Friulan internal history, both before and after the Venetian conquest. Beginning in the thirteenth century, the Savorgnan fortified their position through the acquisition of lands, control of lucrative investments, accumulation of jurisdictions, and cultivation of useful friendships, especially in Venice. Although others feared they would transform themselves into princes, they never acquired a lordship as did the Carrara in Padua, Della Scala in Verona, Este in Ferrara, or Visconti in Milan, but they came close to the kind of covert hegemony the Medici achieved in fifteenth-century Florence.

Considering the aridity of the Friulan plain, it is perhaps not surprising that the Savorgnan based their power in the control of water supplies, especially the water sources for Udine. As lords of a small castle at Savorgnan del Torre, they could regulate the water flow through an essential acqueduct from the Torre River, which made them the ecologic arbiter of Udine. Between 1315 and 1344, with profits acquired in Udine (especially through associations with Tuscans in the woolen-cloth trade), the Savorgnan bought up enormous amounts of land, at first along the Torre downstream from their castle and then in Udine itself. A second concentration in the valleys of the Alps made them predominant in Carnia, where they controlled vast herds of sheep and goats and cut forest timber essential for Venice's shipping. But they also had extensive properties dispersed throughout Friuli in dozens of little villages.

One of the common characteristics of factions in Mediterranean societies was the convergence of friendship and patronage ties with economic transactions. Leaders traded with and lent money and goods to their colleagues and clients. Essential to Savorgnan success in building a vast clientele were their ties to the bankers of Friuli, which allowed the Savorgnan to manage the distribution of credit in Udine and environs. They did not act as bankers themselves but protected first Tuscan and, after 1450, Jewish bankers who provided short-term loans to the poor. The Savorgnan profited from the Jews' business activities by granting the contract that permitted them to live in Udine for a fee and by acting as their protectors, both directly as in 1511 when Antonio Savorgnan prevented the looting of Jewish property during the Cruel Carnival and indirectly through Udine's minor council, which, despite promptings from Venice, failed to curtail Jewish activities in the city.

From their unmatched financial base the Savorgnan wove together a network of political and jurisdictional privileges. In Udine the family considered the right to appoint the city's chancellor "an ancient inherited practice," nearly always had a family member among the deputies, and even had the city adopt the Savorgnan blazon as its own. In the fifteenth and sixteenth centuries the Savorgnan were one of the few Friulan clans to enjoy more than one

feudal jurisdiction. They had twelve. Osoppo was the most important strategically, but within the fiefs of Belgrado and Castelnovo
with some twenty-two subject villages, the Savorgnan were autonomous princes, legally separate from the patria and the supervision of the luogotenente and subject only to the ultimate authority of the Savorgnans' feudal lord, the doge of Venice (see map
"Friuli in the Sixteenth Century"). Their privileges in their fiefs
included the monopoly of salt supplies; the collecting of tolls at the
crossing points of the Tagliamento, Isonzo, Cosa, and Arzino riv-
ers and several smaller streams; the issuing of licenses for keeping
sheep, harvesting grapes, hunting and fishing, and operating a bakery or tavern; and the appointment of podestà, *decani*, judges, and
priests in more than fifty localities. A 1470 census listed 5,328
people under the direct jurisdiction of the Savorgnan.

Even before the conquest, Venice had solidified its position in
Friuli by granting them membership in the Venetian patriciate, a
status that made them, as Mallett and Hale put it, the "most prominent and the most controversial" of all the terraferma families allied
to Venice. Their exceptional autonomy and near-princely powers in Friuli made their loyalty essential to Venetian interests, which
was precisely why the Venetians tolerated and humored them for
so long; but to many other Friulan castellans, their usurpations and
petty tyrannies made them insufferable.[13]

The Savorgnan, however, recurrently divided into mutually antagonistic branches. The repeated schisms of the Savorgnan and
many other Friulan clans illustrate a pattern commonly found in
societies with partible inheritance customs. Where the entire patrimony including castles, lands, livestock, liquid capital, water and
pasturage rights, rents, and levies belongs to the family as a whole,
conflict within the family, even violent conflict, is part of an inevitable and even necessary process that balances resources with
the optimal number of family members. The successful resolution
of tensions might become a source of future clan and family cohesion, but at the point of fission family conflicts disrupted other
social ties of patronage and clientage which normally brought stability to the society as a whole.

During the early sixteenth century, when the factional conflicts
of Friuli reached such a violent peak, the rivalry between the head
of the Savorgnan del Torre di Zuino, Antonio (1458–1512), and

FIGURE 3. Della Torre coat of arms in relief over the main
portal of the castle at Villalta.

the Savorgnan di Monte d'Osoppo, Girolamo (1466–1529), dramatically complicated the position of the clan, confusing the loyalties of the antagonistic factions and threatening the very survival
of Venetian dominion. One of the ironies of Friulan vendettas was
that while revenge assaults and killings were carried on in the name
of clan solidarity, many clans suffered deep internal antagonisms
and recurrent schisms that make a static portrait of the social structure deceptive.

Whereas the Savorgnan had enhanced their influence after the
Venetian conquest, the Della Torre had been among the principal
losers. The centerpiece of Della Torre clan identity became the
magnificent castle of Villalta (Figure 3). With the castle came jurisdictional rights in several villages in the environs and *livello* rents
from properties in twenty-two villages scattered among the surrounding hills. The patrimony also included rents from properties
in Udine and substantial holdings in Muggia. Just as the Savorgnan
had relied on their connections with Venice to further themselves
in Friuli, the Della Torre, especially after the Venetian conquest,
maintained ties with the imperial household in Austria.

Although both the Savorgnan and the Della Torre were lineages whose members recognized a common ancestor, their collective identities as clans were not foreordained. Aristocratic men and women found themselves tossed about by competing vortices of the clan, branch, sibling group, and nuclear family, any one of which could dominate under certain circumstances. The centripetal force of clan or branch cohesion strengthened under outside pressures such as vendetta or peasant rebellion, weakened when the death of the senior male brought the division of a patrimony, expanded its range with a marriage, and lost its power when a superabundance of sons or daughters placed strains on patrimonial resources. The clan and the family were dynamic processes rather than fixed structures and can only be understood in the historical context that forced members to make recurrent, often uncomfortable, choices.

The most important of these choices involved the selection of marriage partners. Knowledge of who married whom helps to fix the position of a family vis-à-vis its friends and enemies and to determine the composition of factions. According to traditional feuding theory, failed or ambiguous marriage alliances could cause animosities that resulted in vendetta violence, just as the end of a vendetta was often signaled by a marriage arranged between former enemies. The theoretical position might be summed up by the admonition to marry one's enemies. But this theoretical supposition about the relationship between feuding and marriage is not borne out by the patterns found in Friuli, in which major families practiced divergent marriage strategies that had important implications for the family's political position but did not characteristically bind together former enemies.

Factional endogamies can best be reconstructed from the alignment of Friulan families in 1511, from which one can determine who was on which side by establishing who killed whom in the Cruel Carnival. The two factions that evolved out of the rivalry between the Della Torre and the Savorgnan differed in their social composition, especially with respect to class. The chroniclers identify the Zambarlani as "all the citizens, all the plebs, and all the city [of Udine] with some castellans." The Strumieri, on the other hand, included "nearly all the castellans, a few citizens [of Udine], and some plebs." Thus, the Zambarlani followed a vertically arranged clientage system with the Savorgnan indisputably at the head, whereas the Strumieri largely consisted of an association of aristocrats who were at least formal equals. Because of the social differences between the factions, the Savorgnan and Della Torre followed distinct marriage strategies with regard to their followers.[14]

Of thirty-five Savorgnan marriages known for the period from 1420 to 1595, none was with families identified as Zambarlani in 1511. Such a finding supports the contemporary impression that the Savorgnan led a faction composed of subordinates from families unsuitable for intermarriage. The strongest form of endogamy in Savorgnan marriage patterns was within their own class of Friulan castellans, a group that produced twelve (34 percent) spouses. These endogamous marriages, however, created a feeble solidarity because most of the families thus allied to the Savorgnan joined the enemy Strumieri in 1511. Even more prominent were exogamous marriages, eight (23 percent) with Venetian patrician families and another twelve (34 percent) with neither Venetian nor Friulan families. Thus, more than half of the known Savorgnan marriages formed connections with families outside of the region, usually from the nobility of northern Italy. None was with Austrians.

Whereas the Savorgnan pattern of exogamies was an adaptation to the Venetian conquest, the more endogamous Della Torre failed to take account of the growing power of the Venetians, as the records of fifty Della Torre marriages between 1147 and 1420 show. In the late thirteenth and early fourteenth centuries, they habitually married among the seigneurial families of northern Italy—the counts of Gorizia and Ceneda, the Carrara of Padua, Soresina of Cortellana, Montefeltro of Urbino, and Della Scala of Verona. In the 1330s, after the tenure of Patriarch Pagano Della Torre, the strategy shifted to one of building connections within Friuli through marriages with other castellan families. Between 1333 and 1420 seventy-five percent of Della Torre marriages followed that endogamous pattern. Of the twenty-five known marriages in the post-conquest period between 1420 and 1511, seventy-two percent were with other Friulan castellan families and sixty-four percent of the total with castellans who were also members of the Strumiero faction. All of the remaining marriages were exogamous, mostly with high-ranking foreign noble families including the Este of Ferrara, Piatti of Milan, Sanguin and Fontellis of Paris, and the Thiene of Vicenza. The only Della Torre marriage into a Venetian family took place after 1511 when one of the sons of the murdered Alvise Della Torre married a Bembo.

The marriage practices of the Della Torre and Savorgnan evolved in opposite directions. From the 1330s through the fifteenth and early sixteenth centuries the Della Torre progressively contracted the geographic range of their marriage connections, becoming more endogamous and declining from a princely family that built alliances of equality among the lordly despots of Romagna, Lombardy, and the Veneto to an aristocratic family of merely local significance with no effective primacy in the region. The Della Torre confined their choices to a very restricted marriage market. In contrast, the Savorgnan progressively expanded their alliances to families in the dominant city of Venice and other towns in the Venetian terraferma while they still retained a strong commitment to other castellans within Friuli. The Della Torre acted defensively, the Savorgnan expansively and opportunistically. The Della Torre, moreover, employed marriage connections to create cohesion among their Strumiero colleagues whereas the Savorgnan avoided marriage to other Zambarlani.

The Friulan patterns parallel those Stanley Chojnacki found among the patrician families in early fifteenth-century Venice. The old families with the most prestigious lineages, the *case vecchie*, formed endogamous marriage alliances much more frequently than the *case nuove*, which were economically ascendant, or the subgroup of the *nuovi*, the *case ducali*, which dominated the highest public offices. Endogamies among old families enhanced the value of social prestige by making it more difficult to marry into them, but at the same time the more exogamous families had a broader range of commercial and political ties which expanded their influence and power.

The gathering of relatives, friends, clients, and allies at the signing of a nuptial contract and at wedding festivities generally served, of course, to solidify their relationships. However, the strengthening of such ties also provoked other clans because the very act of demonstrating collective vigor threatened not only traditional enemies but also anyone not included in the alliance. The mentality of social relations involved a kind of zero sum game in which a gain for one group must inevitably be seen as a loss for another, especially given the castellans' habits of class endogamy, which severely restricted the number of potential marriage partners.

Although marriages have traditionally been seen as a means of building group cohesion and especially as the way to finalize a peace among feuding families, such gatherings also brought out the potential for the feud to reemerge from the peace. Thus, both the Savorgnan and the Della Torre marriage strategies, but particularly the endogamous one of the Della Torre, created enemies as well as friends. The mixed lineage of the inhabitants of many castles and the castellans' characteristic endogamy also worked against a strictly bilateral kinship system that would have sustained distinct lineages and small, cohesive vengeance groups.

Even though the rhetoric of kinship obligations pervaded Friulan society, the fragility of clan structures necessitated the extension of revenge obligations to others who were not strictly agnatic kin. Ad hoc vengeance groups consisted of "friends," a broad category that might include affines and distant cousins as well as persons dependent in some way on the principals in the vendetta. Thus, vengeance groups and the larger factions built around them converged more along lines of dependence than of blood. Whether composed of equals allied through marriage or clients devoted to a powerful patron, both factions relied heavily on the familiars and servants (*famegli, buli, cani della casa*) of the noble lords, subordinates known elsewhere as *bravi* who played a significant role in the vendetta violence of both sides. Originally denoting the squires of knights in battle, the term *familiar* came to be applied to any armed follower of the great lords, and although most of these remain anonymous, those who can be identified primarily seem to have been foreign adventurers hired to serve the grand families. The familiars, often in conjunction with the young men of the aristocratic houses, perpetrated many of the most notorious acts of violence.

Each faction developed a public identity that could not entirely be separated from personal loyalties to Savorgnan or Della Torre but had its own form of representation. The origins of the terms *Zambarlano* and *Strumiero* are obscure, but the best informed contemporary diarist, Gregorio Amaseo, used them as local equivalents of *Guelf* (meaning in this case philo-Venetian) and *Ghibelline*

(meaning proimperial). The partisans of the two factions identified themselves with cheers, "Savorgnan, Savorgnan" countered by
"Struma, Struma" or "Torre, Torre," and a variety of fanciful insignia. Herbs, flowers, or ribbons worn over the appropriate ear,
on a hat, in the hair, on a shoe, or elsewhere served as declarations
of allegiance.

Beginning at least as early as 1468, the Venetian authorities recurrently tried to prohibit all signs of factional affiliation, but partisans invented new ones as soon as the old ones could be identified and made illegal. In May 1480 the provveditore in Cividale
decreed that no one could carry flowers or fern fronds of any sort,
wear blazons, or chant, "Strumer," "Zambarlan," or anything else.
The prohibition applied to all men, women, and children and
threatened a fine of 100 lire and four lashes for violators. The same
month an inhabitant of San Daniele was condemned for dressing a
child in a pair of shoes that had the signs of a faction on them. By
1482 the fine had doubled, and banishment for a year had been
added. Records for 1486 alone show that kerchiefs displayed in a
certain fashion had become a declaration of affiliation, the traditional arbor bows displayed at weddings were employed as insignia,
a servant of Ippolito di Valvasone went to prison for wearing a
carnation on the left side of his cap, and a hunchback was banished
for three years for carrying a vase of flowers on his hump. As futile
as their prohibitions may seem, the Venetians recognized that factions throve on a kind of street theater, where the display of large
followings could intimidate rivals and demarcate turf. Solidarity
had to be shown, publicly and provocatively, in part because without such demonstrations cohesion rapidly disintegrated, and followers reverted to the safety of ambiguous loyalties.

Although the Savorgnan and Della Torre vendetta evolved from
the feudal wars of the late patriarchate and revealed deep structural
contradictions in Friulan society, contemporaries saw the struggle
as an intensely personal affair among people with identifiable names
and faces, with known histories, and with acknowledged friends.
Vendetta was not just a social phenomenon for resolving group
conflict or a form of primitive justice but a medium of collective
memory, a way of structuring clan history around deeds of infamy
and of valor. Vendettas were stories.

The story of the Savorgnan and Della Torre vendetta began in

1339 when Ettore Savorgnan bought from a rich Udinese the castle of Ariis in lower Friuli. Because the Della Torre claimed to possess rights to the castle, they disputed the purchase, and Ermacore Della Torre defended his family's interests by attacking Ettore Savorgnan. By 1346 there had been several brawls between the two clans during one of which Ettore's nephew Pietro lost an eye. Ettore and Ermacore established the pattern that would be repeated again and again in the confrontations between their descendants when each accused the other of planning his assassination and of inciting the peasants.

In the period immediately after the Venetian conquest the Savorgnan and Della Torre lived in relative peace with one another. The quiescence after many years of endemic violence came as a by-product of a peace imposed by Venice, but it is also typical of long feuds for there to be cycles of violence, one phase of which can comprise many years of apparent reconciliation.

During the 1470s and 1480s, a phase of renewed violence started when disputes between the two factions arose which involved an expanded range of clients and friends including even the Venetian luogotenente. During these years the powerful and numerous Colloredo clan matched the Della Torre in animosity toward the Savorgnan. Despite the many ties forged by intermarriage between the Colloredo and Savorgnan, the clans split apart in 1470 when Ghibellino Savorgnan tore down the gallows that the lords of Colloredo and Mels had erected in various parts of their jurisdiction to intimidate the population. The bad blood between the two clans intensified after the Colloredo moved to Savorgnan-dominated Udine where, at about the same time, Tristano Savorgnan, accompanied by his familiars and some of his peasant subjects, attacked the Della Torre brothers during a carnival ball held under the loggia of the city council. By the time young Marin Sanudo visited Udine in 1483 the Strumieri and Zambarlani conflict had reached such a pitch that sections of the city were chained off to members of the opposing faction.

This series of assaults, accusations, and countercharges between the factions was probably precipitated by the destructive Turkish raids into Friuli between 1470 and 1478, which intensified the perpetual Friulan struggle over scarce material resources made scarcer by the raids. The incursions left the indelible impression of unbelievable horror brought on by Venice's long war with the Turks and the dominant city's unwillingness or inability to protect its provincial subjects.

After the Turkish army broke into Carniola and Istria in 1470, irregular bands began to make repeated raids from the Slovenian valleys, pillaging the land and enslaving the rural Friulan population. In 1472 the Turks crossed the Isonzo and blocked up the undermanned and unpaid Venetian army in a stronghold at Cervignano while they plundered right to the gates of Cividale and Udine where women and children mobbed the churches in search of refuge. The approach of the local militia of peasants, more valiant in taking to the field than the Venetian army, drove the raiders off.

In October 1477 a much larger force of Turkish foot soldiers crossed the Isonzo, defeated the Venetian mercenaries, killed or captured several of their captains, and, bypassing Cividale and Udine, marched as far as Pordenone, burning as it went an estimated one hundred villages. The eminent Friulan humanist, Marc Antonio Sabellico, witnessed the carnage from the safety of the castle at Tarcento and described how at night he could see a continuous line of flames across all of lower Friuli.

To divert the Venetians from their siege of Scutari the Turks sent an even larger force into Friuli the next summer, but the Venetian army and Friulan militias deflected the enemy into a circuitous and ineffective expedition into the mountains. In February 1479 Venice and the Ottomans made a truce that ended the immediate threat to Friuli.

Besides disrupting the local economy, causing widespread suffering, demonstrating the incapacity of the Venetian defensive system, and illuminating the irresponsibility of most of the castellans who only looked after themselves, the first Turkish invasion helped stimulate the development of an important new institution, the local militias or *cernide*. During the 1470s, under Venetian encouragement, the villages formed militias, elected captains, and began to drill. Even though these impoverished units often had little more than farm tools to use as weapons and were of limited military value, they built village cohesion by giving the young men some training in handling weapons and in drilling, and expanded the villagers' experience in autonomous decision making.

When the Venetians named a Savorgnan the head of the collective militias, the other castellans felt particularly threatened because they lost direct control of their peasant subjects, who were armed and drawn into the Zambarlano orbit. After the Turkish invasions, the Della Torre became increasingly strident in attempting to counter the perceived threat of Savorgnan-dominated militias.

As the focus of individual loyalties, the factions necessarily supplemented the lineages, especially given the diversity of Friulan settlement patterns, the weakness of clan cohesion, and the endogamy of most castellan families, all of which worked against a strongly bilateral kinship system. In many places the factions came to have a life of their own because individuals allied with one or the other faction to defend themselves against rivals in their own community, expressing animosities that had nothing directly to do with the Savorgnan-Della Torre vendetta. Joining a faction became a means for finding assistance from outside the community, and thus many persons involved themselves for their own reasons in the affairs of the great castellan clans.

The factions thrived from their ability to represent a diversity of interests and to give leadership to the expression of collective grievances. The elaboration of the factions had been activated by outside events, especially the Turkish raids. Even more powerful pressures from outside the region and the appearance of an extraordinary charismatic leader of the Zambarlano faction during the first decade of the new century created an explosive situation.

CHAPTER TWO

Approaching Thunder

The deep structures that had channeled most Friulan social and political disputes into the cultural ambit of vendetta kept the castellan clans in an uneasy balance for some eighty years after the Venetian conquest. However, during the first decade of the sixteenth century external pressures on the region conjoined with a serial crisis in agriculture to bring the factions to the verge of civil war. A youthful, charismatic head of the Zambarlani, Antonio Savorgnan, offered the artisans of Udine and Spilimbergo and the peasants from all over Friuli a leader who seemed to speak for them and who defied the other lords in a succession of public quarrels. His leadership created a vastly expanded network of Savorgnan clients among the peasants, who supported the Zambarlano faction as a means of resisting the escalating demands of Strumiero landlords. A renewed series of invasions by Turkish and then imperialist forces not only devastated crops and increased taxation to pay for the defense against the invaders but stimulated the growth and expanded the fighting experience of the militias, making them a potential armed threat to the knights of the Strumieri. Finally, grain prices fell precipitously over the decade, forcing landlords to attempt to wring more income out of their tenants and to solidify their control of markets. The peasants responded first with legal petitions to the parliament and Venice and then with a violent confrontation that resulted in the sacking of the castle of Sterpo in 1509, actions that reveal the desire among the well-off peasants to gain unrestricted access to the market economy of Udine. During this decade the Friulan factions became more militarized than before, in large part because of invasion and war, a development that intensified the potential for disruptive violence over local political and economic issues.

THE RISE OF ANTONIO SAVORGNAN

The most enigmatic of the enigmas of Friuli, Antonio Savorgnan became the greatest master of the agon of vendetta and its most celebrated victim. Beginning with the death of his father in 1500, his brief tenure as head of his branch of the Savorgnan and of the Zambarlano faction saw Antonio come closer than anyone else since the end of the patriarchate to establishing himself as the prince of Friuli, and yet his behavior could be quite erratic, his loyalties equivocal.

He had the singular advantage of looking like a prince (Figure 4). Although strong and robust, he had a head that seemed too large for his body, even when armored in breastplate. He wore his hair in the close-cropped fashion of the ancient Romans, a style he probably adopted during his student days in Padua, and his broad forehead appeared only more prominent as his hairline receded with age. His huge, aquiline nose and strong chin gave his face a certain angularity made severe by recessed, dark eyes surmounted by bushy eyebrows. He kept his beard short and always looked like a soldier, even though he was educated as a lawyer. The extant copy of his portrait depicts him standing dressed in full armor and pointing with lordly hauteur down at his subject city of Udine, shown in the diminished scale of distant perspective.

Contemporaries had strong opinions about him, and even in tempestuous Friuli his character was especially divisive, his reputation particularly threatening to his enemies. However, he was the only person, aristocrat or commoner, cleric or layman, ever to create a mass following among the peasants and artisans. His admiring nephew, Luigi da Porto, who would become one of the eminent literary men of his day, grew up in the Vicentino and

FIGURE 4. Drawing of Antonio Savorgnan.

as a youth went to Udine to serve his uncle. Luigi described Antonio thus:

> There was in Friuli a very great man of the house of Savorgnan whose authority in that region is still greater than any other, as is his name, called . . . Messer Antonio. Sustaining the Guelf cause, he is of such power in those parts that none of the other lords in Italy are greater in their own states than he nor do they have subjects who are so obedient as the Friulan people and peasants have been, and perhaps still are, to the aforementioned whom they hold in such veneration.[1]

Although widespread, veneration of Antonio was never universal even among those who had their own grievances against other castellan lords. Cividale, ever the archrival of Udine, felt especially threatened by Savorgnan's presumptions. The syndics and deputies of the city wrote to the doge of Venice complaining that "in all his duties he always conducts himself with little honor and intolerable damage to us and our subjects." They went on to ask the doge "to silence the said Messer Antonio so that he can no longer call assemblies of the people of this land or have the opportunity to agitate them as the head of anything, since in all the important enterprises he has always conducted himself poorly and shamefully and to our damage." The animosity of the city fathers of Cividale, however, might best be read as a measure of Antonio's power, inasmuch as they obviously felt threatened by his popularity among and leadership of the poor.[2]

Such was Antonio's influence that even his enemies attributed to him far more power than any man could muster. In their eyes he fostered all the evils of the age. Perhaps the most revealing example of their attitude is found in the magnificently malevolent opening sentence of Gregorio Amaseo's *History of the Cruel Fat Thursday and Other Nefarious Excesses and Horrendous Calamities That Occurred in the City of Udine and Patria del Friuli in 1511*:

In the time of the famous war made by the great league of the Supreme Pontiff Julius II, Maximilian the emperor-elect, Louis XII the king of France, and Ferdinand the king of Spain, Sicily, and Naples with all their allies against only the Illustrious Venetian Republic, the parties and factions of Guelfs and Ghibellines in the Patria del Friuli were inflamed and enraged, much more than they had ever been before, by the forceful instigation of Antonio Savorgnan, Doctor of Laws and son of Messer Nicolò the knight, who through his following of plebeian Guelfs of Udine and peasants of the patria and with all ingenuity and cunning promoted discord and hatred between them and the nobility of citizens and castellans so as then to be able to overwhelm his rivals and enemies and in that fashion to bring down the nobility so that there was no longer anyone who dared raise his eyebrows or open his mouth against even Antonio's slightest gesture, thus assuming for himself much greater impudence than authority, which had been conceded and permitted him on the occasion of that war by the Most Illustrious Signoria of Venice for a good end and with hope of improved results, especially to muster and supervise the militias of the patria, commanding and governing them according to his will, although then he followed completely the opposite end, that is doing no good and a great

deal of evil especially against his own compatriots, searching
to suppress all the rest and to exalt only himself, which was
the most powerful way to alienate the minds of the most faithful, seeing themselves to be more oppressed by the insolent
tyranny of him alone than by all the hostile army.[3]

Amaseo made his assessment of Antonio's character, however, after the lord's death when hindsight offered a certain clarity. At one
time even the vitriolic Gregorio had been a fawning follower of
Antonio Savorgnan.

Born in 1457, Antonio went to study at the University of Padua
at which he earned his doctor of laws degree in about 1485. Hardly
an intellectual, he seems to have been utterly indifferent to the fine
points of the law and to the new humanist learning, which capti-
vated some of his closest associates and his cousin, Girolamo. During his student days his mistress, a certain Paduan woman called
Chiribina, said to have been a nun, bore him a child named in
memory of the boy's grandfather Nicolò. Antonio never married,
and he recognized no other children.

Soon after his return to Friuli he began to represent Pinzano,
Ariis, and Osoppo in the parliament. In 1489 he served as a special
envoy to Venice, where he obtained the approval of new laws requested by the artisans of Udine and with the success of this trip
began to cultivate his reputation as the protector of the common
people. After his father died in 1500, Antonio inherited the leadership of the faction and the family's influence in Udine, where
nothing passed through the councils of the city without his consent
and where he found ample opportunity to exercise his fabled persuasive prowess: "He knew well how to change black into white,"
as Gregorio Amaseo described his rhetorical gifts.[4]

The Savorgnan legacy, however, was a mixed one because poor
management of the family's estates had heavily indebted heirs to
Venetian bankers. Revealing an estrangement from his cousins of
the Monte d'Osoppo branch, Antonio refused to accept full responsibility for these debts, arguing that his father had managed
affairs well and that uncles and cousins had contracted the obligations. But he also blamed the usury of the Venetians for his family's
plight:

And I, Antonio Savorgnan, doctor, with true testimony can tell it straight and have brought up the painful issues. I exhort and pray anyone who will ever read this memorial that if ever for any reason whatsoever he wants to buy anything whatsoever on credit in Venice or to stand surety for a living person in Venice, make any other bad deal and sell one's goods and portions of land rather than begin to take a loan in Venice, because I affirm that from 1475 up until today [July 12, 1500] Messer Tristano and brothers of the Savorgnan and my father have paid in Venice for various loans more than fourteen thousand ducats. And, moreover, in effect no more than eight thousand of these ducats counted toward the principal and the rest went to sterile cows.[5]

Despite their fabled riches in Friuli, the Savorgnan thus had a heavy burden of debt in Venice. Antonio's indebtedness bound him to Venetian policies just as so many peasants bound themselves to the Savorgnan through debt peonage. Probably more important than the formal jurisdictional lines between Venice and the Friuli were these informal and yet quite binding economic moorings that gave Venetian bankers a subtle means of influencing events on the mainland.

Thus, Antonio lived at the center of a vast web of financial, political, and personal ties which stretched from the highest councils of Venice to the peasant villages of Friuli. By 1501 he obtained from the luogotenente a blanket investiture of the fiefs he jointly possessed with his brother. He developed notably cordial relations with Pietro Cappello, who held office as luogotenente in 1506 and 1507, but his most influential Venetian friend was Andrea Loredan, who served in the same capacity in Friuli from 1507 to 1509. The careers of the three men intertwined through the difficult war years that followed. The two Venetians encouraged Antonio Savorgnan's ambitions and became something like Friuli specialists in the Venetian councils, furthering their own political careers through their standing in the troublesome but strategic region.

Cappello and Loredan seem to have been allies in their own right, and their careers moved notably in tandem. After Cappello's term as podestà in Brescia between 1501 and 1503, Loredan replaced him. In a similar way Loredan followed Cappello into the office of luogotenente of Friuli. Both enjoyed a nearly uninterrupted string of prestigious offices.

Cappello served on the Council of Ten or in the college of the Senate almost continuously between his service in Brescia and Friuli. After his return from Udine he held such offices as ducal counselor and *savio* of the college for four years without break, gaining a reputation as a pragmatist in planning Venetian war policy, especially for Friuli and Istria.

Loredan served as a *savio* of the college in 1505 and as a head of the Council of Ten in 1506 and again after his return from Friuli in 1509. Because he was only a very distant kinsman of Doge Leonardo Loredan, Andrea's career prospered not so much from his family connections as from his own abilities and fabulous wealth. During his term of office in Friuli, he earned a reputation as a "most active man" in both his capacity as a judge and as captain of the war effort. The members of the Savorgnan clan even chose him to arbitrate their family quarrels. He and Antonio Savorgnan personally lent money to the city of Udine to pay for soldiers during the campaigns of 1508. Loredan left Friuli with the best reputation of any luogotenente in memory; and in 1511, at the darkest moment as imperial troops closed in, Udine, Cividale, Portogruaro, and Marano sent delegations to Venice to request that Loredan be sent back to organize the defense. This request may have been the only time in centuries that Udine and Cividale agreed on anything.

After his return from Friuli, however, a nasty episode temporarily interrupted Andrea's career. On August 1, 1509, he became one of the three heads of the Council of Ten, the most powerful office in Venice, especially during the war crisis of that summer. Ten days later he was elected provveditor general for the Venetian military in Friuli, but he refused the new office "saying he was in the Council of Ten and a provveditor of the Arsenal" and would have to pay a penalty if he gave up the latter responsibility. In a second vote Francesco Cappello was elected. Nevertheless, four days later one of the state attorneys entered the council to remove Loredan from the ten because he had refused the election as provveditor to Friuli. Failure to accept such an position was against the law, and serving on the Council of Ten no excuse. The statutory penalty included a fine and deportation for six months.

In a personal appeal to the Senate Andrea insisted that he was ignorant of the law, but he was deported anyway—not abroad as the statute required but to the little island of Mazzorbo in the Venetian lagoon where he could stay in contact with political events and entertain friends in his accustomed lavish style. Twice during the deportation allies tried to arrange deals for his freedom, but threats to penalize them as well ended such proposals. Shortly after Andrea's return to Venice, the Great Council elected him to a new office, and by October 1510 he was back on the Council of Ten with his old colleague Pietro Cappello.

Loredan had apparently become used to getting his own way in elections and had made powerful enemies who knew how to use the law against him. Moreover, he was not as enthusiastic about returning to Friuli as the Friulans were about having him there.

Andrea Loredan was certainly not afraid to employ his wealth to promote his own political career. In the election of the podestà of Padua held by the Great Council during November 1510, Andrea came in second in the balloting. Sanudo reported, however, that as the nobles filed into the council hall before the election many stood on the stairs offering bribes in return for votes, and supporters of Loredan were among the most actively involved. The diarist commented that it was "with the greatest shame to the city that in these times when the state has been lost, they made such offers. First of all, in this solicitation for the Padua job one clearly sees that corruption is at a peak and the old families are ambitious. God help this republic; it really needs it!"[6]

A blunter, rougher man than his refined friends from Venice, Antonio found in Andrea Loredan if not a kindred spirit, at least a powerful acquaintance who acted almost as imperiously in Venice's highest councils as did Antonio in Udine's. Antonio would find Loredan's friendship very helpful when the Friulan attempted his *coup de main* against the Strumieri. For his part Andrea stuck by Savorgnan, barely avoiding the destruction of career that befell other Venetian patricians under Antonio Savorgnan's spell.

Antonio's power in Friuli can be measured in many ways: through his domination of the most important deliberative institutions, his range of friends and clients, his reputation as the protector of the poor, and his ability to call upon thousands of armed citizens and peasants. In the 1503 meeting of the Friulan parliament he had four and one-half votes (for Carnia, Pinzano, Osoppo, Ariis, and he shared the vote of Udine with Rizzardo Fontanabuona, one of his partisans). His close associate, Francesco Janis di Tolmezzo, who had been a law student at Padua with Antonio, also controlled three votes. Almost continuously on the Council of Udine, he ranked first on the list of deputies and between 1505 and 1511 proposed legislation more often than any other person.

In most matters, Antonio usually got his way. He pushed through the election of Giovanni Monticolo as chancellor of the commune over the objections of the notaries who quite properly pointed out that Monticolo had not been admitted into their guild. But since Monticolo was Savorgnan's man, he got the job. In 1507 Antonio advocated the reform of the statutes of Udine according to the principles followed in Padua, Verona, Brescia, and Bergamo, and the council accepted his proposal without dissent but never put the reform into effect because of opposition from Venice.

During the first decade of the century, Antonio created a close-knit cadre of factional associates, many of whom were well-placed members of the elite of Udine, and carefully nourished the loyalty of the artisans and plebeians through his advocacy of legislation and reforms that served their interests. As early as 1490 he intervened to support the free market sale of wine, thus breaking the aristocratic monopoly on profits made in its trade. Many of his proposals attempted to alleviate famine and to improve the quality of food available. He proposed that the city buy fodder during a shortage in July 1494 and advocated prohibiting the sale of wheat, millet, and rye to foreigners or to Venice during a later famine. During a meat shortage in 1504 and 1505, Savorgnan accused the butchers of selling at elevated prices meat fit only for dogs and banned the marketing of meat from sick cattle. The next year he accused the guild bakers of selling poorly cooked, nearly rotten bread made from black flour, which had damaged the health of the poor; to improve the bread supply he proposed that the city set up a communal bakery in addition to granting free licenses to private bakers who wanted to compete with the established guild bakeries. Finally, it was Antonio who paid the communal physician to inspect medicines sold by pharmacists to guarantee their quality and Antonio who insisted that the school master accept as students the sons of the artisans and common people without payment.

Savorgnan's advocacy for the poor of Udine built a vast following without costing him much personally because in most cases the financial burden of his reforms fell on the commune. Maintaining the loyalty of peasants, on the other hand, was an entirely different matter inasmuch as his own economic interests and theirs were inevitably opposed, especially in light of the debts Antonio had inherited. Nevertheless, on general policy matters regarding agriculture, even where his own finances could suffer, he backed the peasants over his fellow lords. In 1501 and 1502 he spoke up in defense of the peasants against new taxes and obligatory public work obligations for military purposes imposed by the Venetians, and in 1503 he involved himself in a vicious struggle with the other castellans in the Friulan parliament over their attempts to require tenants to make improvements to their leaseholds without compensation.

In advocating reforms Antonio introduced a new strategy of cultivating clients among the peasantry which contrasted with Savorgnan family traditions of lordship which were far from magnanimous. In 1488 Antonio's cousin Tristano di Pagano had demanded a larger than usual *decima* on wine from the peasants in Vito d'Asio near Osoppo, a demand that precipitated a minor rebellion after which several tenants were beaten and imprisoned. On his own estates, in contrast, Antonio seems to have been a relatively gentle landlord, a fact that enhanced his reputation among the peasants. His motives were not so much benevolent as calculated to acquire clients. Given the absence of any institutional alternative to the system in place, Antonio's personal reputation helped considerably in establishing him as the leader of the peasant movement.

Antonio's policies toward his tenants emphasized the bonds of clientage over economic advantage. During the agrarian crisis of the early sixteenth century he loaned money with great liberality and no rigid expectations of repayment, a policy that allowed peasants to survive during a period of depressed agricultural prices and to counter the effects of a rural rent structure that overvalued the productive capacity of the land. Although Antonio's profits suffered, the loyalty of his followers intensified. In examining the rent-rolls for Antonio's landholdings in Buia, for example, one finds a very high level of personal indebtedness to him. Between 1500, when Antonio became the lord of Buia at his father's death, and 1508 the levels of tenant indebtedness increased steadily, in part because of the poor harvests and disruptions of war but also because Antonio tolerated unpaid debts. In 1508 one peasant had ten outstanding loans. Most of these were advances of wheat, rye, oats, and millet made in June just before the harvest, but there were also loans of wine, straw, tools, shoes, and pieces of cloth.

Antonio's paternalism, in effect, subsidized his tenants during the most difficult parts of the year and maintained a policy of repayment which contrasted sharply with that of other castellans, such as the neighboring Colloredo, whose rent-rolls have been studied. Savorgnan certainly knew what he was doing because the rent-rolls list a monetary value for all commodities and quote current market values of both loans and repayments in kind. His estate managers, therefore, had a keen sensitivity to the market economy and to values as determined by price, but they did not exploit these loans to make a profit. By lending to tenants and others on such a vast scale, Antonio acquired dependents rather than profits. Despite the systematic record keeping and other modern techniques, his practice was closer to a potlatch than a business enterprise. Antonio's loan practices redistributed wealth, revealing an objective more social than economic, the accumulation of what might be called social capital, which would have been squandered by precipitously demanding timely repayments.

Besides his advocacy of popular issues in the councils of Udine and the parliament of Friuli and the easy credit he made available to his tenants and followers, Antonio cultivated the rural militias more systematically than any of his predecessors. Venice's 1487 decree naming Antonio's father, Nicolò, the permanent captain of the Friulan militias provoked a riot when it was read in the parliament because the other castellans could easily envision the extraordinary power the Savorgnan would acquire from such a position. But Nicolò had never made his captaincy a reality, and the militias existed largely on paper until the wars of the first decade of the new century, when Antonio transformed them into a private army.

Antonio's opportunities came from changes in military practice stimulated by the Swiss victories of the late fifteenth century and the invasion of King Charles VIII in 1494. The Swiss example encouraged the integration of mercenary troops among soldiers recruited from the local population with an eye to providing professional officers for the militiamen. Venice called these units *ordinanze* and commissioned an officer, the *contestabile*, for every one hundred men and a corporal for every twenty-five. Because recruits were not paid in peacetime, the only incentives to join came from the exemption from labor services such as carting and work on fortifications, the opportunity to obtain weapons, and whatever rewards or punishments local recruiters or a lord such as Antonio Savorgnan could offer.

Antonio and his cousin Girolamo came to monopolize the recruitment of militiamen so that in 1510 when Venice tried to create its own *ordinanza marchesca* in Friuli quotas fell short because the available men had already enrolled under the Savorgnan. Militiamen performed admirably on occasion but were prone to desert at harvest time or when their home villages were threatened. Later in the century a Venetian rector observed that not even "another Mars" could discipline these ragged bands, and although Antonio Savorgnan succeeded in bringing together hundreds of men from many villages, he was no Mars himself.

Estimates of the number of men Antonio could muster varied greatly from five hundred to six thousand, but a reasonable guess might put the maximum ever in the field at about fifteen hundred. Supplies for the peasant militia often came from the larders of Antonio Savorgnan himself, as can be seen in 1508 when he lent flour and wine to the communes of Buia and Maiano to provide for their men leaving for Gorizia on the campaign. In July 1509, when foreign armies controlled much of the terraferma dominion, Venice could spare only two hundred extra mercenaries to defend Udine. In addition to these professionals, fifty artisan militiamen were available to guard the castle of the luogotenente, leaving the manning of the town walls to the peasant militias. Savorgnan mustered the peasants at two locations in the environs of Udine, but during a heavy rain many of them wandered away. Evil rumors spread panic among those who remained. One peasant who was on the run told Leonardo Amaseo that he was fleeing not because anyone was actually chasing him but out of fear that someone would.

Amaseo commented, "it is a bad business to defend the patria with peasants, and this comes from bad government." The next spring Antonio called up a huge but undisciplined horde to expel the enemy from the castle at Cormons, but they performed with little honor and fled in the face of any opposition.[7]

However unsuccessful their efforts against foreign enemies, the militias under Antonio Savorgnan altered the balance of factional forces in Friuli. In building up the militias he not only relied on his own peasants but made clients out of the feudal subjects of his traditional Strumiero enemies. Although recruits from the tenants of the Strumiero lords may have considered their adventures away from their home villages dreary, they learned how to follow a leader other than their landlord, one who did not demand forced labor or extra rents and who might even provide a weapon, food, and wine. In causing the peasants to step outside of their normal social roles for a brief period and experience a certain autonomy, a certain breath of freedom, the wartime musters created a liminal state, which contributed to the vast uprising of 1511. Although we have no direct information about Friuli, in other regions of Europe militia companies usually also acted as festive companies, organizing carnival revelries and often initiating riots, as the Friulan militias would do in 1511.

Liminal states and liminal groups—those periods such as festivals and those persons such as young soldiers who had not yet acquired the responsibilities of adult life—often stimulated reform in premodern Europe. By participating in liminal experiences promoted by Antonio Savorgnan, the peasants of Friuli began to build bonds outside of their own villages. They became a rebellious political force, the Zambarlani.

Antonio Savorgnan's expansive incorporation of artisans and peasants into the Zambarlani disturbed not only the Strumieri but also his equally ambitious cousin Girolamo. Hindsight has produced stark contrasts between these two men: Antonio the cruel, wicked, and audacious tyrant whose character opposed Girolamo's, the pious, heroic, and faithful "paragon of true soldierly temperament." But matters were hardly that simple. The tensions between them were, in many ways, the inevitable result of the clan's inheritance patterns, which forced them to share large parts of the Savorgnan patrimony. Each struggled to carve out of this collectivity his own portion, creating a rivalry that intensified during the wars with the empire. Both instinctively served Venice, but neither was above making overtures to the emperor when it seemed useful. Both relied on the same circle of men for their principal servants and allies. Whereas Antonio's chief aid was Francesco Janis di Tolmezzo, Girolamo's was Francesco's brother, Giacomo, who even suffered imprisonment in Girolamo's service. Both Savorgnan captained their own companies in the militia. In 1509, as a reward for their service to Venice, they jointly received the fief of Castelnovo, a possession that soon drove them apart because Girolamo felt slighted by Antonio's quick grabbing of booty and ransoming of prisoners who surrendered with the castle's conquest.

Until his death, Antonio remained the dominant figure of the two. His personality, which was sometimes courageously magnanimous, especially toward his clients, and sometimes treacherously mean-spirited, his constant calculations of advantage and disadvantage, and his arrogant ambition help explain the intensity of the factional struggle during his lifetime. A clash between the Zambarlani and Strumieri may have become highly likely because of the conjuncture of war and an agrarian crisis, but the timing of their battles, not to say the intensity and form of their violence toward one another, had a great deal to do with the elusive character traits that made Antonio Savorgnan a brilliant and yet deeply flawed leader, the only Italian nobleman of his age to guide a mass movement of peasants, a movement that would produce the greatest conflagration in Friulan history.

INVASIONS, 1499–1509

While Antonio Savorgnan was making himself a prince without title, a storm was gathering over Friuli. Unresolved and opposing legal claims to the patriarchate and the disputed division of the region into territories occupied by Venice, the empire, and the counts of Gorizia, who remained closely tied to the Hapsburgs, had been building pressure since 1420.

Two new developments released the pressure. Maximilian Hapsburg's grandiose ambitions lured him to reassert imperial rights in the regions of northern Italy conquered by Venice. At the same time the Turks attacked Venetian possessions on several fronts. Friuli was the only place among Venice's far-flung lands which suffered assaults by both of the republic's enemies. The Turks laid waste to the countryside in 1499, and before recovery could take hold, Emperor-Elect Maximilian and Venice escalated their conflict by moving from clandestine interference in the affairs of each others' dominions and border skirmishes to open warfare.

Until these wars, the most important of the empire's enclaves in Friuli were Pordenone in western Friuli, Latisana and Belgrado on the lower Tagliamento, Castelnovo in the mountains north of Spilimbergo, and Codroipo southwest of Udine on the road to Venice (see map, "Friuli in the Sixteenth Century"). Also outside of Venetian control was the county of Gorizia, which dominated the Isonzo River valley and extended westward to include Cormons and southwestward to Aquileia itself.

The counts of Gorizia and many of the Strumiero castellans had feudal or marriage ties that enmeshed them in a web of anti-Venetian loyalties. As early as 1438, the luogotenente prohibited Venetian subjects from accepting titles, offices, or positions from the counts, and in 1467 the Senate forbade feudal investitures from them; but the lure of Gorizian and imperial fiefs continued to nourish Strumiero hopes for the removal of the Venetians.

The proximity of the enclaves facilitated employing them as refuges for those banished from the Venetian dominions, making it profitable for the Austrian *gastaldi* who administered them to welcome exiles in return for a fee. Assassins found these enclaves particularly convenient because if they could manage to ambush an enemy close to a border, a secure haven might be only a few steps away. Pordenone, situated in the midst of the western plain without any natural borders, was particularly notorious as a roost for bandits, with those exiled from Venetian Friuli living in the town and others exiled from imperial territories congregating on the Venetian side of the border in the castles at Porcìa, Torre, Cusano, and Zoppola.

When Count Johann of Gorizia died in 1468 the county passed to his son Ludwig, who lived in Lienz because he feared the Turkish threat to Gorizia. Insecure and unlikely to leave an heir, Ludwig agreed to cede Gorizia to Maximilian Hapsburg in exchange for safer lands across the Alps, a transfer that intensified the legal and military confrontation in Friuli between Venice and the Hapsburgs.

The Venetians argued that the county had been a fief of the patriarch of Aquileia, and therefore should pass to them when Count Ludwig died no matter what he himself desired. Venice's case was based on the fact that after the conquest of the patriarchate the doge had invested Ludwig's ancestor with the county in a grand public ceremony in San Marco. By participating in the investiture ceremony the count had recognized the republic as his feudal lord. Pope Alexander VI supported Venice's claim, pointing out that fiefs can not be reassigned by vassals. Maximilian, on the other hand, argued that the German emperors had originally invested the patriarchs with their territories, which the Venetians had illegally usurped. By insisting on irreconcilable positions, the two sides committed themselves to a fight.

In the summer of 1499 Venice focused its attention on an invasion of Milan planned with its new ally, France. The enterprise enfeebled the eastern frontier defenses despite recurring reports in August of numerous imperial detachments in the vicinity and rumors from Bosnia that a large Turkish force anticipated invading Friuli as soon as the weather cooled off. On August 26 a delegation of Friulans spoke to the Venetian college of the Senate about the very poor condition of Udine's fortifications and the lack of sufficient troops to defend against the expected Turkish assault. But with offensive ambitions elsewhere, Venice was in no position to offer any assistance. On September 28 a force of more than ten thousand Turks camped outside of Gorizia. Sanudo recorded a rumor that they had with them thousands of huge attack dogs, two or three for every man, a story that spread panic. Crying for help, peasants from the surrounding countryside flocked to the Venetian fortress at Gradisca, but the provveditor, Andrea Zoncani, refused to help, saying reportedly, "I don't want to get myself killed." Except for a few stradiots who disobeyed orders (probably because their own families were threatened) none of the Venetian forces put up the slightest resistance when Skander, the Turkish general, and his troops entered Venetian Friuli.

The invaders formed a fifteen-mile-wide front of infantrymen who advanced to the Livenza River, destroying or looting everything in their path and spreading panic as far as the Marghera ferry stations to Venice. Reports of the numbers of their victims are untrustworthy, but the figures certainly imply massive devastation: twelve hundred slaughtered at Cordenons, one thousand killed in a field outside of Roveredo, two thousand massacred or taken prisoner from the Aviano district. The village of San Martino outside of Aviano lost 420 of its 500 inhabitants. Near Valvasone the Turks put to flight a poorly armed and even more poorly led company of peasant militiamen and brought back some 260 heads on their lances. Detachments of Turks lingered around Valvasone for four days, and while the nobles locked themselves up in their castle, approximately five hundred of their subjects hid in woods and ditches. During the night two bands of Turks rode up to the castle gate and plumbed the depths of the moat but found it too deep to ford; lacking the necessary artillery for a siege, they were forced to retire. Before recrossing the Tagliamento, Skander divided his captives into two groups in anticipation of a final sickening spectacle: the young men and women who could be sold into slavery were taken away, and the remaining old people, estimated at between fifteen hundred and two thousand, were beheaded on the banks of the river. After an investigation, Venetian officials estimated that during the eight-day rampage the Turks killed or captured more than ten thousand people and burned 132 villages. This singularly horrible invasion etched itself in the collective memory of the Friulans. The village of Vigonovo, for example, continued to mourn its dead every year on September 30 until late in the nineteenth century.

The results of these terrible eight days can hardly be overestimated. Some of the peasant villages in the Turks' path never recovered. As the ensuing decade brought increasing fiscal demands both from the landlords and the Venetians, many villagers found themselves faced with starvation, others were forced to give up their leaseholds, and many gravitated for protection to the Zambarlani of Antonio Savorgnan. The Venetians' failure to provide efficient frontier defenses undermined confidence in their leadership, particularly because they seemed to be locked in a permanent struggle with the Turks, who could again assault Venice by invading Friuli. The empire was at peace with the sultan, a fact that made Maximilian's claims to Friuli ever more alluring to his local supporters.

Even before the Turkish invasion, a Friulan castellan with a humanist education, Jacopo di Porcìa, composed a learned critique of Venetian rule in Friuli, *De reipublicae Venetae administratione*. Porcìa advocated the complete reorganization of the Venetian military in particular by rejecting the reliance on mercenaries along lines Machiavelli would later recommend for all Italy. Porcìa followed the feudal traditions of his family and class by arguing that experienced Friulan knights be systematically integrated into the forces and preferred over young, inexperienced Venetians. However, despite the merits of Porcìa's views, Venetian politicians completely ignored his advice and relied even more on mercenaries and the Savorgnan militias.

In addition, until the Turks came to terms in 1503, their continued threat prevented Venice from countering Maximilian's intrigues in Friuli. When Count Ludwig finally died on April 12, 1500, Maximilian sent representatives to Friuli to seize his inheritance, and the Venetians, still faced with rumors of another Turkish invasion, did nothing to stop them. The initiative and the lands of Gorizia thus slipped out of Venice's grasp. The way was now open for Maximilian to act out his fantasy of reviving the German empire of Otto the Great by using Friuli as his base for the reconquest of imperial Italy, lost so many centuries before to the Lombard League. In both Venetian and Austrian Friuli factions were encouraged by the trouble brewing between La Serenissima and Maximilian. Even the castle at Gorizia was divided into two parties when the imperial counts arrived to take possession after the death of Ludwig.

Antonio Savorgnan, dismayed by the arrival of the Hapsburgs on his doorstep, pointed out that the prospect of Austrian domination frightened the peasants in particular because they assumed that an imperial victory would lead to a reintroduction of serfdom. The same prospect encouraged the Strumiero lords. At the Treaty of Blois in 1504 Maximilian and King Louis XII of France secretly agreed to conquer and divide up the mainland territories of Venice, and concentrations of imperial forces in Villach alerted Venice to an impending invasion throughout 1506 and 1507. Maximilian requested permission to make an armed march through Venetian territory on his way to Rome for his coronation. Venice refused and amassed its forces in the Veronese, anticipating an invasion through the Brenner Pass.

War came in early 1508 resulting in a quick Venetian victory in the Cadore and, after a brief siege, the capture of Gorizia itself.

The imperial enclaves of Pordenone, Castelnovo, Codroipo, and Belgrado fell as prizes to the victorious captains, including the Savorgnan cousins.

Although Venice celebrated a stunning victory, several signs already foretold future troubles. Despite new revenues from the conquered towns, the cost of the campaign and the expenditures necessary to defend the new territories put Venetian finances under a tremendous strain. Supporting the army in 1508 consumed one fifth of the entire Venetian state budget even though the campaign had been relatively brief. As early as May, Antonio Savorgnan and Andrea Loredan had to pay out of their own pockets the troops of Francesco Sbroiavacca to keep the men fighting for another month.

Maximilian, the one truly humiliated, began to plot his revenge. On December 10, 1508, he and King Louis of France signed a treaty in Cambrai which broke the truce with Venice of the previous June. Soon after, the marquis of Mantua, the duke of Ferrara, Pope Julius II, and Ferdinand of Aragon joined the new league, officially formed against the Turks but secretly designed to divide up the dominion Venice had conquered during the previous century. The treaty assigned spoils in advance to each signatory. Among other spoils Maximilian would get Friuli.

When news of the League of Cambrai arrived in Venice, the government undertook hurried preparations in an attempt to stave off the inevitable, but on May 14 disaster struck. The French crushed Venetian forces at Agnadello. Bartolomeo d'Alviano, one of the victors for Venice the previous year, was taken prisoner. As fast as the news could spread, town after town capitulated to the enemy, and in a few days Venice lost almost all its mainland empire. Excited by the news, Maximilian proposed to go beyond the treaty by taking the city of Venice itself and dividing it into four quarters to be administered by the four principal allies in the league.

Venetian forces regrouped for a strategic withdrawal to the edge of the lagoon, and a nervous Senate voted to abandon without further fighting more than thirty-six subject towns. Such defeatist behavior did not encourage Venice's supporters on the mainland, and until the Council of Ten seized the initiative and began to dictate a new policy, towns such as Verona, Vicenza, and Padua stayed in the enemy fold.

In Friuli imperial troops recaptured the towns lost the year before and ranged throughout the countryside without opposition, threatening to besiege at any moment the cities remaining in the Venetian camp. Imperial heralds approached the walls of the fortified cities and demanded that they send representatives to Padua to make a formal submission or face sacking and burning. Udine remained loyal despite the abject fear felt throughout June and July. The Savorgnan, Della Torre, and many others sent their wives and movable property to the safety of Venice. On June 14 rumors of a pending attack spread waves of panic through the city. We are told that the populace began to run hither and yon through the streets, fighting among themselves with sticks and clubs. As soon as calm prevailed in one area another tumult broke out elsewhere. Five or six times during the night a suburban village's tocsin rung in response to approaching phantoms, echoed in Udine by a call to arms. Fits of fear became so common that Luogotenente Giovanni Paolo Gradenigo was forced to decree on the twenty-eighth that "the first person who speaks about surrendering to the king of the Romans, no matter what social position he has, will be hung, and whoever accuses him will have a one-hundred ducat reward from the public treasury." The general nervousness seriously undermined the discipline necessary to defend the city when the enemy finally did arrive. A false alarm or even a drunken brawl would draw militiamen in the direction of the noise, abandoning the gate they were assigned to guard. To protect their palaces, the great families brought in heavily armed *bravi* who aroused the suspicions of the citizens worried that their city might be betrayed from within.[8]

The situation was just as bad if not worse in Spilimbergo, where the deep distrust between the consorts and the citizens led each to suspect the other of betrayal. Leonardo Amaseo recounted in his diary "that all Spilimbergo turned upside down. There are evil people everywhere."[9]

The uncertainties of the spring and summer of 1509 opened an extraordinary period of internal disintegration in Friuli which lasted for more than two years. All the social tensions between peasants and castellans, between Zambarlani and Strumieri, between Antonio Savorgnan and his many enemies, and between Venice and its Friulan subjects came into the open. The war introduced the possibility that the whole system of patronage and allegiances would be changed by an imperial victory, which would certainly have meant the destruction of Antonio Savorgnan and his friends, unless, of course, they switched to the imperial side first.

As the external controls by the Venetians loosened from the spring of 1509 to the winter of 1511–12, Friuli became a society governed almost entirely by its factions and serves, therefore, as a revealing historical laboratory for the scrutiny of vendetta and factional relationships. During this period, Friuli suffered from cycles of violence, generated by the internal logic of vendetta, which alternated periods of fearful social tension with demonstrations of pacification and unity. The war often quickened the periods of tension, and the Venetians tried to draw out those of domestic peace. But the cycles had a life of their own, often operating quite independently of the pressures of war and the policies of Venice.

The first signs of renewed factional conflict appeared in June, when many castellans, despite their assurances of loyalty to Venice, conspired with the imperialists, inhibited the Venetian defense, or abstained from fighting. Most, in fact, never took up arms until it appeared as though the Austrians might be defeated. Soon after the fall of Padua in June, Antonio Savorgnan presented the luogotenente with a list of castellans whom he said had been dealing with the enemy and should be sent to Venice for the security of the patria. The list included the houses of Colloredo (except for Camillo), Mels, Strassoldo (except for Giovanni), Candido, Gorghi, Arcoloniano, Brazzacco, Cergneu, Frattina, Zucco, Cucagna, Partistagno, Bertolino, Castello, Soldonieri, Sbrugli, and Guarienti and the individuals Martino Valentinis and Francesco Pavona. Among the great families of the Strumieri the only names missing were the Della Torre, who were left off, according to Gregorio Amaseo, because Savorgnan knew the list was a fraud and he did not want "to put too much wood on the fire the first time around." Later in the summer, however, his cousin Girolamo, who had no reason to make Antonio look good, implicated Alvise Della Torre in treasonous activities. Despite Amaseo's opinion, the list has a certain credibility, especially given the decidedly tardy appearance of these castellans on the field of battle. Nevertheless, the traitors named were all Antonio's personal Strumiero enemies, and one cannot blame the luogotenente for having some doubts about Savorgnan's motives.[10]

Quite unlike his predecessor Andrea Loredan, who had be-
friended and defended Antonio, Giovanni Paolo Gradenigo suspected the Strumieri less than the Zambarlano leader himself. Late
in June a rumor spread that Antonio's brother, Giovanni, had gone
to negotiate with the imperialists. In response some nobles attempted to elect a citizen to govern Udine over Antonio's head,
but a member of Antonio's inner circle, Giovanni Monticolo, sabo-
taged the election. Even the Austrians' failure to attack Udine for
so long was attributed to Antonio Savorgnan's supposed dealings
with them. Instead of forwarding Savorgnan's list of purported
traitors, Gradenigo wrote to the Council of Ten about his own
suspicions of Antonio. The council replied that although it appre-
ciated the luogotenente's vigilance,

> every day we see and understand the actions of the above men-
> tioned Lord Antonio we neither are persuaded to believe
> these charges nor do we expect from him anything that is not
> faithful and that does not conform to that which he and all his
> house have always shown and done for our state. And this
> single doubt should not permit you to show any ambiguities
> and suspicions about his faithfulness to this patria because it
> could well push him to some thoughts alien to his nature and
> disposition, which would be dangerous for the following he
> has in the whole patria.

The council thought the rumors about Antonio originated with
his enemies and ordered, "you must use every sweet and kindly
office with the said Lord Antonio in such a way that he knows that
we and you love and admire him." Although Gradenigo repeated
his suspicions, the council again warned him against alienating the
head of the Savorgnan clan in any way. Given the ambiguity of the
situation in Friuli, the confidence of the council in the loyalty of
Antonio Savorgnan seems remarkable, even foolhardy, but it recognized better than Gradenigo that Venice had few alternatives to
trusting Antonio given the strain on its military resources. Moreover, Antonio's friend and patron, Andrea Loredan, was on the
council that summer, and his influence in defending Antonio was
undoubtedly strong.[11]

While imperial and French armies roamed almost at will across
Venice's mainland territories and Friuli disintegrated into its com-

ponent parts, the Venetians worried about what had gone wrong. There were many diagnoses, some of which were not far off the mark. Girolamo Priuli confided to his diary that the attack and failure to defend the mainland dominion were the fault of his fellow patricians. They had been victims of their own arrogance, which had led them to neglect justice, live in a splendor fed by bribes, avoid civic duties, rely on mercenaries rather than fatigue themselves in mastering the arts of war, indulge in sexual exploits with nuns and young boys, and search for the easy life in country villas rather than bear the hardships of maritime trade. Although some mainlanders, such as Luigi da Porto, were fatalistic, blaming the stars and indecipherable fortune, most critics from the terraferma were inclined, at least in their first reactions, to blame the Venetians themselves, echoing Priuli's themes of haughtiness, pride, and obliviousness to the truth. Despite the fact that some saw precisely what had gone wrong, reforms faltered, and Venice stumbled through the next eight years of war, separating its enemies from one another by either bribing them or playing upon their mutual suspicions.

The Pillage of Sterpo

While the Venetians agonized over their own failings in provincial administration and international diplomacy which had brought on the disaster of 1509, a peasant uprising took place in Friuli in July of the same year. The uprising, which culminated in the burning of Sterpo castle, was fueled by an agrarian crisis that began with the Turkish invasion of 1499 and was sparked by the War of the League of Cambrai. The disruptions of the war finally permitted the peasants from this tiny village and its environs to confront their lord in a way that anticipated the more general agrarian revolt that was to occur in 1511.

One needs to distinguish between the agrarian structures that had impoverished rural Friuli for centuries and the more immediate precipitants of the violent attacks on castellan property and privilege. The ubiquity of malaria, absence of irrigation projects, frequent flooding, lack of roads and bridges, indebtedness, and manifold financial exactions from foreign overlords had plagued the region for centuries. During the fifteenth and sixteenth centuries high taxes on milling forced many peasants to haul their grain long distances to one of the exempt mills in the imperial enclaves, the patriarchal towns of San Vito or San Daniele, or the Savorgnan fief at Belgrado. Although these long-term conditions produced a rural economy with little ability to cushion crises, they did not alone stimulate rebellion. However, during the first decade of the sixteenth century, several other kinds of developments made some kind of rural disturbance likely. First, a dramatic drop in agricultural prices prompted landlords to increase income from agrarian holdings by monopolizing access to markets and guaranteeing control over the labor force, actions that led to a growing insecurity of tenure for leaseholders. In addition, war pressures forced the Venetians to increase fiscal and work obligations and rural billets for mercenaries. And finally the Zambarlano faction under the leadership of Antonio Savorgnan offered some kind of redress of grievances.

Although peasants had been threatening violence against the castellans since at least 1503, no actual attacks took place until 1509 when peasant militiamen destroyed the little castle at Sterpo, an imperial fief granted to the Colloredo lords and surrounded by Venetian territory. Perhaps second only to the Savorgnan in the extensiveness of their holdings and closely allied to the Della Torre through several marriages, the Colloredo clan took its name and collective identity from the vast fortified complex at Colloredo di Monte Albano in the morainic hills. Like the Savorgnan, they held properties both in the Carnic alpine valleys from which they collected mutton and cheeses and in various places on the Friulan plain which provided them with grains, poultry, and wine. Unlike the Savorgnan, however, they owned little in Udine besides their palace.

The lands of Albertino Colloredo's branch were concentrated among the marshes on the left bank of the lower Tagliamento. The Colloredo also held six jurisdictions including Sterpo, all located on the lower plain. In 1502 Albertino obtained from his grandfather Febo Della Torre additional lands, the fortified house, and landworks in Sterpo; in 1508 he conceded them to his own son, Teseo. They remained in Colloredo hands until 1959. Because Sterpo was a fief of the count of Gorizia, Albertino carefully arranged to have Emperor-Elect Maximilian ratify Teseo's succession. During the campaign of 1509, moreover, Albertino and his

FIGURE 5. Sterpo; moat and castle rebuilt after 1509.

son Odorico both served with the imperial forces, more openly declaring their allegiance than did most of their fellow castellans; Odorico died in 1510 fighting at Cormons on the imperialist side. The open affiliation of Albertino and his sons with the emperor became one of the principal motives in the 1509 assault, which combined an act of war with a rebellion over economic grievances.

A document drawn up in 1502 for the imperial court describes Sterpo (Figure 5). Situated on wooded land between the Bua and Roia, streams which converged just below it, the castle had a circle of walls, themselves encircled by a moat fed by a ditch from the Bua. The only entrance was through a tower that guarded a bridge over the moat and the Roia. The modest castle buildings consisted of a cooking shed with attached pigeon roost, a three-room house with two roof terraces, a barn, and a minuscule chapel. The haphazardly built defensive works were uneven in height and strength. On the chapel side of the entrance tower the walls consisted of an earth embankment that merged into a more substantial wall of stone and rubble. Between the barn and the house there were no barriers at all, but in the final section between the house and the entrance tower stretched a foot-wide wall about five or six feet high. Outside the walls on one side a natural swamp had been excavated to make a deep pond, and on the other the moat was deep enough to prevent both men and horses from wading across. The water barriers formed the real protection from intruders, and the uneven walls seem to have been intended to provide cover from shot and bombardment. Outside the moat a second, higher circuit of walls offered some safety for the people of the village and their animals, and if the additional, partially finished towers, walls, and ditches had been completed there would have been better security and more room for livestock. Near these walls clustered a handful of rough-hewn, thatched hovels for the tenants. As insubstantial as these fortifications may seem, during the Turkish invasion of 1499 they succeeded in providing a refuge for the peasants and livestock from many nearby villages.

Compared with the grander castles of the hill country around Udine, humble Sterpo must have appeared almost ignoble. The swampy, mosquito-infested terrain and the climate, miasmal in summer and murky cold in winter, offered few allurements for pleasant living. Sterpo's principal attraction came from a location that made it a convenient place for gentlemen to stop over on the route between Udine and Venice.

Nevertheless, in the seven years before the peasant rebellion Albertino Colloredo and his sons attempted to transform Sterpo into the centerpiece of a more unified estate, even into a local market town. They required peasants from their widely separated properties to cart their rent payments to Sterpo, to mill their grain there (in an open challenge to the nearby Savorgnan mills at Belgrado, which charged cheaper rates), and to fulfill most of their *corvée* obligations in improving the fortifications and ditches around the castle.

When rents came due in 1509, the Colloredo tenants faced a

disaster. Barely more than one in ten had harvested enough to pay a full rent, and about two thirds would pay nothing at all that year. The precise motives for failure to pay in 1509 are hidden behind laconic notes in the rent-roll: "agreed that he need not pay," and the more common phrases, "he owes past rents," "he owes for last year," "he owes all the past rents," "she owes," "he owes," "they owe."

Payments had been trickling in right up to the day of the assault, but many tenants were obviously not going to be able to pay. The military situation, however, provided both an excuse and the necessary organizational structure and leadership for measures against the landlords. The rural militias under the general captaincy of Antonio Savorgnan had been called up during the month in anticipation of the imperial army's siege of Udine.

On July 14 under the pretext of needing to drill, a company of militiamen attempted to gain access to the castle at Valvasone, but a wary lord raised the drawbridge against them and ordered them to drill outside in the village streets. On July 30 Asquinio and Federico Varmo brought several hundred militiamen from Belgrado and Ariis to imperial Sterpo on the pretext that they needed to search the castle for munitions reportedly stored there to aid the enemy. Asquinio and Federico were influential leaders of the militias of the lower plain and well-known as clients of Antonio Savorgnan. Three of Antonio's closest associates, Ippolito Valvasone, Francesco Cortona, and Vicenzo Pozzo, joined the local forces. Although Belgrado and Ariis were Savorgnan jurisdictions, Albertino Colloredo had at least eighteen tenants in Belgrado and environs, but of course there is no way of knowing if any of them joined the militiamen at Sterpo. In any event, the leaders told the militiamen that Albertino Colloredo was a "rebel and had assembled a great deal of munitions to requisition to the enemy for use against Saint Mark." At the time only Albertino's son, Nicolò, and four retainers manned the castle. When they saw the peasants approaching, they raised the drawbridge quickly enough to block entry. Negotiating across the moat, the Varmo captains apparently convinced Nicolò that they merely wanted to search for weapons and would not harm him or the castle, but when he lowered the bridge, the peasant militiamen swarmed across. They seized the tower, sacked the castle, and set it afire. During the following days they and other local peasants tore the remains down to the foundations. Nicolò was captured and taken as a prisoner to Udine.[12]

The destruction of Sterpo castle permanently ruined the Colloredos' plans for the village. The rent-roll of 1513 notes "that the castle, mills, and houses that were in that place were ruined at the time that the nobles were persecuted by the peasants." Soon after the event Gregorio Amaseo estimated the damage at ten thousand ducats, but in 1530 when the heirs were finally able to submit claims for restitution, the estimate increased to fifteen thousand. The 1530 document lists as destroyed the castle "ruined down to its foundations," two towers, one mill, a house for the overseer, and other houses. Taken as plunder were 400 *stazi* of wheat, 100 of rye, 160 of spelt, 111 of millet, 13 beds, and blankets, sheets, table linens, wine, carts, cattle, horses, pigs, geese, and a deep-red cloak lined with the fur of a marten.[13]

Just as dramatic was the decline in the number of Colloredo tenants after 1509, a decline revealed by tracing the names of tenants from one rent-roll to the next. In Sterpo proper the number dropped from 29 in 1509 to 13 in 1510 and 1512 and only 6 by 1513. In the surrounding villages the number also lowered precipitously from 129 in 1509 to around 80 in the following years. But most of the tenants who disappeared from the Colloredo rolls were the least successful farmers, many of whom had obtained leases on marginal, perhaps newly cleared land. In fact the expansion of the number of leaseholds in Sterpo between 1502 and 1509 may indicate that the Colloredo were usurping parts of the common land for arable, which is precisely what the peasant syndics had been charging for years.

The Colloredo lost nearly all that they had acquired at Sterpo, not only the castle fortifications and their own houses, but much of the income from their tenants, this at a time when their military obligations to the empire left them hard-pressed for cash. In the other villages, as in Sterpo, many of those who had owed back rents and who were burdened with debts disappeared from the rolls, and it seems likely that these indebted peasants, relegated to the inferior or smaller leaseholds, were the ones who looted and destroyed Sterpo castle and the rent-rolls listing their debts. Nevertheless, someone, perhaps Nicolò Colloredo himself, escaped with the 1509 roll, from which the situation can be reconstructed.

Although Luogotenente Gradenigo condemned the attack and conducted an investigation, the Venetian signoria tacitly excused it, probably because Albertino Colloredo was a public rebel and the leaders of the assault had Antonio Savorgnan's protection. No one ever suffered punishment. The Strumieri vainly demanded justice, and the Colloredo pursued legal channels to have their jurisdictional rights reestablished. About a year later, Pope Julius II excommunicated those who had pillaged Sterpo, but inasmuch as Sterpo lacked a priest no one suffered much from the distant indignation of His Holiness.

The attack on Sterpo castle, however, had wide-ranging effects in Friuli. Their success in challenging the Colloredo helped the peasants better articulate their needs and emboldened them to put together a list of demands, presented to the luogotenente in November. Sterpo also represented a crossing of the Rubicon for the Friulan factions. Both sides later looked to this event as the beginning of an almost inevitable slide into factional civil war.

The peasants' November demands, the Eleven Articles or "supplication from every village in the patria," broaden the picture of general rural discontent of which the attack on Sterpo was only the most violent example. First, the most pressing demands of the twenty representatives who spoke before the luogotenente concerned the distribution of the Venetian *gravezze* and other taxes, which they argued were corruptly collected by deputies who made the peasants bear an unfair portion of the burden. Pointing out how loyal they had been in opposing the enemy during the past year, how they had shed blood and lost their property, they requested that a chancellor be appointed at their own expense to audit the accounts. Second, they complained that frequently the luogotenente had required them to sell their grain to him at a fixed price but later he would resell it at a higher price, defrauding them of any chance to make a profit. Third, they requested that there be a limit to the amount that itinerant judges (*gastaldi*) could charge communities when they came to represent the luogotenente in court cases. Fourth, notwithstanding the many prohibitions to the contrary, they wanted the right to sell bread, wine, and other necessities at market prices in their own villages. Fifth, noting that many lords had usurped the commons for their own use, thus making it impossible for the peasants to graze their animals, they asked that these communal lands be returned to their original state. Sixth, many villages had suffered considerable expenses when soldiers had passed through in transit, and these villagers wanted some consideration in the distribution of future taxes. Seventh, other villages had been pillaged by the stradiots serving Venice, and these victims deserved compensation. Eighth, some villages on the east side of the Tagliamento had already been given exemptions from some taxes because of storm damage to their crops, but the luogotenente had ignored these exemptions, which they wished to have restored. Ninth, inasmuch as many persons in the countryside were indebted to Jews from Udine who had sent out agents to confiscate collateral at a time when repayment was impossible because of the war, the peasants wanted one or two accountants paid by the debtors to examine the books and calculate the debts. Tenth, because many poor peasants had been paying extraordinary taxes, had borne the expenses of the war, and more often than not had lost their crops to the enemy, they wanted a moratorium on paying debts, "except for payments they wanted to make." And last, because some creditors had even sequestered crops in the fields of debtors, the peasants wanted all creditors to be required to go to court before they could confiscate unharvested crops.[14]

The Eleven Articles of the Friulan peasants are almost exclusively concerned with short-term economic problems engendered by the war and attempts to gain fuller access to the markets. In every case, they demand justice and fairness, envisioning practical reforms of society rather than a turning of the world upside-down. Theirs is a conflict within the social system, an attempt to make it work for themselves. Moreover, the complaints in the Eleven Articles are mostly about abuses by Venice and its agents—the luogotenente, his *gastaldi*, and soldiers fighting Venice's wars—or by the merchants of Udine, especially the Jewish bankers. The only antifeudal provision is the perennial complaint about the alienation of commons for private use. Thus, in many ways these articles represent a set of problems which did not entirely correspond to the situation in Sterpo. The burdens of indebtedness and the ravages of war were the same, but the articles address issues that would have been most important to the substantial farmers and independent peasants who sold produce on the Udine market and who dominated the village assemblies that wrote up the list of demands. The small cottagers of Sterpo who risked slipping into the fetid pool of day laborers suffered more from the exploitation of the Colloredo lords than from the bureaucrats of Venice and bankers of Udine and had to rely on their own collective force rather than legalistic petitions.

The articulate authors of the Eleven Articles, however, anticipated the peasants and townsmen who launched the great rebellions in the south Tyrol and upper Swabia during the 1520s and who went beyond their Friulan fellows by employing religious language to envision a different, more godly society. Protestantism provided a new law by which to measure the world. In contrast to the famous rebels inspired by Luther, neither the rebels of Sterpo nor the supplicants to the luogotenente made even the most conventional references to God, the Virgin, the saints, or the Bible. Their mental horizons limited what they thought could be done because no common religious or ideological aspirations bound together these various peasant groups, each with divergent economic grievances. But Antonio Savorgnan did. Speaking of all the castellans of Friuli in the aftermath of Sterpo, a contemporary commented, "the men of their jurisdictions do not want to obey their lords any more, and they recognize no other lord than Messer Antonio Savorgnan." The idea of a loyalty based on personal choice rather than tenant obligation was a revolutionary new concept, akin to the doctrine of election in its effect on the peasants. The peasants and their leader freely entered into a reciprocal relationship of mutual help which undermined the traditional hierarchy of feudal society. By giving shape to the peasants' desires, Antonio Savorgnan promised the only kind of salvation imaginable in Friuli, the salvation of revenge.[15]

CHAPTER THREE

The Tempest of 1511

The gradually intensifying pressures of the Savorgnan-Della Torre vendetta, the polarization of the Zambarlano and Strumiero factions, the turbulence of war between Venice and the League of Cambrai, and the accumulated economic grievances of the Friulan peasants merged to create a terrible tempest during the carnival of 1511. What began as a clash in the streets of Udine between the followers of Antonio Savorgnan and the youthful enthusiasts of the Strumieri rapidly spread beyond the city and became the largest and most destructive peasant uprising in Renaissance Italy. The composite sources of the violence, finally let loose by the gathering for a festival of thousands of armed men, produced oddly hybrid forms of violence, in which participants improvised murder and mayhem, pillage and arson according to the ritual structures of vendetta practices and carnival.

Under the factional leadership of the Zambarlani, crowds in the city collectively murdered the Strumiero leaders whereas in the rural areas the faction soon dissolved into its component communities. There rioters pursued their own specific grievances against individual Strumiero landlords and limited themselves to pillage, arson, and a few rapes. The complexity of the forms of violence and the specificity of the objects of attack reveal how opportunity had created a strange coalition of Friulans who acted in concert not so much because they shared common objectives as because they shared a common culture of violence and found their mutual enemies suddenly vulnerable. After the Cruel Carnival the fragile Zambarlano hierarchy quickly disintegrated from the centrifugal forces of its own violence. The vendetta-revolt of 1511 followed more the logic of violence than the leadership of men or the dictates of a political agenda.

GIULIETTA E ROMEO

Since the Sterpo assault, "all the poor castellans have stayed in their castles in great fear," as a contingent of Strumieri put it, "anxious not to be cut to pieces by the peasants and burned out as happened at Sterpo." The threat was not an idle one. In March 1510, peasants from Zompicchia, led by the militia captains who had been at Sterpo, attacked Alvise Della Torre, the Strumiero leader, and other castellans on the road from Venice where they had gone to complain about Antonio Savorgnan. Although the Strumieri escaped, the incident provoked several days of street fighting in Udine. Commenting about Venice's inability to pacify the factions after the Zompicchia confrontation, Gregorio Amaseo wrote that "one could accurately say that the lovely state of Venice lost her virginity on this one." [1]

With the Strumieri and Zambarlani testing and accusing one another, Antonio Savorgnan threatening a coup, and the enemy pillaging the countryside, ravished Venice allowed great pressures to build up in Friuli. An inept shuffle of provincial administrators did not help matters much. In October 1510 the latest vice luogotenente, Antonio Giustiniani, who had "in the turbulent past and dangerous times" earned a high reputation for himself back home, asked to return to Venice to take up a new position on the Council of Ten. Granting his request became problematic when the luogotenente himself, Alvise Gradenigo, who had been recovering from wounds received at the siege of Cividale in 1509, announced he could not yet assume his office. Despite the misgivings of a few, the Senate agreed to make some temporary arrangement. It sent Giustiniani's brother Orsato, without salary, expense account, or title, to govern Friuli until Alvise Gradenigo could resume his duties. During his brief stay Orsato failed to keep the disputants under surveillance.[2]

When Alvise finally arrived in Udine during the first week of the new year, one of the saluting cannons misfired, injuring five men, an accident "reputed by all to be the worst portent, as subsequent events would show." That very day, partisans of one faction killed a miller from the other. Gradenigo issued the usual New Year's decree against petty crimes such as blasphemy and impersonating priests and friars, to which he added provisions designed to prevent factional violence, such as orders against assembling without permission, assisting exiles, carrying weapons at night, and fighting. Public officials, surgeons, and gravediggers all had to report any injury or death that came to their notice. The government made its intentions clear, but that was about as far as it could go. In fact, the luogotenente faced the rapid deterioration of public order and lacked sufficient time to reestablish the delicate personal ties necessary to hold together the capricious collectivity and to keep the factions from one another's throats.[3]

In January when Venice finally lured Pope Julius II into a separate peace with a rich bribe of salt from the Comacchio beds, Venetian politicians relaxed with a false sense of security. Although the new peace brought some quiet to the southern front, Maximilian's mercenaries raided eastern Friuli with impunity from their winter quarters in Cormons and Gorizia. They specialized in nighttime sorties that terrorized helpless civilians, plundering, murdering, and burning whole villages while the Venetian army slept safely in garrisons and refused to go out on night patrols because of the difficulty of tracking the enemy in the dark. Even though the damage was limited to a small area, the surprise appearance of probable death and certain ruin, one night here the next there, thoroughly panicked the peasants and demoralized even those protected by city walls. Officials sent numerous letters and a delegation to Venice to plead for assistance, and finally on February 3 Giovanni Vitturi was promoted to provveditor general. On February 11 the Udine city council voted to send him on retaliatory strikes against the Cormons raiders.

During the months of Venice's weakness and inaction each faction built up its forces. "Occasioned by that war, during which the authority of the glorious state of the Most Illustrious Venetian signoria ceased because it was overwhelmed," commented the diarist Gregorio Amaseo, "everyone took license"; they "were prompted to push the government around and to abuse their adversaries." Antonio Savorgnan, or so his enemies asserted, provoked matters during the *interregnum* between luogotenenti by hiring fifty *bravi* in Venice and elsewhere and sending them to Spilimbergo to assist his followers there against exiles who were returning with forged safe conducts. The prickly castellans of Spilimbergo reacted quickly, secreting into their towers during the night two hundred peasant retainers from Zoppola and Fanna and securing the city gates. The *bravi* managed to talk their way out of town and retired to Udine where they spent their time swaggering about and daily provoking Savorgnan's enemies.[4]

Toward the end of December, the *bravi* killed a Strumiero retainer, and on New Year's Eve Nicolò Maria Caporiacco, a member of Nicolò Colloredo's company, was assaulted and murdered in his own house. On Epiphany the Savorgnan thugs happened upon the unarmed, sixteen-year-old Francesco Candido, attacked him, and chased him into the courtyard of his father's palace. The Epiphany outrage prompted Teseo Colloredo and Sebastiano Monfalcone, perennial mainstays among the Strumieri, to hire their own squad of fifty foot soldiers.

On January 25 Antonio Savorgnan, feeling secure and knowing that the Venetians needed him more than he needed them, tried a daring bluff. Claiming that the four leading Strumieri—Giacomo Castello, Alvise Della Torre, Teseo Colloredo, and Francesco Cergneu—"undoubtedly await Mysia and the coming of the Germans and are the worst enemies" of Venice, Savorgnan asked the signoria either to remove them or him from Friuli. Otherwise, he warned, the peace could not be maintained. Ignoring his advice, Venice exiled no one, encouraged all of the principals to reconcile themselves, and implored them to unite against the common enemy. His bluff having failed, Antonio and his retainers left Udine on February 15 to avoid a confrontation during the dangerous carnival holidays and went to Marano where, following a request from the Council of Ten, he was to supervise work on the fortifications.[5]

While he was gone, both sides continued to build up their forces, each claiming that whatever it did was merely for its own defense.

Strumiero brigades formed under the leadership of the Candido, the Brazzacco, the Sandanieli, the Frattina, Sebastiano Monfalcone, and Francesco Pavona. The most noteworthy, however, were Teseo Colloredo and Nicolò Della Torre, who strutted about Udine with a band of forty men brandishing weapons, "bragging, and threatening." Giacomo Spilimbergo put together a force of five hundred infantrymen and fifty cavalry to defend his relatives and friends, and throughout the land people commented on the fact that in time of open war the castellans had failed to provide any contributions of soldiers but now found it so easy to put armed companies together.

For his part, Antonio Savorgnan sent his favorite, Dr. Francesco Janis di Tolmezzo, back to Udine to organize the Zambarlano artisans and to gather a large company of peasant militiamen and followers to be billeted in Chiavris, a village on the outskirts of Udine in which the Savorgnan operated one of their mills. The ostensible reason for the mobilization was to guard the city against Austrian raiders. Other groups of Savorgnan supporters gathered in San Daniele, Venzone, Spilimbergo, Cividale, and elsewhere. On Sunday the twenty-third the luogotenente in Udine desperately tried to prohibit anyone of any rank from carrying arms day or night, but despite the assertion that the edict would be enforced "without respect of any person," no one was arrested.[6]

It is difficult to tell just what the factional leaders, let alone their many followers and friends, had in mind in these days before Giovedì Grasso. Later, with benefit of hindsight and under the necessity of justifying themselves, each side would accuse the other of following out a prearranged nefarious plan. Apologists for each charged the other with elaborate conspiracies devoted to taking advantage of Venetian irresolution and to fulfilling ancient dreams of total revenge.

The situation was, in fact, far less starkly clear. Charges of conspiracy were in part outright fabrications and in part self-delusions, guesses filtered through prejudice about what the others must have been up to. At the beginning of the week each faction looked toward Giovedì Grasso, the principal carnival day of revelry, as the time when the throngs of outsiders gathered to feast and play in Udine would give the other side special opportunities. Everyone wanted to be prepared for the worst. Although the events that followed could hardly have been fully planned by anyone, they could not have been entirely accidental either. Two pieces of evidence, a letter supposedly written by Alvise Della Torre and the surprising success of the Zambarlani, point to foreknowledge that there would be some sort of showdown on carnival Thursday.

On Tuesday the twenty-fifth there was no overt violence, but brigade after brigade of armed peasant militiamen marched through town chanting "Savorgnan, Savorgnan" in open violation of Gradenigo's decree and in obvious provocation of the Strumieri. Many citizens hastened up the hill to the luogotenente's palace and urged him to do something. In the meantime, Antonio Savorgnan, forced, he said, by pleas from his friends that as long as he stayed away the entire populace of Udine was unprotected, returned from Marano accompanied by only five retainers. He knew "for certain" that the Strumieri conspired to kill him, but "wanting to come back to town in order not to lose reputation during the present war," he alerted some of his subjects along the way, and when he arrived in Udine a great gathering of followers protected him. He immediately conferred with Gradenigo to explain his reappearance, and although Antonio wanted first to consult with the signoria in Venice, the luogotenente insisted that he disband his followers immediately and accept a peace with the Strumieri. Antonio finally agreed, asking only to defer the peace pact until the next day. The luogotenente also convinced the Strumiero leaders to dismiss their men and join in a pact.[7]

By Wednesday a large crowd of outsiders, mostly Antonio's peasant clients and militiamen armed and ready for combat with someone, had arrived in town. Mingling with local artisans, they were unlikely to disband quietly and leave the city the day before the most Dionysian festival of the year. Antonio knew this. In an attempt to make the peace pact work, or so he later swore, Antonio invited about one hundred citizen and artisan leaders to his palace to persuade them to join him in an honest peace with the Strumieri. At sunset the luogotenente gathered the deputies and elders of Udine in one room, Antonio Savorgnan and his friends in another, and in a third the Strumiero leaders, Alvise and Nicolò Della Torre, Giovanni and Giovanni Battista Candido, Teseo Colloredo, Francesco Cergneu, Giovanni Leonardo Frattina, and Sebastiano Monfalcone. After separately haranguing each group, Gradenigo brought the

principals together to solemnize the peace. They embraced and
kissed one another on the mouth in front of a group of distinguished witnesses. It is not certain that the host was broken and
shared at this peace ceremony, creating the "terrible obligation" of
Florentine peace pacts, but the pledge was a serious matter, and
those who blamed Savorgnan for breaking it thereafter called him
Antonio Iscariot.

The pact may not have been, as partisans of both sides later
claimed, an empty ritual that masked the devious intentions of
some of the participants, as much as an utterly inadequate resolution of a perilous situation. Alvise Gradenigo had neither guaranteed the safety of anyone nor had he the manpower to divide up
the many dangerous groups and force them out of the city. And
that very night the Austrians mounted another raid.

During the evening the leaders of each faction gathered separately to assess the prospects for a lasting peace and found themselves pessimistic about the chances that the other side would keep
the pact it had sworn to preserve. To some, the peace may have
just bought time, but none could have avoided the appearance of
keeping the peace. Antonio Savorgnan, at least formally, dismissed
his followers. One of these, Sebastiano Vicentino from Paperiano
near Fiumicello where Antonio had some properties, later testified
that he arrived that day with twenty armed men and went to the
Savorgnan palace. He recalled that after the peace Antonio's son
Nicolò thanked them for their support and announced that in the
morning they were to go home. They were then billeted out for
the night. Antonio seemed sincere about the peace, but he sent
a message to the luogotenente asking him to advise Alvise and
Nicolò Della Torre and Teseo Colloredo to leave town the next
morning and to spend carnival on their estates to prevent any "outrage," indicating that he must have known that even if he had
wanted to, he could not control his followers. Unfortunately none
of the three lived to confirm whether or not he received any warning from the luogotenente.

That evening, however, witnessed a sweet interlude. The Savorgnan clan, their friends, and guests gathered for a ball that lasted
late into the night at the house of Maria Savorgnan, widow of
Girolamo's brother Giacomo and sometime mistress of the famous humanist, Pietro Bembo, who was also a mentor to Luigi da

Porto, the nephew of Antonio Savorgnan. Singing to the accom-
paniment of a clavichord, a rare sixteen-year-old beauty cast a de-
licious spell over the evening. Even sour Gregorio Amaseo interrupted his long invective against the Judas Antonio to recall her
enchantments, and at least one young soldier fell in love with her,
probably on that evening. She was Maria and Giacomo's daughter
Lucina, the second cousin of Antonio. The love-smitten soldier
was da Porto, who had already earned local acclaim for his courage
in the guerrilla skirmishes against the imperial mercenaries on the
eastern frontier and would later achieve lasting fame for his literary
and historical writings. Luigi was close to Antonio, who had entrusted the youth with delicate and difficult missions.

As Cecil Clough has cleverly argued, the memory of this magical evening, framed as it was by anxiety and blood, became the
seed for a great story. Years later, half-paralyzed by a battle wound
from which no one thought he could recover, Luigi sat in his villa
in the Vicentino and wrote a *novella* about love and hate set among
the towers of Verona, which he could see from his convalescent's
window. He titled it *Giulietta e Romeo*. Shakespeare, of course,
would later transform Luigi's story into a far greater play. He dedicated the *novella* to none other than Lucina Savorgnan, by then
married off to another of Antonio's nephews, Francesco, and the
dedication barely disguises in Petrarchan dress Luigi's lost love for
her. Perhaps in memory of his mentor's past love affair with Lucina's mother, he sent one of the first copies to Pietro Bembo for
comment.

Although da Porto's *Giulietta e Romeo* was a literary creation
rather than disguised history, and fortunately neither Lucina nor
Luigi met Juliet's or Romeo's fates, their separation was a sad and
probably inevitable one. Although they were not members of opposing factions as were the star-crossed lovers, they belonged to a
badly divided clan; Girolamo Savorgnan was Lucina's guardian,
and Luigi had the misfortune to meet her when his uncle and patron Antonio's relations with Girolamo were at their nadir.

During the evening the Strumieri celebrated carnival with a banquet hosted by Alvise Della Torre. In an after-dinner palaver Francesco Cergneu recommended that each lord remove himself to his
country castle as the best way of guaranteeing safety and as the
only way of making the peace work. Francesco was an unlikely

pacifist; unlettered and quarrelsome, he was known for his soldierly abilities, having commanded the reluctant feudal cavalry at
the defense of Udine in 1509, and for his animosity toward Antonio Savorgnan, who in turn described Francesco as "seditious,
wretched, and beggarly." [8]

The voice of reason which he uncharacteristically offered was
quickly hushed. Opposed to Francesco's counsel was Teseo Colloredo, who had first hired foreign *bravi* back in January and who
arrived that evening with a large company of armed retainers. Both
Francesco Cergneu and Teseo Colloredo included themselves in
the inner circle of leaders around Alvise Della Torre, and each had
his own constituency. Teseo argued that he would not allow himself to be dishonored by fleeing, and he soon convinced the others,
isolating Francesco, who reluctantly agreed to stay.

That night Alvise Della Torre wrote a letter to report the news
of peace to the lords of Spilimbergo, who still waited at their castle
with a large following of *bravi*. Later the letter became the critical
piece of evidence used to document Strumiero bad faith. Everyone, even partisans of the Della Torre, accepted its authenticity. In
it Alvise abused the Zambarlani and minimized their threat: "this
beast of Antonio Savorgnan . . . has been put to such flight that he
does not dare show his face." According to the letter, although
Savorgnan brought eight hundred peasants in by various roads,
when he saw how well prepared the Strumieri were he ran to the
luogotenente to beg for a peace. Alvise, averring that he himself
had accepted the peace only for convenience's sake because he did
not believe it would last long, asserted that the other side wanted
it not only as a deception but to gain reputation. Finally, warning
the Spilimbergo lords to keep their eyes open and to stand united
with him because their mutual enemies wished to rob them of all
power and honor, Alvise offered the military services of his own
friends and servants. Alvise entrusted the letter to a servant of
the Spilimbergo lords, who was to slip out of Udine when the
city gates opened at dawn. Neither messenger nor message ever
arrived. [9]

THE CRUEL CARNIVAL OF UDINE

The next day was Giovedì Grasso. In normal times gluttonous,
drunken Fat Thursday was the favorite festival in Udine, but in-

stead of playing light music, as Giovanni Battista Cergneu would later put it, the Udinesi gathered for war. Antonio Savorgnan would also later recall several Strumiero predictions of a slaughter for that day, declarations of intent which shifted blame from himself to the victims of the massacre. It was reported that public physician Leonardo Gubertino, a passionate devotee of the Strumieri, had said a few days before, "I have studied this matter and I find that on Giovedì Grasso there will be revenge by massacre which in Udine will be extensive, and many people will be killed." The recollections of others suffered from the excessive appositeness of hindsight. Former grand captain of Udine and future prisoner for treason Giovanni Candido declared on Thursday morning that his enemies "long to have a delightful Giovedì Grasso, but they are going to eat the bitterest fritters they have ever eaten in their lives." And finally but least probably the *enfant terrible* of the Della Torre clan, Nicolò, declaimed as he slipped on his woolen gloves to go outside on the last day of his life, "today we are going to have a Sicilian Vespers." [10]

The Strumiero prognostications alluded to the faction's own alleged plan to help imperial troops capture the city while the Zambarlano militiamen debauched themselves in festive revelry. There is some evidence to support the idea of a Strumiero conspiracy with the imperialist captains. Antonio Savorgnan cited several witnesses who reported that one hour after sunrise fifteen hundred enemy cavalry and infantry equipped with ordnance appeared outside Pradamano. Their captain asked among the peasants if the gates of Udine were guarded and if riots had broken out yet. Many others repeated this intelligence uncritically, but Strumiero survivors always denied any such conspiracy and even accused Antonio of having plotted with the enemy.

To counter the supposed imperialists' threat, Antonio called out the militiamen and his other followers, a combined company of twenty cavalrymen and an estimated fifteen hundred armed infantry who sallied forth from the Aquileia gate to meet the enemy (Figures 6, 7, and 8). The ringing tocsin closed the shops and brought artisans to arms at posts on the outer walls of the city. After wandering about for some three hours and failing to engage anyone, the militias returned to Udine and as they entered the gate chanted, "Savorgnan, Savorgnan."

In the meantime Alvise Della Torre's messenger to Spilimbergo had been captured, and the letter secreted in his boot was brought to Savorgnan, who hurried with this document of insult and possible bad faith to the luogotenente. While the two were conferring they heard a tumult rise up from the city below.

Most of the Strumiero nobles had already gathered at Alvise Della Torre's palace for another banquet or returned there when they heard that the messenger to Spilimbergo had been captured. Nicolò Della Torre joined his uncles Alvise and Isidoro; Teseo Colloredo and Francesco Cergneu, who had debated on strategies the night before, were there together with Giovanni Leonardo Frattina and his nephew Apollonio Gorghi; Giovanni Battista Candido, the cousin of Nicolò Della Torre; Antonio Arcoloniano; Sebastiano Tomasi di Monfalcone and his son Felice; Agostino Partistagno and his four sons Ercole, Girolamo, Francesco, and Alessandro; Francesco Guarienti and his son Troiano; young Bernardino Pavona; and others, mostly youths, boys, and retainers. Outside a pro-Savorgnan crowd of between two and four thousand, consisting mostly of artisans and plebs from Udine but also including about three to eight hundred peasants, surrounded the palace and began a siege that wore on for hours until the defenders escaped. The crowd then plundered and burned the palace; later some twenty-one witnesses would testify that they saw looters take out a large chest full of money and carry it to Savorgnan's house.

Meanwhile in the vicinity of the burning palace a manhunt began for the escaped Strumiero nobles. The leaders of the hunt included several "attendants and dogs of the house of Savorgnan": Giovanni di Leonardo Marangone di Capriglie called Vergon ("lime-twig," a stick smeared with a sticky substance made from holly bark and used to catch small birds, was a nickname applied to a deceitful, predatory person), Bernardino di Narni, Guglielmo di Marco Floriti da Venzone called Tempesta (the storm), Giovanni Pietro Fosca, Zuanetto di Pietro del Pizol called Il Piccolo (shorty), Matana (stingray or in Venetian a migraine headache), Smergon (loon, which was noted for its ability to dive into water to escape hunters, was used as a nickname for a crafty person), Viso (the face), and "the Ferrarese."

The blame for much of what followed fell on the heads of these men because either they served as useful scapegoats or they were act-

Noble

FIGURE 6. Drawing of Antonio Savorgnan and his militiamen
outside Udine on the morning of Giovedì Grasso, 1511.

ing on their own initiative. Vergon and Narni served as the "principal executioners" of this "dog pack," and the former boasted of
personally striking down some of the most important Strumiero
nobles. Both would later disappear, leading many to speculate that
Antonio Savorgnan had them killed because they knew too much
or had held back too much loot; others said they killed each other
in a fight over spoils. The ten, however, could not confirm the
deaths, and although two unidentifiable bodies turned up in a well,
in 1515 the ten banished Vergon, whereabouts unknown. Tempesta, who had precipitated the battle by confronting Nicolò Della
Torre earlier in the day, would escape four days later to Feltre, face

FIGURE 7. Udine; Palazzo del Comune (1448–56).

FIGURE 8. Udine; casa Veneziana (fifteenth century) was one of the few
palaces that survived the events of 1511.

banishment from the Venetian dominion, and eventually be executed in Rome. Piccolo and Matana would later suffer exile, but of
this group only the Ferrarese, a painter who served as Savorgnan's
falconer, would be unlucky enough to land in a Venetian jail,
where he would languish for four years until he was drawn and
quartered in 1515.

Four others who were not actually retainers of Savorgnan also
became known as instigators on Giovedì Grasso. Simone Scraiber,
a scrivener and procurator from an honorable family, suffered the
same fate as the Ferrarese despite an attempt by a group of armed
peasants to rescue him as he was being dragged off for confine-
ment. Alvise Spilimbergo and one Antonio, retainer of the gentleman Giovanni Vitturi but also a crony of Tempesta, suffered banishment, and a mysterious Morgante was eventually executed in
Cividale. There were also numerous accusations that Antonio Savorgnan's half-brother Pietro and Antonio's bastard son Nicolò
both participated personally in the fray.

These men constituted, to use Canetti's apt phrase, the "crowd
crystals," that small unified body of men who served to precipitate
a crowd. The most ardent in the resulting group hunted down and
killed, the less valiant merely watched gang murder. Most would
enjoy the safety of anonymity, the collective nature of their actions
transforming assassination into an unofficial public execution. The
killers saw themselves as the executors of justice, as acting in the
name of Venice and the lord Savorgnan to do what the officials
wanted but could not do themselves. An apparent confluence of
interests, those of Venice which wished to check the philoimperi-
alists, those of Savorgnan who longed to crush his hereditary enemies, and those of the poor who feared that the castellans sought
to return them to servility, made massacre possible.[11]

Stimulated by these men, the crowd systematically searched
through neighboring houses for the Della Torre and their allies.
Isidoro Della Torre, wounded in the flight from the Della Torre
palace, found refuge with the Sbroiavacca. When the crowd invaded the house, they found Isidoro lying on a bed and attacked
him twice. The second time Girolamo Arlatto, a member of the
Udine city council, struck him on the head with a hatchet and left
him for dead. Unlike most of the other victims, Isidoro made a
final confession and, pardoning his enemies before his death three

days later, became a Strumiero martyr: his corpse "filled the room with a most sweet odor to the extreme amazement of those around him and only he among all those killed was buried in the ancient sepulcher of his ancestors." [12]

Isidoro Della Torre's brother, the hearty sixty-year-old Alvise, head of the faction, met a far more miserable fate. He and Apollonio Gorghi hid in the wine vault of the palace of the patriarchal vicar, which is where the Ferrarese and some others discovered them. A shoemaker named Giacomo Vicentino later testified about what happened. Alvise's end was not dignified. He offered a large treasure in exchange for his life, but when Vergon entered the cellar he ignored the proffered ransom and simply slit Alvise's throat. Antonio Savorgnan, who had not known what was going on, came upon the scene and found Vergon torturing Alvise as the latter slowly bled to death; Savorgnan vainly ordered his retainer to stop. The men with Vergon were mostly peasants from Zompicchia, where Alvise had been attacked the year before. They stripped him of four hundred ducats and his clothes and dragged his still half-alive, naked body by the foot into the streets, chanting "here is the traitor." His death was a collective execution in the fullest sense: he was trampled and stoned and his corpse desecrated in the mud.[13]

After dark the looting and burning spread. Next door to the Della Torre, the palace of Francesco Cergneu went up in flames, quickly followed by part of the Guarienti house on the same street. The throng sacked the house of Sebastiano Monfalcone, who had marched the Strumiero *bravi* through the streets of Udine only days before; he found refuge among the nearby Franciscan friars, as did Leonardo Gubertino.

Worse fortune visited Soldoniero Soldonieri. Driven from his house by the flames, he and his two daughters, one a widow and the other a maiden, "among the most beautiful in the city," ran into a band of men who were out searching with lighted torches for refugee nobles. The assailants dispatched several Soldonieri familiars and attacked the already badly wounded old man, but the daughters threw themselves on top of their father to protect him. The younger was herself hurt when the men tore a strand of pearls from her neck. They left the three bathed in the father's blood. The daughters found refuge for their dying father in a neighboring house. Later Simone Scraiber came to find him, and although Soldoniero begged to be allowed to die in peace, Scraiber insisted he had to be moved for his own security; Scraiber's men carried him in a chair followed by the two daughters and a widowed sister. All went well until the little procession reached the cemetery of San Francesco where the captors threatened to cut off Soldoniero's head right there unless given one hundred ducats. One of the women ran to a friend and produced a rich silver belt, but after dividing up the silver pieces from the belt, Scraiber reneged on his promise and whistled for his followers who rushed out and murdered the old man anyway.[14]

Although Antonio certainly permitted, if not encouraged, the extinction of all the adult males in the Della Torre clan, he opposed certain excesses, epitomized by the fate of Soldoniero and his daughters, as can be seen by his actions during Thursday night and the succeeding days when he saved the lives of several Strumiero nobles and sent out trusted servants to contain the spread of violence in the countryside. The crowd and its leaders had their own agenda, which they pursued in the name of Antonio Savorgnan but which went beyond his orders.

Antonio's character manifested many complexities, and his position at the pinnacle of a vast but fragile patronage system necessitated the pursuit of seemingly contradictory actions. For example, Antonio later testified that he himself went to the house of Ascanio Sbroiavacca, in which many nobles had found refuge, and brought to safety in his own palace Francesco Cergneu and his son-in-law Troiano Guarienti, Giovanni Battista Candido, Agostino Partistagno and his three sons, Felice di Sebastiano Monfalcone, and Antonio di Francesco Gorghi. He also personally rescued three of the Brazzacchi from the house of Giovanni Zucco and conducted them to the monastery of San Pietro Martire. Savorgnan's intervention saved some twelve nobles in all. Thus, whatever fate he had desired for the Della Torre, he certainly did not organize a systematic massacre of Strumieri.

However, some of Savorgnan's followers found Tolmezzo's aphorism, "dead men don't fight back," more to their liking than Antonio's apparent caution. When the rioters swarmed into his palace, Federico Colloredo fled to the Roncho gate tower, but a peasant revealed his hiding place. The Ferrarese arrived to talk Colloredo into surrendering by offering a safe conduct to Savor-

gnan's palace, and after a long resistance Federico saw no alternative and surrendered. Despite their promises his captors killed him
and badly mutilated his body as they had the others.

In feeding their own appetite for revenge, the Colloredo family
would long remember one particularly shameful detail about the
murder. The Ferrarese's gang refused to allow the corpse to be
buried, leaving it in the open for a pack of dogs to tear apart and
eat. More than fifty years later this particular detail would still be
recalled with a shudder, held up and thrown back at the Savorgnan
at every opportunity.

The denial of burial to the victims resulted more from systematic choices than from the hazards of chance. Apollonio Gorghi's
crying mother had not been allowed to recover his body, Alvise
Della Torre was left in the open for three days, and several bodies
were abandoned to Udine's roaming pigs and dogs. In late March
the stink from a well drew an investigation. Authorities extracted
three bodies, one of a strangled woman identified as a servant of
the Castello family and two of unidentified men who some specu-
lated were the missing Savorgnan *bravi*, Vergon and Bernardino di
Narni, but who were probably Strumiero victims hidden from
proper burial. The rioters threw other corpses into caves, wells,
and latrines, probably less in an attempt to cover up evidence of
killings that had been openly committed in the streets than to deny
proper Christian burial to the hated nobles and to condemn their
souls to wander among the armies of the dead. During Thursday
night a Paduan priest, Bernardino Manzatore, gathered as many
bodies from the streets as he could and placed them in a newly
built tomb in the façade of the cathedral. Venetian officials came
that night to examine the dead; the next morning many filed by
to take a look, but the corpses were so badly disfigured they could
not be recognized.

The carnival killers revealed a particular *modus operandi*: they
murdered, mutilated or dismembered, prevented the burial of their
victims, and fed the remains to street scavengers. More than just
cruel brutality, this pattern evolved out of carnival itself and reveals
the peculiar bond between the body-centered nature of carnival
imagery and the style of vendetta murder. In revenge as in carnival,
the human body and its parts produced the vocabulary and syntax
for symbolic communications.

The luogotenente finally called for outside help from Teodoro Del Borgo, who rushed his one hundred heavy cavalry units from Gradisca to Udine, arriving about three hours after sunset on Friday. As roguish pantomimes displaced murder and fire, more troops marched into Udine, and by Ash Wednesday Antonio Savorgnan's old Venetian friend, Andrea Loredan, then serving as a head of the Council of Ten, arrived and promptly began an investigation.

The Cruel Carnival of Udine consisted of a series of collective murders, mostly by the henchmen of Antonio Savorgnan backed by a large crowd of artisans and peasants, and the victims were exclusively members of the Strumieri. Despite its intensity the looting and violence were confined to specific targets chosen more by the dictates of vendetta than by military necessity. The urban riots had lasted little more than two days, during which some seventeen to twenty-two palaces were sacked or burned, and between twenty-five and fifty of the most influential nobles and their retainers were killed. With the show of force the artisans retreated and the peasants left town, but at the same time the flames of discontent spread into the countryside where more looting and burning put the remaining castellans to flight.

CASTLES BURN

The peasants who wandered out of Udine spread word of their successes. The news encouraged many others across the countryside to take advantage of the castellans' sudden vulnerability that had been created when many of the aristocrats went to Udine to aid the Della Torre, leaving the rural estates occupied only by women, children, and servants. At least in the early stages, the pillagers included others besides local peasants: those forced out of Udine, roaming bands of retainers and clients of Antonio Savorgnan, Udinese artisans, and errant militiamen. But as the disturbances spread, assaults came more often from local peasants acting alone without any outside leaders. The henchmen of the faction yielded to local community leaders. Although the example of Udine stimulated violence elsewhere, each rural community pursued its own particular grievances.

On the left bank of the Tagliamento, within the broad amphitheater of hills, the most intensely concentrated attacks on noble

FIGURE 9. Villalta; main tower gate of the castle.

property took place. In this cluster of villages and castles near Udine, where communal and feudal jurisdictions intertwined and the population density was high, peasants could actually hear the uproar from the villages down the road or across the shallow valleys. There the rebellion spread like wildfire.

The castles of Villalta, Moruzzo, and Brazzacco shared a common fate, created by their geographic situation and the personal connections among their castellan families. Here clustered some of the most prominent Strumiero families whose jurisdictional privileges contrasted with the autonomy of a commune, which was nearby, and the paternalistic lordship of Antonio Savorgnan, who also had a large fief in the area. From neighboring mounds each of the castles guarded important roads.

No one harmed any of the noble inhabitants of these three castles, and those who forced entry restricted themselves to plundering. A considerable amount of movable goods disappeared, including household furnishings, clothing, foodstuffs, and a chest from Brazzacco containing a rich hoard variously estimated at between one and three thousand ducats. The actual physical destruction of the castles, frequently exaggerated by contemporary partisans of the Strumieri, varied greatly from place to place. Amaseo reported that at Villalta "most of their [the Della Torre] castle was looted and ruined," but by September 1512, if not before, the building had been reoccupied. As at Sterpo peasants quite systematically burned rent-rolls and other seigneurial records. The Della Torre later swore that their inability to document their jurisdiction over two nearby villages stemmed from the fact that most of their papers were burned in 1511.

From the environs of the Della Torre stronghold at Villalta, disturbances spread to the properties of the allied Colloredo clan. The Colloredo holdings formed an odd hodgepodge created by centuries of acquisitions and losses through dowries, inheritances, sales, and purchases. The family records boast about the influence the consorts enjoyed in the places in which they collected rents from most of the land and had jurisdictional privileges. It was in these areas of concentrated Colloredo power that some of the most intense disturbances broke out: in 1509 in Sterpo and in 1511 in Colloredo di Monte Albano, Susans, and, less forcefully, Mels.

On Friday, February 28, the day after two members of the family had been killed and their property pillaged in Udine, Colloredo and Susans came under attack. At Colloredo the consort Tommaso fled with his family; local villagers held Gregorio Colloredo captive for some time, but the other consorts suffered only losses of household furnishings and supplies of food, much of which was later returned. The assault seems to have concentrated on the movable property and portions of the castle belonging to Albertino, the consort whose fortress had been destroyed at Sterpo. His house at Monte Albano was burned to its foundations. Regarding Susans, the consorts recorded in a rent-roll for 1513, "we had in the place where the castle had been a palace or house that was burned at the time of the looting of 1511 a little after Giovedì Grasso when the nobles were persecuted by peasants and everything found in that house was stolen." Vines were also cut and a supply of lumber burned.[15]

In the same area an episode in defense of the castles of Mels, Pers, Caporiacco, and Arcano, which fortified positions overlooking a stream named the Corno, generated another of the famous stories of Giovedì Grasso. Tenants from the nearby villages threatened these four castles with looting and burning, but intervention by Antonio Savorgnan's agents halted the onslaught, at least temporarily. According to his own account, Nicolò Monticolo went to Pers to rescue some of his relatives. While in flight, Tommaso Colloredo met Nicolò at Pers and persuaded him to return to Colloredo di Monte Albano. There Nicolò released Gregorio Colloredo from captivity, restored to the family much of their pillaged property, including eleven beds (the valuable symbol of aristocratic comfort), and organized a guard consisting of a knight of the luogotenente, a priest, and four men from Buia, the nearby collection of hamlets under Savorgnan control. Nicolò later wrote that had he not intervened the castle would have been leveled to its foundations.

After returning to Pers, Nicolò met Bernardino Pers, a Strumiero nobleman, and rode toward the smoke rising from Arcano. There they heard that the castellan's wife, Regina, had fled into the woods, finding refuge in a cave. More than sixty armed peasants hunted for her, some watching from hill tops, others, like "dogs after a scent," searching for her through the dells. The two gentlemen finally found her refuge and brought the distraught woman and her sister-in-law to safety.

Again Nicolò and Bernardo set off toward distant smoke and at Caporiacco found the humble house of the consort Giovanni Antonio aflame and nearby, crying on the bank of a ditch, his disheveled wife holding an infant. She joined the other refugees in a cart, which headed for the relative security of Pers. Once they had arrived, Regina Arcano asked Nicolò to return to save some of the valuables that she had hidden in a tomb in the Arcano church. When Nicolò arrived there he discovered the chaplain and four peasants dividing up Regina's things. He chased them off and brought back the salvaged property. Nicolò said of himself using the third person that "Monticolo went on to save the castle of Pers and the castle of Mels, which were not touched because he is a very close friend of Antonio Savorgnan and known by everyone as a person of great authority and power, who was nevertheless much loved, and when he was not there anymore, these two castles were not only looted but destroyed." [16]

Monticolo pictured himself as a chivalrous knight saving innocent ladies from house fires, freezing cold, and ruffian rapists. His story has a narrative structure that is almost too pat, and his assessment of the amount of damage to these castles is not entirely sustained by other sources. His tale begins with his intervention at Colloredo di Monte Albano to rescue a prominent noble and to save the property of one of Antonio Savorgnan's most bitter enemies. There follows the remarkable episode of the beautiful lady hiding in a cave from vengeful rustics, and then a maudlin scene of the weeping mother abandoned on the bank of a ditch, and finally the victory over impiety when Nicolò retrieves his lady's treasures from the greedy chaplain and his fellow grave robbers.

There is an element of truth to all of this inasmuch as others reported that Monticolo intervened in some way, but his own version of the events best serves as an example of the transformation of experience into a chivalrous fantasy. In like fashion, most of the indigenous aristocratic sources minimize the autonomy of peasant actions, attributing all *virtù* and leadership to nobles. In contrast to such heroic illusions, the peasants' own materialist values and the absence of a broad reformist, revolutionary, or millenarian ideology limited their objectives and prevented coordinated political action.

The tide of insurrection in the area stopped at the circuit of hills in the sprawling Savorgnan territories around Buia. After the outbreak in Udine, Antonio Savorgnan wrote to his captain for Pinzano and Buia ordering subjects not to harm any person, to steal any property, or to burn anything. Here Antonio was obeyed. No Savorgnan fief was touched in the aftermath of Giovedì Grasso, although Antonio's orders to his captain imply that he was not so sure himself how far matters would go. Some of his men from Buia went to Colloredo di Monte Albano to guard the castle there, and a group of peasants on their way to sack Gemona got as far as Buia but did not dare defy Savorgnan's men who guarded the road there.

Peasants took up arms all across the plain, sacking noble property in Varmo and around Codroipo with its satellite village of Zom-

picchia, which had been restive for the past year since Alvise Della
Torre had jailed those who had assaulted him there. With far fewer
castles than in the hill region, the lower plain witnessed more dif-
fused disturbances. As we have seen, two of the most influential
Zambarlano leaders came from the lower plain, Asquinio and his
nephew Federico Varmo, who organized the assault of Sterpo. Asquinio had been captain of the militias of Varmo since early in
1509, had rounded up three hundred men for duty in December
1510, and would provide some four hundred during the summer
of 1511. Federico would later be described the "head of the infantry of the patria," and Amaseo pictured both Varmos as Antonio
Savorgnan's devoted followers, who served as the "heads of the
popular classes of the city and the peasants from outside." [17]

Many of the peasant bands in Udine on Giovedì Grasso came
from the lower plain, and in particular from Fiumicello, Zompicchia, and Pradamano, areas long friendly to the Savorgnan and directly menaced by the enemy, a fact that made the inhabitants all
the more enraged by rumors of Strumiero treachery. In this region
in which castellan power was weakest and Zambarlano influence
strongest, the peasants followed the militia leadership in contrast
to the hill country in which the villagers behaved more autono-
mously. The settlements in the hills had better developed community institutions and greater residential stability than in the
lowlands, in which high mortality from disease must have led to
frequent changes in tenancy.

In contrast to the short-lived, war-provoked panic found in the
eastern lowlands, the disturbances across the Tagliamento came
much closer to a revolution, especially in Spilimbergo. The previous December, *bravi* had been hired to support the citizen faction
in Spilimbergo, leading the consorts to bring in retainers as a coun-
ter-measure. Exiles also filtered into town during the early winter
months while the chief consorts schemed with the Della Torre.
Even without Udine's example, Spilimbergo could well have ignited on its own during carnival. On Monday, March 3, the servants
and hired guards (*famegli e provisionati*) of the consorts abandoned
the castle, leaving the noble families unprotected and forcing them
to flee south to Zoppola, where they found temporary refuge along
with many other castellans. While they were gone their subjects and
peasants (*li popolani et villani loro*) set fire to several of the houses

in the castle, the smoke from which Nicolò Monticolo saw while on his rescue mission across the river. Damage was extensive but selective, some nobles' buildings remaining intact. However, the looting went beyond the castellan complex to include local merchants.

As was the case in the fifteenth century, Spilimbergo remained a dangerously fissured community in which class conflicts cut across factional affiliations and the consorts themselves were deeply divided. Besides the castellan-commoner split, the Strumiero-Zambarlano cleavage was perpetuated by successive generations of Spilimbergo nobles, who contributed members to both sides, although most followed the clan's traditional affiliation with the Strumieri and took spouses from among the Della Torre, Colloredo, and Cergneu. Those members attracted to the Zambarlano badge seem to have been disinherited or alienated from their kin in some way.

Because of the clan's numerous branches and highly fecund spouses, the consorts as a body were weakened by a subdivided patrimony, by the competing claims from collateral branches, and by the paucity of resources to satisfy the younger men, many of whom had to seek their own fortunes. Some of these turned to making their livings as bandits. In January 1511, Simone di Francesco di Antonio received a warning from the heads of the Council of Ten that he must cease harboring armed bandits in his quarters in Spilimbergo castle and using them to protect him from the citizens of the town. Other castellans disassociated themselves from him by sending a delegation to the luogotenente.

When Simone failed to follow orders, the ten fined and then banished him. At first he refused to leave; when he finally did depart he only went across the river to San Daniele, where he remained just as troublesome. By the summer of 1511, at least three consorts were under the ban, two of them surviving by robbing peasants. Although the consorts of Spilimbergo would produce one of the most illustrious female painters of the Renaissance, supply a rector of the University of Padua, and host the Emperor Charles V at their massive complex, several of them lived as thieves and adventurers whose relations with their own family and town were often violent.

Aftershocks from the 1511 carnival radiated from the secondary epicenter at Spilimbergo, threatening castles as far away as Por-

FIGURE 10. Zoppola; the castle.

denone. The consorts of Spilimbergo and those of the nearby castles fled, in the words of the provveditore of Pordenone Alvise Bondimier, "screaming to heaven as if mad"; as a puny remedy he sent his chancellor on a tour to threaten the gallows for those who did not desist from violence. The chancellor complained that he could not find any leaders among the crowds to receive the decree and reported that extensive damage had already been done by Monday evening at Spilimbergo, Zoppola, Cusano, and Valvasone. Nobles at Porcìa, Brugnera, and even Pordenone closed their gates to menacing crowds. No more able to take effective action than had the luogotenente in Udine, Bondimier raged in his letters to Venice that the rustic dogs acted more cruelly than Turks.[18]

The consorts of Valvasone, Salvarolo, Cusano, Spilimbergo, and others who had sought refuge at Zoppola soon abandoned it and fled to Pordenone, where they found the castle in ruins from the imperialists' recent siege, a fact that obliged them to push on to Porcìa where they formed a council of war. The counts of Porcìa recruited eight hundred peasants from Cordenons and some sixty to seventy knights to hunt down the pillagers. Their reprisals were vicious. They massacred between fifty and one hundred peasants, took many prisoners, and hanged one as an example at Zoppola. The peasant bands fled "like geldings frightened by a wolf," abandoning the field to the castellans. Most of the fighting ceased

FIGURE 11. Zoppola; peasant housing near the castle.

within a week, but in several places, notably in Spilimbergo, it continued for months.[19]

Deeply disquieted by the news from Friuli, the Council of Ten acted quickly to pacify the region. Choosing expediency over justice, the ten chose one of their own number, none other than Antonio Savorgnan's protector and friend, Andrea Loredan, to go to Udine to stop the violence, arrest the culprits, and restore property. Loredan once again showed himself to be an active partisan rather than an objective arbitrator, offending with his highhanded methods the resident Venetian officials as well as all but the most dedicated partisans of the Savorgnan. Staying for barely two weeks, Loredan left after paving the way for the complete exoneration of Antonio Savorgnan and arresting only two minor figures among the Zambarlani. Very little property was returned. In fact, it was twenty-three years before any serious attempt at compensation for damages was ventured.

When they pictured the peasant crowds, contemporary witnesses imagined only two stark alternatives: either mobs wandering like vagabonds without master, intent solely on plunder, or the opposite situation of gullible rustics manipulated by some treacherous noble. Most observers remarked on the spontaneity and apparent lack of organization in the peasant violence. A noble who later gloried in the brutal crushing of the peasants probably reflected the views of many of his peers in arguing that the peasants went on a rampage "without any cause." Other witnesses confirmed the view that the crowds lacked leaders. One quite frank account states that the peasants "went about without any head at all to guide them in plundering and burning and with the goal of castigating and breaking the rebel castellans, and these were the very subjects of the castellans." Although many of the participants were locals who joined the assault on their own lords' castles, others certainly moved from castle to castle, pillaging where they could, as did those who went on from Spilimbergo to Valvasone, Zoppola, and Cusano. The crowds must have been large otherwise they could not have overwhelmed the castles so easily. Twelve hundred were reported at Zoppola and two thousand at Porcìa, but the assertion that a horde of between four and five thousand wandered from castle to castle is certainly exaggerated.[20]

Many of the anti-Savorgnan sources maintained that Antonio coordinated even these far-flung disquiets. However, even Amaseo had to admit that Nicolò Monticolo succeeded in quieting the peasant Zambarlani, saving lives, and preventing even greater destruction. Monticolo himself asserted that "if Antonio Savorgnan had not had some of his friends ride out, all of the castellans would not only have been plundered and ruined but some of their families would have become extinct. Such was their flight that they abandoned houses, goods, and their own wives with little children in order to save themselves. It was a horrible thing to see."[21]

Although these contrasting opinions create a picture of fragmentation and ambiguity, the rural situation can, in fact, be clarified considerably. In Udine Antonio Savorgnan's agents were visible everywhere and were at the forefront of the attack. It is beyond doubt that they provided the leadership in the streets, identified at least some of the quarry, and did much of the killing themselves. However, the situation in the countryside was quite different. There were very few murders. In fact the only persons killed during the rural outbreak were peasants caught in the castellans' counterattack. The violence of vendetta which predominated in the city almost completely disappeared in favor of highly selective plundering, threats to the dependents of the absent nobles, and vague expressions of long-standing peasant grievances.

The indigenous strengths of the peasant crowd, built around leaders from village councils and the militia, the decade-long experience of collective protest against the parliament, and the memory of the success at Sterpo nineteen months before, collapsed the vertical hierarchy of the Zambarlano faction into localized, fragmentary peasant communities. In the countryside neither nobles nor priests, with one obscure exception, led the rebels, and the known intimates of Antonio Savorgnan protected rather than threatened lives and property.

When Antonio himself attempted to stop the violence, he relied heavily on the indigenous village leadership to do so. He asked two men, Jacomo del Fara and Rosso di Bagnarolla, described as among the "first peasants" in importance from across the Tagliamento, to go home, disperse their people, and stop the pillaging. The starkly popular character of the rural revolt underscores the diverse interests that had been attached to the Zambarlano faction, which was the only effective voice against the castellan-dominated parliament and the only defense against the imperial marauders. Given the limited amount of information available to the peasants and the nature of rumors, such as the one that the Strumiero castellans sought to aid the enemy, the rural rebels need not have had any central directives; they merely seized an opportunity and justified their rampages by labeling their victims as traitors.

During all the violence in Udine and across the countryside attackers exempted women for the most part. As far as can be determined only one woman, a servant of the Castello clan, died in Udine. In another incident, the crowd beat and kicked Angela Gorghi while she was attempting to rescue her son from certain death. In the rural areas assaults on women seem to have been limited to two or three rapes. The general exemption of women from physical harm reflected the theoretical exclusion of women from vengeance killing and confirms the pattern of the careful selection of victims and targets. Although the rapes may have merely been crimes of opportunity, they certainly served to dishonor further the Strumiero lords who proved themselves incapable of defending their own wives.

Selectivity characterized both the Udinese and the rural disturbances in the sense that only aristocrats with close ties to the philo-imperial inner circle of the Strumieri came to grief. The only exceptions were the few merchants of Spilimbergo whose shops were looted. The attacks were most intense in the hill regions that fanned out to the north of Udine and in the arid scrub of Spilimbergo. By contrast, in the lowlands antinoble agitation was less extensive and less successful; nevertheless, several lowland villages contributed bands of armed militiamen who wandered off elsewhere (particularly to Udine) and joined in the fray. The most likely targets of attack, then, were those castellans who had abused jurisdictional rights and who were particularly rich. In fact, the peasant looters were far more successful in obtaining valuable property than the Austrian raiders who had precipitated the conflagration.

CHAPTER FOUR

The Problem of Meaning

For those who witnessed and survived the Cruel Carnival or even heard about it after the event, ascribing meaning to the collective killing and pillaging remained an embittering concern. Contemporaries could find an obvious explanation in the long history of the Zambarlano-Strumiero vendetta, but the carnival slaughter seemed so unprecedented in magnitude and involved so many people from outside the narrow ambit of castellans and their familiars that evoking the age-old quarrels between the Savorgnan and Della Torre was inadequate to the task. The meanings attributed to the deaths and destruction came after the fact as persons from various cultural levels with diverse interests and objectives saw very different things in the Cruel Carnival. Just as it had no single cause, the Cruel Carnival had no single meaning, and in the ensuing years the process of imposing meanings on the event became not only a problem of interpretation but the justification for future violence and the substance of political discourse as well.

To understand fully how social position conditioned the assigning of meaning to the Cruel Carnival, the background of the factions should be considered. The language of class distinctions which contrasted peasants and nobles and which was employed by the notaries, chroniclers, and humanists who produced most of the records often masked the fact that the constituent elements of the Zambarlani were usually small communities consisting of internally differentiated groups of neighbors and villagers who had their own abbreviated hierarchy of leaders in the form of *decani* and militia captains.

By 1511, the travails of a decade had drawn the urban poor and rural tenant farmers of these microcommunities into the Zambarlano orbit. The Turkish incursions and the wars between Venice and the Emperor Maximilian escalated Venetian fiscal demands. In addition, changes in the manorial economy led many of the Strumiero landlords to exploit their properties more efficiently by denying tenants compensation for improvements to their leaseholds, by usurping common pastures, and by eliminating many of the guarantees of permanent tenancy which peasants had traditionally enjoyed. Forced by the terms of their leases to pay rents in kind and chronically behind in doing so, peasants could not take advantage of the opportunity for capital accumulation provided by access to the market for agricultural produce in Udine and were, instead, drawn into accepting usurious loans.

Both the artisans and the peasants found solidarity in their neighborhoods or villages and support from the Zambarlani. Such neighborhood and village microcommunities offered the corporate identity and leadership structure necessary for collective action and for incorporation into the larger structure of the faction. Although relations among the communities had historically been competitive, on the eve of and during Giovedì Grasso the communities acted in concert against a common economic and military foe, primarily because of Antonio Savorgnan's patronage and the comradeship of the young men in the militias. The Friulan communities may have been weaker than communities in many other parts of the Mediterranean, but they were still the necessary basis for any larger popular movement.

Particularly characteristic of Friuli was how rural life penetrated deeply into the city and the few towns, making neighborhoods similar to country villages in structure and values. Even in Udine a large portion of the population consisted of peasant cultivators, and artisans often worked as part-time farmers and invested in live-stock raising. Thus, the economic concerns of the peasants also motivated many city dwellers.

The smallness and rural nature of the Friulan communities help to account for their limited political expectations, so lacking in radical ideological alternatives or millenarian enthusiasm, unlike even isolated, mountain-bound Belluno, where in 1501 peasant agitators followed a certain mendicant friar who had preached about the common man's God-given rights. When the Friulans went so far as to articulate their desires, the men of the villages and neighborhoods wanted at most local control over their own affairs. To be sure, the Venetian rectors imagined a cataclysmic upheaval, warning the Council of Ten about "the plebs who always want new things" and recalling "the last few days during the revolution of that patria" or the "revolution of the heavens"; and yet the revolution about which they wrote consisted of limited demands for fiscal reform and unity against invaders rather than a transfor-mation of the social system or eschatological expectations of col-lective salvation. Of course, an endless stream of delegations had made political demands to the parliament and to Venice, but the real revolution in Friuli, rather than a political or religious one, was a moral and cultural one in which the men and women of the villages and *borghi* employed the body metaphors of carnival and vendetta to express their desires for revenge. Giovedì Grasso epit-omized the restricted potential of the vendetta-revolt for political change, a potential that could not be expanded until the desire for revenge was channeled into a coherent political movement.[1]

Whatever had been the concerns of the villagers and neighbors of Friuli before Giovedì Grasso, the violence of the day trans-mogrified their grievances into new representations or ideas that coalesced on at least four different cultural levels. The primary level used traditional motifs of carnival as a form of communica-tion. Significant actions conveyed messages through improvised variations on the accepted forms for the butchery of bodies. Here deeds spontaneously and ritualistically communicated in a form which historians have widely recognized as characteristic of the poor in premodern Europe. These were the immediate messages formulated by the men who did the killing in the streets of Udine.

On a second level participants, survivors, and interested parties in Venice and Udine sought to influence the determination of guilt. Friulans incorporated the Venetian organs of justice into their own struggles, using judicial procedures as an extension of their private and factional quarrels. Although anyone could make a denunciation, serve as a witness, or face charges, the politicized Venetian system of justice, far from being an impartial arbiter, facilitated collective scapegoating in the interests of a powerful few.

The two final levels were the products of hindsight and literacy, attempts to place Friulan events in a cosmological or historical context. Some envisioned Giovedì Grasso and its aftermath apocalyptically, a human vendetta that either fulfilled or precipitated the divine vendetta. Finally, after years of reflection a few humanists and aristocrats wrote up historical narrations of the events, interpreting Giovedì Grasso for outsiders and future generations.

As time passed and individual memories faded, literate sophistication became more important. Time was on the side of those capable of committing their ideas to print although when they did so, they divorced themselves from the catharsis and corporality of the actual Giovedì Grasso, reinterpreting the event to serve a personal or ideological agenda and suppressing entirely the original messages of the participants themselves.

THE CARNIVAL BODY

Carnival has received so much attention from scholars of the Renaissance in recent years because it was so richly complex, subtly interwoven into the fabric of daily life, and therefore resistant to a single or simple interpretation. Relying on a Europe-wide repertoire of images and motifs, carnivals absorbed meanings from the social environment and from certain universal human processes. One of those processes was killing—the killing of animals, the killing of humans. Carnival helped sustain certain beliefs about killing which were shared by both vendetta practices and hunting. (These beliefs will be examined in the next chapter.) Carnival, vendetta, and hunting were distinct activities, but in the act of killing and in talking and writing about killing the boundaries among the three blurred, so that a vendetta could easily become a carnival riot or adopt the cultural trappings of the hunt.

Whatever the local manifestations, carnival images revolved around the paradox that human life sustained itself through death.

Carnival celebrated the necessary deaths: the death of the old season and the birth of a new (carnival as a wake for winter), the killing of animals for meat (carnival as the time for the slaughter of hogs), and the death of Christ soon to be commemorated during Holy Week (carnival as an unloosening of the forces of the underworld). One of the characteristic ways in which carnivals represented the struggle between life and death involved a fight, typically a staged fight between personifications of Carnival and Lent, but the games and mock combats that institutionalized this fight could seldom be controlled entirely by authorities, and carnival festivities often tested the boundaries of order by becoming chaotic.

A related carnivalesque emphasis on gluttony and drunkenness celebrates fat times and recognizes the inevitable recurrence of the opposite condition of lean times; thus, the fight between Carnival and Lent is also a fight between the Fat and the Lean. Given the long history of Savorgnan patronage of the peasants and artisans on the one hand and castellan hostility to agrarian fiscal reform on the other, it is not far-fetched to imagine that in the minds of the poor, the Zambarlani took on the role of the Fat and the Strumieri the Lean. Giovedì Grasso, or Fat Thursday, became the natural, almost inevitable, extension of the local factional struggle when the crowd assimilated popular images of the two factions to carnival archetypes. Actual and mock combat, vendetta and carnival fighting, merged entirely on Giovedì Grasso, and participants stripped away accumulated strictures to concentrate on the central theme of the festival: the act of killing.

While eliminating hated nobles and ransacking their houses on Giovedì Grasso, peasants and artisans also represented their feelings of anger and contempt by employing natural symbols derived from human and animal anatomy. Carnival and vendetta shared a fascination with body imagery because both provided a cultural justification for killing and a formula for disposing of carcasses and corpses. As elsewhere in premodern Europe, Friulans acted out social conflicts in patterned ways that constituted rites of violence, various forms of which came together in a burst of murderous fights on Giovedì Grasso. By exploring contemporary attitudes toward the body and its slaughter, one might better approximate, for that is all we can hope to do, what the Friulan rites of violence meant.

Carnival expressed popular discontent by serving as a means of examining social categories, particularly for the illiterate and weak. The playacting, masking, and satiric mimicry associated with normal, nonviolent carnival helped define social roles and clarify status distinctions because, as Richard Trexler has pointed out, individuals characteristically shaped their identities during the late Middle Ages and Renaissance not so much by following social norms as by imitating others. Carnival commented on imitation by paying homage to the orderliness of personal conformity to group models and also by subverting the order in the process of uncovering it. For example, Rabelais illustrated the power of miming by showing how Panurge's ability to use and interpret hand signs helped him understand and convey meaning better than those whose exclusive reliance on spoken language resulted in a failure to communicate fully. Gestures constituted a universal yet grammatical language because they were derived from the natural movements of the body, and the people closest to nature, peasants, understood these signs better than the élite, whose cultivated speech masked their ignorance of the language of the body, a primary source for the language of carnival.

Animal bodies also contributed to the repertoire of carnival body images. In part because the seasonal chores of hog butchering and making sausages took place at carnival time, the festival was especially concerned with the acts of slaughtering and butchering animals, or as Emmanuel Le Roy Ladurie aptly put it, the language of carnival amounted to saying it with meat. Body parts provided the vocabulary, ritual the syntax.

These corporeal images contributed to the typical carnival process of mimicking established mores and culture. Carnival revelers parodied hierarchic order by transgressing established social distinctions through grotesque juxtapositions including cross-dressing, imitating animals, and torturing or killing animals that symbolized some social group. Transgressions in any area had implications for the others, so that such apparently innocuous activities as men masquerading as women or blacksmiths butchering hogs drew attention to the legitimacy of political authority.

In its lexicon of humorous transgressions, carnival was usually quite conservative, helping sustain the social order by representing and explaining it, and when necessary by reforming or purifying it. Especially in communities in which civic organizations such as guilds, confraternities, and festive clubs were highly developed, transgressions reinforced hierarchy precisely because they were temporary and controlled. In the Schembart carnival of Nuremberg, for example, the vigilance of the city council guaranteed a festival that was, according to Hans Sachs who witnessed it in 1539, a "mirror of a bygone revolt, to remind the common people never to participate in such rebellious madness" as they had when they had assaulted the magistrates in 1348. The Nuremberg carnival, moreover, hosted several kinds of dramas for different cultural levels which transformed social tensions into relatively harmless play.[2]

In Venice between 1521 and 1526, the often pointed carnival comedies by Ruzante served as a form of social protest; but after the playwright went too far by associating himself with dangerous political ridicule, he lost his patrician patrons. The Venetian authorities were particularly adept at containing the subversive potential of carnival, in part by turning aggressions outward as they did with the annual carnival butchery of a bull and twelve pigs sent as tribute, in fact, from Friuli.

However, during times of war or grave social tensions, carnival transgressions could provide a language of protest and a model for violence, especially in feudal Friuli. Without a legitimate prince who transcended factional loyalties, without effective religious institutions that encouraged collective rituals, without a miracle-working shrine that focused the quest for supernatural assistance, the Friulan hierarchy lacked symbolic cohesion, and thus Friulan society was susceptible to having its holidays go wrong.

During the 1511 carnival in Udine, the dominant social organizations of militia companies and factions guided the crowds in their festivity, but the pervasive sense of threat remodeled festivity beyond play and any organization's control. In contrast to the elaborate metaphoric images displayed in the carnivals of more sophisticated areas, carnival in Friuli was hardly subtle: its metaphors of Fat and Lean were the factions themselves, its performances less a substitute for direct action than an incitement to it. The Giovedì

Grasso was characterized by a poverty of symbolism and a brutal directness, as when the Savorgnan retainers forced Alvise Della Torre to his knees to beg for his life in an inversion of the normal gesture of respect accorded a man of his rank. After the conflagration the Zambarlani masqueraded in the clothing of their victims and reveled in wearing the hats of the dead aristocrats, the most obvious insignia of rank. These acts of status inversion derived their power from negation and from the lowering of the high born. There were few symbols with which the rioters could identify positively, except perhaps the flag of the Savorgnan. Most powerfully, the Zambarlani gave form to vendetta justice by mimicking the customs of official justice, as Luigi da Porto noted: "I saw the goods taken in that sacking sold at the stands in the piazza of the city, as if such confiscations had been against rebels of Venice and the property sold by commission of the Senate."[3]

The Giovedì Grasso rioters sent their most graphic messages through the disposal of the corpses of their victims, which was performed in ways fraught with symbolic meaning. At least three people were thrown into latrines or wells. The killers left the body of Alvise Della Torre in the streets for three days, and the mother of Apollonio Gorgo had to plead with the Zambarlani to allow her to bury her son's body, which they wanted to leave in the street. Others were systematically dismembered. When Amaseo described Vergon and Bernardino da Narni as "bloody butchers," he was speaking quite literally: they cut up their victims "like beef." Dismemberment deprived the victim of his body, the very source of masculinity and social honor, just as a refusal to bury him denied salvation to his soul.[4]

Dismemberment also had a broader social significance. Mikhail Bakhtin noted that medieval and Renaissance satires typically linked the mutilation of the body with the dissolution of society by adhering to the myth that various social groups originated in the parts of God's body. According to the logic of carnival, hacking up the bodies of dead aristocrats was a way of carving up the body politic.

The lacerating of the bodies of the dead can also be understood as an expression of the widespread belief that corpses retained some sensitivity. Such beliefs were encouraged by religious pictures and sculptures, especially Last Judgment scenes, which explicitly showed the agonized bodies of the dead condemned to Hell. Confirming the theology of corporeal sensation, physicians and legal experts justified many forms of postexecution torture such as drawing and quartering, and they authorized the *jus feretri* whereby the supposed reaction of a dead body in the presence of its murderer would be accepted in a court of law as a valid proof of the identity of the guilty party. In medical schools well into the eighteenth century, dissections continued to produce uneasy emotions about the pain of the dead, which the University of Bologna, for example, respected by relegating public dissections to carnival, when recently executed criminals were available, and the masked audience could watch the procedure as a kind of theatrical performance appropriate to the season. There may also have been a way in which damaging corpses acted as a kind of sympathetic magic, a way of tormenting the victim's soul in the other world and his living relations in this one.

And yet the tortures inflicted on Strumiero corpses did not quite do and say enough to satisfy the Zambarlani. In perhaps the most infamous episode of Giovedì Grasso, the Ferrarese lured Federico Colloredo out of hiding with a promise of a safe conduct but then "killed him and slashed him with so many wounds that one could see all of his insides, which were eaten by dogs; the remains were not allowed to be buried." This most thorough act of revenge drew its evocative power from the horror of dogs and pigs eating humans, a transgression that obsessed the Udinesi. An ordinance of 1490 mentioned a fence built around the public gallows so that "dogs and other animals can not enter in that place to lick up human blood." An edict from 1520 stated that pigs invaded the cathedral of Santa Maria daily and despoiled graves, and reports of animals rooting in cemeteries continued throughout the century. Titian's late sixteenth-century painting of *The Flaying of Marsyas* summoned similar horrors. The image of animals eating human bodies was not only a festive inversion but a perverted fact of life recalled with dramatic effect on Giovedì Grasso. In murdering Federico Colloredo, the Zambarlani degraded him on many levels: by hacking at the corpse, they inflicted additional agony on him; by making him the meat of beasts, they transgressed his status as a man and likened his fate to that of executed criminals; by shaming him in the public streets, they humiliated his surviving relatives;

and by disfiguring his body, they destroyed the collective body of castellans he represented. In his death the methods of carnival and vendetta merged completely. More than any other deed, the fate of Federico epitomized for future generations the Cruel Carnival and the cruel revenge of 1511.[5]

The Giovedì Grasso killings, thus, followed certain patterns that generated messages by the forms they took, forms borrowed from vendetta and carnival. Violence in Udine was neither an anarchic expression of "millennial antinomianism" which lacked rules, nor was it entirely planned. The combination of structure and spontaneity discloses the operations of shared beliefs about dying which made it possible for killers to step into defined roles, as if they improvised the lines of stock dramatic characters.

For many Friulans, especially from the peasant classes, death was neither accidental nor natural but was the result of a fight between phantom forces composed of the shades of the dead who enacted revenge among humans by employing living agents. Revenge, in fact, motivated all deaths, even the most apparently innocent ones. Evidence for such beliefs can be found in the Friulan lore about the armies of the dead and the *benandanti*, who fought night battles for the survival of the crops. Parallel beliefs also appear in other feuding cultures such as Corsica, in which all deaths were blamed on the *mazzeri* who went "hunting" at night in dreams or as doubles. As a time of killing, carnival made the living vulnerable to the forces of the dead, and living men with living grievances had little trouble acting as the doubles of the dead.

In the immediacy of the carnival of 1511, I would suggest, something like the above beliefs about bodies and death infiltrated the minds and influenced the behavior of the humble crowd and killer *bravi* who roamed the streets of Udine. In the weeks after the violence and at a slightly higher cultural level, a more extended process of assigning blame began.

Assigning Blame

On Giovedì Grasso the Zambarlani had scapegoated the Strumieri by describing them as agents of foreign invaders, and after the riots Strumiero survivors sought to reverse the process by attributing the massacres to the will of Antonio Savorgnan. Paralleling these operations were attempts by the Venetian judiciary to determine guilt. However, judicial procedures broke down while investigating Giovedì Grasso, largely because the very act of identifying criminals brought the whole Venetian system of terraferma rule into question. As a result, the indigenous scapegoat mechanisms of the vendetta biased assessments of responsibility.

Within a matter of weeks the Venetian Council of Ten began a general investigation of the Giovedì Grasso disturbances, and in early April the city council of Udine met to elect four delegates to go to Venice to explain what had happened. The chosen four were known Savorgnan associates personally selected by Antonio, who did not allow their formal instructions to be put up for debate in the council. The instructions dismissed all charges of collusion among the attackers of the Strumieri but somewhat inconsistently asserted that the slaughter had been a defensive military action. In their private comments delivered along with their official report, the delegates praised Antonio Savorgnan and emphasized that the common rabble rather than he were responsible for what happened. Subsequently, Antonio Savorgnan himself went to Venice where he testified in secret for more than a week. The investigation finally produced some limited results. The ten issued arrest warrants for Vergon, Tempesta, Matana, the Ferrarese, Piccolo (the familiars of Savorgnan), Pietro Savorgnan (Antonio's half-brother), Alvise Spilimbergo, Simon Scraiber, and one Antonio, familiar of Giovanni Vitturi. A proclamation demanded that all the carnival loot be returned. Only Scraiber and one of the familiars were executed in Venice. The rest were exiled *in absentia*. Most of the Zambarlano élite including seven of the eleven deputies of the council of Udine, chancellor Nicolò Monticolo, and the nine *decani* of the *borghi* of Udine completely escaped blame. Antonio Savorgnan had come under strong suspicion, but as head of the militias and victor over his factional enemies he remained too powerful to be charged with any crime.

For his part, Antonio described himself as in the grips of a kind of madness on Giovedì Grasso. When the luogotenente had asked him to intervene during the riots Antonio had explained away his refusal saying, "I am so angry that I am beside myself and do not know what I am doing." Impelled by his mad blood, Antonio abdicated all responsibility as if his anger had blotted out his reasoning faculties, pushed him beyond the reach of self-restraint, and

subjected him to the governance of pure emotion. His words derived their force from the integrity of burning anger, as if authenticity of feeling justified even the most outrageous crimes. His passion replicated Benvenuto Cellini's numerous boastful accounts of
violent exploits, petty quarrels, and vicious retaliations told in his
Autobiography as assertions of his own identity. The artist was saying, it seems, "I hate, therefore I am." By refusing to accept responsibility on the grounds of his mad passion, Antonio had to
accuse some of his own men, and when investigators came uncom-
fortably close to his inner circle, a few of the minor players were
sacrificed. Antonio turned over to the Venetian authorities the
lowest among his personal retainers and a few lowly peasants but
protected the important client brokers of militia captains and *decani*
who tied the Savorgnan to the rural villages and neighborhoods of
Udine.[6]

In contrast, after the event the Strumieri continued to blame
Antonio Savorgnan and his friends, diverting attention from the
Strumieri's own potential treason and their own unmanly failure
to defend themselves and their dependents despite their considerable military resources. Amaseo wrote that even among the twelve
apostles there had been a betrayer and called Savorgnan Antonio
Iscariot and Mohammed, a snake charmer whose friends, "hoping
for impunity from punishment, attributed all [the violence] to the
public anger which proceeded from jealousy of the state, thus calling down the divine vendetta onto the whole city just to free a
single Judas." Some Strumieri even extended the blame to Venice
itself, which they thought had put Savorgnan up to the task of
cleansing the region of its obstinately imperialist aristocracy.[7]

It would take a generation before any serious attempt was made
to provide some compensation for damages suffered in 1511. Although the castellans and their heirs continued to clamor, Venice
could not risk alienating first Antonio and later Girolamo Savorgnan, who financed his own military efforts on behalf of Venice
with the inheritance he received from Antonio's estate. After Girolamo's death in 1529, which coincided with the Peace of Bologna,
Doge Andrea Gritti finally began to listen to the Strumiero claim-
ants and decreed in 1530 that some thirty thousand ducats should
be paid over a period of fifteen years from the estates of the heirs
of Girolamo and Giovanni Savorgnan (Antonio's late brother, whose

sons had inherited part of Antonio's patrimony). As soon became obvious, that sum was utterly inadequate, and so a board of arbitrators was set up to examine claims for compensation. The claims amounted to 158,369 ducats, only half of which were certified by the arbitrators, and only a fraction of which were ever paid.

Besides the need to restore property, the cataclysms of 1511 left many things unresolved: the Strumieri would spend a decade avenging their dead, and Venice would seek to break up the factions. But the most pressing need was to provide explanations. Simply put, what had all this violence and destruction meant?

THE APOCALYPTIC

Once justifiable anger had excused the principals and a few expendable henchmen and rustics had suffered punishment, contemporaries indulged themselves in speculations about the deeper causes of their misfortunes. In early sixteenth-century Friuli, everyone believed that deaths were announced by omens, that great events must have great causes, that divine agency influenced natural events, and that clues to divine will could be discovered in astrological conjunctions, miraculous signs, prodigies, and visions. Even Machiavelli and Guicciardini, the most skeptical historians of their time and the most likely to ascribe human causes to human affairs, believed that prodigies signaled future events. Divine vendetta against human sinfulness was adduced by many as the explanation for the difficult years surrounding 1511, and prodigies foretold God's revenge, which would take the form of apocalyptic disasters such as war, civil strife, earthquakes, and plague, each of which might be ameliorated by human acceptance of the suffering they brought and by acts of propitiation. The relationship between God and humanity was cast, thus, as a series of cosmic exchanges in which humans projected onto God their inner fears and hopes.

Aware of the violent consequences of abusive words spoken among humans, authorities throughout northern Italy since the late fifteenth century had concerned themselves with how blasphemy provoked God's ire. One of the first reactions to the events of Giovedì Grasso was a proclamation against blasphemous utterances, which were to be punished by a fifty-lire fine and the cutting out of the profaner's tongue. Venetian authorities had first expressed worries about the consequences of cursing in 1500, when the Council of Ten issued a decree against blasphemers in response to the news of the fall of Modon to the Turks, but during the War of the League of Cambrai, the tendency to see a close relationship between private sins and public retribution intensified. Because communications with the divine were modeled on human patterns, care had to be taken not only to avoid insulting God but also to discern what he was saying in return.

God's intentions had to be read in obscure signs, the meaning of which, indeed the awareness that they had even appeared, only became clear in retrospect. In 1508 during the days when troops were leaving for the battle of Cadore, reports of the moon dripping with blood, lightning striking church towers and killing several people, and wolves attacking children and adults were read as auguries of divine anger to be expiated by "litanies and sacrifices." As Venice's conflict with the papacy and France escalated, some interpreted the mosaic and pavement designs in the basilica of San Marco in a Joachite fashion to prophesy the loss of Venice's empire; although these prognostications may have only been remembered or made up after the disasters at Agnadello, they provided satisfying retrospective explanations of disturbing events. A pamphlet published in Bologna with a backdated publication date of 1511 enumerates the signs and prodigies that announced the imminent punishment of the world and especially of Italy: will-o'-the-wisps appeared above the fields of Agnadello, two angels displayed unsheathed swords over Padua, the heavens spewed forth fire, and a three-headed child was born in Florence. The cataclysm in Friuli became one of many events in a series of portends and disasters which dominated the public imagination during the Italian wars, but Friulans seem to have been particularly open to prophetic interpretations of their affairs. Members of the Amaseo family, Friuli's most prominent humanist dynasty, collected prophecies from numerous sources both by acquiring parchments of old ones and by copying down new ones when they heard them. The notary Antonio Belloni, who wrote an account of the Giovedì Grasso killings, also left a Latin prophecy among his papers.

Reports of astral conjunctions and signs of divine wrath were commonly used to explain Giovedì Grasso. Antonio Savorgnan refused to heed the pleas of the luogotenente because, "more than anything else the evil constellation of that day inclined him in that direction." Accidents to looters signified divine justice and admonished others; the falling of a lighted torch indicated "how the light of justice must be extinguished"; and a few weeks after the massacre, two angels holding bloody swords hovered above the bell tower of San Francesco, which was next to the Savorgnan palace, "and between them appeared a great pillar of fire in manifest sign of vendetta." Jacopo di Porcìa employed a similar image to describe Antonio Savorgnan's motives: "hatred is a fire, which is extinguished not by water but by great quantities of blood." In April a twelve-year-old peasant girl reported that while collecting firewood she saw the Virgin and an angel, who requested that the girl follow a regimen of fasts and avoid blasphemy. This stock vision, similar to many others recounted in contemporary sources, stimulated her neighbors to organize processions and a Mass in a collective response to the sign of favor bestowed on them in a time of tribulations. In the months after Giovedì Grasso many persons trembled with dire expectations, creating a collective receptivity to, even need for, apparitions.[8]

However, natural catastrophes produced the most telling signs of divine indignation over the killings of Giovedì Grasso. A month after the riots, an earthquake caused extensive damage throughout Friuli and as far away as Venice, where senators rushed from the Ducal Palace when they felt the first tremors, strong enough to shake loose ceiling mosaics in San Marco. In Udine half of the luogotenente's castle collapsed, killing two women, and the many falling buildings produced a cloud of dust so thick that Gradenigo complained he could not see well enough to write his daily dispatch to Venice (Figure 12, *lower plate*). The mountain towns were most gravely damaged, especially Gemona, which was left in ruins. The Venetian patriarch attributed the catastrophe to God's anger with Venice's homosexuals; he was supported by legions of female prostitutes who reported that business had been particularly bad.

In Friuli many were certain that God was furious with them because of the impieties of Giovedì Grasso. "Moreover, the sword of divine justice, which in the heavenly hand moves slowly to avenge, trembled over our land of Friuli." The bishop of Udine organized the clergy, confraternities, luogotenente, and assembled citizens in a sacred procession to the rubble of the Della Torre palace, where he left a piece of the host in an overt linking of the

FIGURE 12. Drawings of Udine. *Upper plate*, pits for the plague dead; *lower plate*, earthquake damage.

ruin of the Della Torre with divine wrath against the whole city. The breaking of a cross during the procession frightened the crowd almost to the point of riot. The Strumiero survivors portrayed the earthquake and broken cross as an act of divine retribution against Savorgnan and the rebellious peasants, and even the Zambarlani saw God's hand in the disasters, although they imagined them to portend future calamities.[9]

Within weeks of the earthquake, plague infested Udine. Although the deadly disease had briefly appeared the previous autumn, Gregorio Amaseo convinced himself that its reappearance in the spring of 1511 came from the failure of the Friulans to avenge the innocent blood spilled on Giovedì Grasso. He examined the standard naturalistic theories of contagion, corruption, and astrological influence as possible causes and even recognized how bad weather had produced a poor harvest that elevated mortality rates over the summer, "but whatever cause was precipitant, by universal judgment it was reputed to have been the result of the divine scourge" brought on by the actions of Antonio Savorgnan. As proof, Amaseo reported that when Antonio returned from Venice on June 15, mortality quadrupled, forcing most of the healthy to abandon Udine to the dead and dying. Many of the poor perished in the streets from hunger or disease without the succor of medicines, prayers, last rites, or even a decent burial. As the graves filled, a terrible odor arose from the putrefying, unburied bodies (Figure 12, *upper plate*). Only when Antonio Savorgnan finally left Udine at the end of the summer did the plague abate. Thus, in the opinion of Amaseo and, by his report, of many others, Friuli's Iscariot had betrayed the land to the apocalyptic horsemen of war, sedition, earthquake, pestilence, and famine, who scourged the land to cleanse it of the pollution brought on by Giovedì Grasso.[10]

For contemporaries these disasters represented a double-edged sword because they could be both the results of human sins and portents of additional tribulations soon to befall Friuli. In the many accounts of those troubled times, Friulans searched to identify the agents of evil and to recruit cosmic forces in the struggle between local factions. Projecting their anger with their enemies onto God and assimilating their own values of vendetta to biblical ideas of divine justice, many saw the visions and disasters as the measure of events, the lens through which explanations filtered.

THE WILL TO NARRATE

God's judgment alone did not suffice. The survivors of Giovedì Grasso sought to enlist the judgment of history as well. For them the function of history was to preserve a record of past injustices, creating a peculiar relationship between violence and memory. Perhaps because pain assists recollection, the deepest, most haunting myths and rituals of many cultures recall bloody sacrifices, cruel tortures, and the deaths of innocents. Narrations about vendettas memorialized the travails of ancestors, preserving anguish for years and in so doing establishing a sensitivity to linear time reaching back for generations. The bearing of a grudge may well be one of the well springs from which historical consciousness flows, from which the decisions and actions of individuals in the past become for succeeding generations matters of fascination, matters in need of explanation, matters that motivate necessary deeds.

In preliterate feuding societies, various mnemonic devices kept alive the awareness of past slayings that required revenge. The feud sagas of the medieval Icelanders not only recorded the past but, through a stereotypical narrative form, provided a model for the resolution of future disputes. In Somaliland, Southern Greece, Albania, and Corsica, women sang haunting dirges to incite male kin to vengeance, and in some parts of Albania and Corsica a stone cairn erected on the spot of a murder reminded the men of their obligations every time they passed by. In Albania widows preserved vials of their husbands' blood, which they showed to their young sons to teach them to avenge the death of their fathers. Italians usually preserved memories of vendettas through stories told in an oral tradition that has survived in some regions well into the twentieth century.

During his enforced exile in Basilicata during the Fascist period, Carlo Levi heard the stories of ancient murders that ennobled the hatreds still obsessing the principal families; through repeated tellings that were far more common than any act of violence, these stories became the substance of vendettas and, more recently, of politics. If one were to ask where in society vendetta actually exists, how it is preserved, how its rules operate, one might best find the answer in the stories of past deeds, the selective memories that merged into new grievances and new enemies. The roots of vendetta intertwine with a kind of history that is an expression of the will to narrate.

Just as a Florentine merchant might keep a *ricordanza*—a "memory book" designed to inform his sons about the family business, marriage connections, and political alliances—or a Venetian patrician might write a chronicle of his city to instruct his fellows and progeny about the republic's mythic truths, so did Friulan aristocrats write down accounts of their relations with their blood enemies. Besides preserving a memory of events, these narratives justified past deeds, provided a basis for future retaliatory or legal actions, and protected family honor; in short they fashioned a version of events which served the needs of the family. Some of these accounts can be found among the family's private papers and were never intended for publication, but the anguish produced by Giovedì Grasso with its many unpaid debts of blood stimulated a new genre of works variously called *narratives, descriptions, histories, historical letters,* and *chronicles,* circulated as part of a campaign of exculpatory explanation and literary revenge. During the half-century after 1511, narrative assassinations became as much a part of the pursuit of vendetta as actual murders.

Some nine different accounts written after the events constituted the first generation of Giovedì Grasso narrations. In the intensity of its eyewitness descriptions, the *History of the Cruel Fat Thursday* by Gregorio Amaseo has no peer. Much of the attraction of the Friulan Giovedì Grasso for modern historians from Leopold von Ranke to the present author comes from the singular power of Amaseo's little history.

Belonging to a family long involved in the affairs of Udine, Gregorio participated in the events of 1511, a fact that makes his *History* especially valuable as a document of emotions. The Amaseos originated among the *popolo* of Udine, practicing in earlier generations the trades of barber, furrier, and pharmacist. Through the patronage of the Savorgnan, they attained communal office, bought lands, abandoned trade, entered the liberal professions, and by the early sixteenth century adopted a family crest and spurious descent from an ancient Bolognese noble family. Classic parvenus, they maintained a high consciousness of their privileges, worried about slights against their honor, wrote contemptuously about artisans, and tried to act like nobles.

Their attachment to the Savorgnan went back to the patriarchal civil wars, during which Domenico Amaseo saved Tristano Savorgnan from assassination by warning him in the middle of the night of a pending attack, later welcoming him triumphantly into Udine after the success of Venetian arms. "As a result the house of Savorgnan has been more obligated to the house of Amaseo than to all the rest of the patria and most of all has preserved the friendship up to the present because *amicus Socrates, amicus Plato, sed magis amica veritas.*" Even after 1509, when they became alienated from

Antonio Savorgnan, the Amaseos repeatedly tried to reclaim the connection with the Savorgnan on the basis of its antiquity. "I am not one of the new friends," Gregorio reminded Antonio, "ours is an old friendship of more than one hundred years duration." [11]

Three brothers, Leonardo, Gregorio, and Girolamo Amaseo, were among the grandchildren of Domenico and became the leading humanist intellectuals of their generation in Friuli. Leonardo married into the Monticolo family and produced eleven children. By examining the godparents of these children, one can discern the range of Amaseo friendships from the end of the fifteenth century to 1510 when Leonardo died. Three members of the Venetian patriciate stood at the font for Amaseo babies, as did several prominent officials of the Venetian citizen class including a secretary of the procurators, a ducal secretary, a collateral of the signoria, a chancellor of the luogotenente, and a notary of the *auditori nuovi*. After 1502 Antonio, Giovanni, and Girolamo Savorgnan all acted as godparents. Leonardo solidified his alliances within a Zambarlano network consisting of Venetians (especially Venetian professionals who worked in Venice at about the same social level as the Amaseos did in Friuli) and of the leading figures among the Savorgnan. However, these connections began to unravel in 1509 when the council of Udine, fearful that Antonio Savorgnan might be about to transfer his allegiance to the imperialists, elected Leonardo as the head of the city. Thereafter, Antonio considered the Amaseo brothers as traitors to his interests. The next year, Antonio blocked the appointment of Gregorio as a delegate to Venice and openly showed his ill favor to the brothers, who were unable to get even their Monticolo in-laws to help. The brothers' pleas and recollections of ancient friendship with the Savorgnan betrayed their bitterness at being rejected. By the time of Giovedì Grasso, Gregorio found himself in a dangerously ambiguous position, and although he still tried to reclaim Antonio's friendship, in private he was an acerbic critic of the Zambarlano leader.

After Leonardo's death in the summer of 1510, leadership of the family passed to Gregorio. One of the responsibilities he inherited was the continuation of Leonardo's diary, a vast record of the events of the war years begun for motives similar to those of Marin Sanudo, who also thought he was living through momentous times. In addition to recounting episodes in the war, the Amaseo diary chronicled the Friulan vendetta and reported opinions about the conflicts.

The brothers shared in the impulse that was widespread among intellectuals to explain the turmoils provoked by repeated foreign invasions and to capitalize on the confusion by obtaining commissions from governments that needed exculpation. In 1499, after France and Venice occupied Milan and the Venetians proposed to recruit the French for a new crusade against the Turks, the youngest Amaseo, Girolamo, published a book prophesying that the combined Christian powers would finally defeat the infidel, recapture Jerusalem, and impose a universal Christian monarchy that would usher in a new Golden Age. Borrowing the hexameters and rhetorical form of the classical epic, he revived late medieval prophecies and flattered the French king. However, in 1507, when Gregorio formally presented his brother's book to Louis XII in Milan the anticipated commission to write a history of the French conquests failed to materialize. Nevertheless, the brothers continued to keep the diary, which would have served as the source for a proposed Latin history if a patron had ever been found.

Both Gregorio and Girolamo had been students of the famous Friulan humanist Marcantonio Sabellico and struggled to maintain their positions as schoolmasters during the difficult war years. However, Gregorio brought his own personal liabilities to the family struggle for recognition. Frequently reproved for neglect of his duties, he lost his teaching position in Udine in 1489 when arrested after a nun became pregnant with his child. His resulting prison sentence was commuted to a six-month exile. Despite many misadventures including capture by papal troops, Gregorio moved in the highest literary circles of the Veneto and maintained a lively correspondence with other humanists. He eventually became a lecturer in Latin letters in Udine but failed to obtain a similar post in Venice in 1512. In addition to keeping up the family diary and writing his history of the Cruel Carnival he published a commentary on the history of the patriarchate of Aquileia.

Gregorio intended his polemical pamphlet history of Giovedì Grasso for a regional readership inasmuch as he composed it in Venetian rather than in Latin or Tuscan. Written in an unpolished style between March 1513 and February 1514 and giving a recounting of daily events, the *History* merely extended the family diaries in which Gregorio outlined his standards of evidence by noting that he recorded what happened "in large part according to the common gossip of the streets and in part from true information, mostly regarding events that took place in the patria and known positively by us and written down without any ornamentation and with little diligence." The *History* betrays slightly more humanist erudition than the diaries. Its precise beginning recalls the foreign invasions of Italy; a relentless thesis blames Antonio Savorgnan for planning a premeditated and diabolical massacre; and a sweeping conclusion explains all of the misfortunes of Friuli as the result of a divine vendetta provoked by the impieties of the Judas Antonio. The vitriol of Gregorio's language and the sensory immediacy of his descriptions allow the reader to begin to feel what it was like to witness the Cruel Carnival. Amaseo's *History* is reliable in recounting most facts correctly, even agreeing on matters of substance with Nicolò Monticolo's pro-Savorgnan version, but his stated goal not to offend anyone but to write a history motivated solely by a zeal for justice, liberty, the common good, piety, and peace was at best disingenuous. As might have been expected, he offended some people greatly.[12]

Because of his words, Gregorio became as much the object of retribution as those who had actively participated in vendetta murders. During the imperial invasion of 1514, some of the surviving partisans of Antonio Savorgnan proposed to take advantage of the situation to abduct Amaseo secretly, to gouge out his eyes and cut off his tongue and hands "so that," as Gregorio lamented, "I could neither see, nor speak, nor write about my cause." Particularly enraged when he read the *History* in a copy supposedly stolen from Gregorio himself, Antonio's surviving son, Nicolò, threatened to tear the humanist to pieces but missed his chance because, Amaseo thought, God prevented it. "If one still needs another example, then this result fully demonstrates the appearance of the divine vendetta." Gregorio's transition from an ardent Zambarlano to the most adamant literary enemy of Antonio Savorgnan and finally to an open propagandist for the Strumieri was epitomized by the funeral eulogy he gave in 1527 for Giovanni Della Torre, an encomium that led to a series of death threats against Gregorio. Once the memories of the eyewitnesses faded or died with them, Amaseo's *History* became the most important source of the collective memory. Even fifty years later, what Amaseo said had happened justified antagonisms and determined the appropriate forms of revenge.[13]

With the exception of Nicolò Monticolo's pro-Savorgnan version, the other accounts produced in the wake of Giovedì Grasso suggested various combinations of diabolical, providential, and astrological explanations. Giovanni Battista Cergneu and Giovanni Candido emphasized the persuasive power of Antonio Savorgnan's envious, iniquitous, and slanderous tongue among the ignorant. Several authors noted the coincidental revolts against nobles in Dalmatia, Slovenia, Hungary, and southern Germany but offered little to explain the waves of peasant rebellions other than malevolent celestial influences. Whatever the explanations, these narrations provided a literary substitute or postponement for exacting blood revenge. Referring to the Giovedì Grasso murderers, Giovanni Candido vowed, "I will annihilate them like the dust of the earth and crush them like the pieces of brick in the piazze." Of course he did nothing of the sort but contented himself with assaults of the pen.[14]

Friulans could not escape further travails. Although the factions would begin to dissolve after Giovedì Grasso, obligations of revenge remained, especially for the brothers and sons of victims whose honor was hardly restored by the scapegoating of a few lowly thugs. But revenge was not just a matter of keeping score. In retaliation for the 1511 carnival with its systematic butcheries of the Strumieri, avengers had to debase Antonio Savorgnan thoroughly.

CHAPTER FIVE

Retaliation

The events of the Cruel Carnival, continuing pressures of war, and tardy political reforms initiated by Venice eventually broke up the long-standing Friulan factions. Antonio Savorgnan's assassination followed a year of tensions and intrigues during which Venice again lost its hold on Friuli.

The murder was accomplished in a notoriously macabre fashion that reveals the deep cultural connections between vendetta practices and hunting, an activity that created a peculiar identity between killers and hunting dogs and formed a hierarchy for valuing the body parts of animal prey and human victims. A symbolic vocabulary derived from hunting enriched vendetta symbolism and paralleled the body imagery of carnival, which had influenced the forms of killing on Giovedì Grasso. Through a process of multiple projections, killers invested their hunting dogs with their own anger, a process that allowed them to see violent human emotions as being like the madness of a rabid dog or the wildness of a wolf and thus as something beyond human control. In addition, by feeding parts of the bodies of their victims to dogs and treating dead men as the objects of a hunt, avengers dehumanized their enemies, making them quite literally dog meat. As was the case with carnival, which emphasized the forms of butchering, vendetta imagery found its richest source in the processes for transforming bodies into meat, especially in the hunt.

In the years immediately after the war, factional killings waned as Girolamo Savorgnan failed to recapture his cousin Antonio's popular following. As a result of Girolamo's limitations as a leader and Venice's reforms of the governing institutions of Udine, the Zambarlano coalition of peasants and artisans collapsed. The course of Friulan history after the Cruel Carnival reveals how the carnival killings and the retaliatory assassination of Antonio Savorgnan produced a deeply resonant catharsis, the memory of which evoked intense emotions, and so weakened the patronage system that Friuli underwent fundamental changes.

ASSASSINATION OF ANTONIO SAVORGNAN

During June and July 1511, Venice encountered serious difficulties in its defense of Friuli from the Austrian invasion. Combatants had become so weakened by famine and plague that the surviving troops languished in their garrisons, and most of the fighting consisted of minor skirmishes and nocturnal raids. In addition, Venice found its financial resources drastically depleted. The provveditore for Friuli, Giovanni Vitturi, had not received regular payments for his men for months, and Venetian soldiers began to riot and loot in nearby Treviso. Antonio Savorgnan's repeated pleas for assistance were answered with testimonials of the doge's confidence in him rather than with troops and money. As a result he was able to rebuild only a portion of the fortifications at Marano. By the end of August the entire responsibility for the defense of Friuli had fallen on his shoulders.

Friuli seemed doomed. The region had been stripped of troops because the Venetian captains had insisted that the enemy would find it impossible to ford the Piave after all the available boats had been destroyed. They were wrong. In September the enemy crossed with ease. As the traditionally philo-Austrian nobles contacted imperial agents to transfer their allegiance in anticipation of the collapse of Venetian rule and in hopes of avenging themselves on Antonio Savorgnan, the Zambarlano townsmen and peasants tensely waited out events. Short of men and bereft of artillery, Antonio abandoned the fortified town of Sacile, and within hours the counts of Porcìa and Polcenigo offered their fealty to the empire. In Spilimbergo the exiled castellan Giovanni Enrico Spilimbergo captured the Venetian provveditore Giacomo Boldù and turned him and the town over to the Austrians, who then threatened Antonio's flank as he retreated toward Udine.

Faced with an untenable military situation and the probable sacking of Udine, Savorgnan agreed to receive imperial messengers who offered him extremely generous terms including the retention of all his properties and fiefs and a permanent alliance with the emperor. Antonio accepted, abandoning in a day the Savorgnan allegiance to Venice, which had lasted for more than a century. On September 20, accompanied by the imperial prefects, he entered Udine, hastily abandoned by the Venetian luogotenente, who had left behind all his artillery. With the help of these valuable pieces, Maximilian's captains quickly took the strategic fortress of Gradisca on the Isonzo, thereby completing their surprise conquest. Although none of Antonio's actions was without controversy, least of all this epic treason, most contemporaries agreed that he switched sides to save Udine from the destruction imperial armies had recently visited upon other towns.

All Friuli fell into enemy hands except for the lagoon fortress of Marano and the rock of Osoppo, which held out under Antonio's cousin, Girolamo. Despite his many protestations of loyalty to Venice, even Girolamo contemplated treason, traveling to Austria to negotiate terms with Maximilian. What transpired between them is unknown, but Girolamo returned to Osoppo dissatisfied, possibly because the emperor favored Antonio over him.

The Venetians were finally prompted to decisive political if not military action by the reversal of fortunes in Friuli and the surrender of Antonio in whom they had placed such high trust. The Council of Ten immediately confiscated all of his property and that of his brother Giovanni and Giovanni's sons Francesco and Bernardino, who were considered rebels because they were in imperial territory. Moreover, the ten offered a reward of 5,000 ducats and release from any previous sentence of banishment to anyone who successfully assassinated Antonio. Since its founding in the aftermath of the Querini-Tiepolo conspiracy of 1310, the council had indulged in the occasional political assassination, but the ten recognized that the scheme to kill Savorgnan was special. The assas-

sination contract, signed by three Strumiero lords who desired revenge for the Cruel Carnival, is the only document in the "most
secret" file of the secret archive of the council, which apparently
wanted a quick solution to the Savorgnan threat which could later
be publicly disavowed and blamed on the feuding Friulans, especially if the emperor became overly concerned.

In reaction to Antonio's betrayal, his former supporters in the
Venetian councils suffered political reprisals, none more so than his
most powerful advocate, Andrea Loredan. Despite the fact that on
the day before Antonio's double-cross the citizens of Udine had
sent a delegation to Venice asking that Andrea Loredan command
the city's garrison and despite the fact that on the very day of the
capitulation Loredan had loaned more money than anyone else to
provide for the troops in Padua refusing to leave their barracks
without pay, Loredan bore the brunt of the political backlash
against the Friulan traitor. On September 30 the bid of Loredan
and the other architects of Venice's policy in Friuli to be reelected
to the Senate was rejected, a particularly humiliating defeat inasmuch as established patricians were virtually guaranteed reelection.
In fact, not a single Loredan remained in the Senate. Throughout
the autumn Andrea Loredan and Pietro Cappello lost every office
for which they were nominated; it took nearly a year for Loredan's
career to recover and even longer for Cappello's.

Meanwhile, the enemy experienced its own dreadful problems.
One of the few documents preserved from the imperial side re-
counts the travails of the army occupying Friuli during the autumn
of 1511. Despite their rapid successes, the troops began to mutiny
because of a lack of pay and food, which could not be expropriated
locally because the region had already been so badly ravaged. Attempts to impose heavy taxes on the inhabitants alienated Maximilian's supporters among the castellans and townsmen, and it soon
became evident that the army could not safely winter there. With
the retreat of the French army under Gaston de Foix in Lombardy, Venice could concentrate its efforts on recapturing Friuli.
Imperial occupation forces stayed barely three weeks before they began to withdraw, leaving behind only a token garrison at Gradisca.

Faced with a debacle, Antonio Savorgnan tried to provoke an
uprising on his behalf in Udine, a desperate measure that failed
and forced him to retire to Gorizia, leaving all of Friuli, except

Gradisca, to return peacefully to Venetian authority. Antonio's son Nicolò broke the calm by sacking a few Strumiero castles. Throughout the winter both father and son menaced the borders with small guerrilla armies, but in the end Antonio and his followers faced a complete reversal of their fortunes. The turncoat sent repeated messages to Venice pleading for a safe conduct or a pardon and offering to help Venice capture Gradisca and Gorizia, but the Council of Ten refused to make the slightest concession to him. Girolamo's unbending hostility toward his cousin steeled the resolve of the council, which could not afford to antagonize the new Savorgnan lord, who now possessed all of Antonio's old fiefs and served as Venice's new client prince in Friuli.

During that winter, with the support of Girolamo and the ten, Artico Prampero plotted to lure Antonio into a trap at the mountain fortress of Chiusaforte, and wishful thinking produced recurrent false rumors that Antonio had already been murdered. As the emperor began to rebuild his forces, Venetian politicians were repeatedly gripped by fears that Antonio might return to lead a broad-based revolt. To head off the dangerous prospect of a revival of Antonio's popularity, the Venetians opened negotiations with the emperor in the early spring. On April 6, 1512 Maximilian signed a truce with Venice, an act that now made Savorgnan an unwelcome liability for the emperor, who wanted him to leave Gorizia, where he could cause trouble. Abandoned by all but his son and a few retainers, Antonio made a final retreat through the melting snow across the mountains to find refuge in Austria.

Savorgnan remained in seclusion in Villach, a pleasant town just across the Carnic Alps on the road to Graz and Vienna. There his enemies found him.

A band of Strumiero lords who had signed the assassination contract with the Council of Ten secretly entered the town with the complicity of Maximilian's representative in Villach, an exiled Friulan castellan named Federico Strassoldo. The assassins confessed to a mixture of motives. Girolamo Colloredo, the son of Albertino lord of Sterpo and the brother of Teseo, murdered on Giovedì Grasso, came along just "for revenge" (*per far la vendetta*) whereas Agostino Colloredo sought to reacquire the possessions he had lost the previous year. Peasants had sacked Giovanni Giorgio Zoppola's estate and raped two of the women of the family, and rioters had looted and burned the palace of Giacomo Castello, one of the three ringleaders of the Strumieri in Udine. Giovanni Enrico Spilimbergo had lost a brother on Giovedì Grasso, but for Giovanni Enrico, who had ridden abreast of Antonio Savorgnan when the imperial armies entered Udine in September and was one of the great men of the new imperial coalition, opportunism must have been the strongest motivation. After Antonio's move to the imperial flag had proved foolhardy, Giovanni Enrico again sought to stay on the good side of fortune by negotiating with the ten to assassinate Antonio, receiving in return a revocation of his life sentence of exile.[1]

The Friulans bribed two imperial captains in charge of security to be absent on the morning of May 27 while Antonio attended mass in the gray Gothic cathedral. The attackers concealed themselves at the foot of a stairway leading from the churchyard. After mass, as Antonio descended the stairs, the assassins and some ten *bravi* sprang out and drove their intended victim back into the cemetery. In the fight that followed, Giovanni Enrico Spilimbergo delivered the telling blows (Figure 13). Agostino Colloredo recounted the events:

> It was by divine miracle that Antonio Savorgnan was wounded: his head opened, he fell down, and he never spoke another word. But before he died, a giant dog came there and ate all his brains, and one cannot possibly deny that his brains were eaten. His familiar did nothing about it. . . . Since I am a priest, that is a canon of Aquileia and Cividale, I did not want to participate in that homicide, so I stayed at home.[2]

The macabre detail of a dog eating Antonio's brains became for contemporaries the most revealing point of the whole assassination, one that most subsequent accounts included or embellished. A Spilimbergo family chronicle improved on it by adding a pig:

> It is noted that when Messer Antonio Savorgnan was killed in the square of Villach . . . a pig and a dog came along from which he could not be protected until they had eaten the brains that had fallen on the ground. There are many people who do not believe this, but I have been assured of it by trustworthy men, among others by a surgeon, son of an Italian

FIGURE 13. Drawing of the murder of Antonio Savorgnan
in 1512 in Villach, Austria.

surgeon from Tolmezzo, who said that his father saw this happen with his own eyes. While this account is widely known, I
do not know from whom it originates, but I know well this
father and his son who, as I said, are faithful and good men.[3]

In his chronicle of the war years, Cergneu further refined the details by alluding to Dante's *Inferno*:

He never arose from that place where by divine will a pig
drank his blood and a dog ate the brains. Such was the just
end to the deeds of the new Judas who was sent to the lowest
circle of Hell in the first place among traitors.[4]

All of the assassins escaped except for Gregorio Colloredo, whom
the Austrian authorities captured when he stayed behind to destroy
a bridge.

The very day on which firm news of Antonio's assassination
arrived in Venice, the ten lifted Spilimbergo's banishment and
granted him a safe conduct, valid for one hundred years, to move

freely about the patria. When they presented themselves to the heads of the council, the killers tried to put an honorable face on their deeds by refusing the full reward and accepting only enough money to cover their expenses for bribes, hired *bravi*, and lost horses. The ten obligingly and uncharacteristically paid them off immediately and granted them and their relatives the right to bear arms wherever they went as protection from the anticipated retaliations of the Zambarlani. The erstwhile imperial governor in Villach, Federico Strassoldo, spent three years defending himself in Austrian courts against charges of his complicity in the murder, and although never convicted, his involvement ruined his career as an imperial courtier. From the confiscated wealth of Antonio Savorgnan, the ten began to pay a modest annual stipend to the heirs of Alvise Della Torre and to repair frontier fortresses, but the bulk of the estate remained under the control of Girolamo Savorgnan.

Dogs of Revenge

The phenomenon of the dog eating Antonio Savorgnan's brains demonstrates how useful animals can be for understanding human violence. The incorporation of animals into human affairs in Friuli contrasted with the ritual process of incorporation found in Venice with the annual execution of swine during carnival; in the Friulan vendetta animals actually participated in killings when men permitted or encouraged dogs to eat human victims. The Friulan experience might best be understood as an example of what Emmanuel Le Roy Ladurie has called the "spontaneously nominalist" mentality of the Renaissance, a mentality that was "better adapted to handling objects . . . as it saw fit than dealing with abstract concepts such as class struggle, reforms, etc."[5]

In his study of Menocchio, the heretic Friulan miller Carlo Ginzburg observed a similar characteristic. Menocchio treated the many metaphors that he employed in his speech in a "rigorously literal" fashion, thinking through problems by identifying one term of a comparison with the other, a mental process he followed when he envisioned the primal matter of the cosmos as cheese and the first men and angels as worms spontaneously generated from it. The characteristic nominalist logic involved strings of analogies, attaching like to like in an attempt to explain chaotic and violent events. In examining their own violence, even the educated Friulans who wrote the chronicles and histories employed animal metaphors nominalistically; to recapture their meaning, one must begin by trying to appreciate Friulan and Renaissance attitudes toward the animals in question, dogs in particular.[6]

The very lexicon of factionalism identified certain men as dogs. Antonio Savorgnan's principal retainers were the "familiars and dogs of the house" or the "dogs and comrades," an appellation distantly echoed by Shakespeare, who described "a dog of the house of Montague." Although the modern reader might dismiss these appellations as common insults, they seem to have had more substance than that: a subordinate might accept the label by referring to himself as "your dog and slave" when writing to his lord. The term implied that these men obeyed their master with the devotion of hunting hounds and that they were of a lowly condition. For example, when the Zambarlani realized that they could sack the palaces of the enemy nobles, "they became alert like dogs at the chase," and the peasants who attacked the castellans were likened to barking or rabid dogs.[7]

The eating dog more specifically brought out specters of apocalyptic revenge. In the days immediately after Antonio's treason, a defamatory sonnet circulated in Venice which ended with a vision of the traitor hanging by his foot from the gallows while dogs and crows pulled apart his body. Years later Giovanni Candido conjured up a list of horrible fates that he said befell those who had directed the carnival riots of 1511: some were dismembered, others broke their necks, many were thrown into deep wells where they drowned, still more were imprisoned or exiled to live a miserable life in foreign lands, a great many died of starvation, and "many seeking death became like rabid dogs and gave up the ghost." "The others, who were few, remained sick in spirit awaiting God's justice [la divina vendetta], prophesied by David." Few of the events Candido reported ever took place, but the list of imaginary fates provides a useful index of contemporary ideas of revenge.[8]

Friulans also talked about their own offenses by employing animal metaphors, especially comparisons with dogs and pigs, which explained human violence by showing how men had crossed the line into bestiality. In fact, analogies to these animals pervade the dialects of the Veneto, most significantly as blasphemies and insults. Comparing God or the Madonna to a dog or a pig, as in Dio *cane* and *porca Madonna*, juxtaposed the most sacred with the most profane, dragging all that was good and true into the filth, promiscuity, and senseless aggressiveness of these everyday animals. "You were baptized in a pig trough," as the dramatist Ruzante put it, might be the paradigmatic Veneto insult. Pigs and dogs were always in the streets of Udine and Spilimbergo, just as they were in every other European town, and their habits of eating offal and the remains of the unburied dead infested the thoughts of those who witnessed vendetta brutalities. To them the two species became the signs of shame, the contraries of the honorable, socially correct man, whose enemies in a vendetta could most thoroughly dishonor him by making him the food of street scavengers.[9]

The identification of men with dogs had ancient and widespread precedents in which men were said to metamorphose into dogs and dogs became men. Early medieval law considered domestic animals part of the household and subject to the same legal protection accorded to free persons, including *wergild* if killed. The legal personification of animals survived most clearly in the unwritten laws of twentieth-century Montenegro and Albania, in which the regulations of blood feuding made careful provisions for house dogs. Albanians trained and kept attack dogs, which could be handled safely only by the person who fed them; the dogs were unchained at night to guard against intruders. If a house dog killed someone at night, the victim's clan had no rights of revenge inasmuch as the law assumed that any man abroad in the dark was a robber or an enemy. If, on the other hand, a traveler killed a dog near its house in the dark, the dog's owner could seek to take blood from the killer's clan because, according to the laws of the Kanùn, "at night a dog is equivalent to a man." In fact, in some places, clansmen deemed the killing of a dog more serious than the murder of a man, as revealed in the notorious case in which twelve men forfeited their lives in recompense for one dog. In contrast, if a dog attacked a traveler on the public path or during the day, the victim's clan could then seek retribution from the dog's owner because under those conditions the animal was considered an offensive fighter for his clan rather than an exempt house dog deployed for defense.[10]

In a similar fashion in nineteenth-century Corsica, the killing or even criticism of a dog could lead to violent retaliation, so complete was the identification of the owner with his dog. Although we cannot know whether or not Friuli had a similar unwritten law during the Renaissance, many Friulans kept attack dogs for defense, and the language employed to describe feuding families reveals an attitude toward the dogs of a house similar to that of the modern Albanians. In addition, both Turkish and German invaders used dogs as combatants against unarmed civilians.

Some of the habit of personifying dogs survived even in the refined aristocratic regulations governing the duel. Stefano Guazzo reported that most disputes leading to duels arose from quarrels over gambling, women, or dogs; in Ferrara, at the time Ariosto was the poetic luminary of the court, a courtier challenged another to a duel because of the contempt the latter had shown the challenger's dog. The theorists of dueling noted that it would be infamous to attack a fallen duelist who had lost his weapon because even a shameful dog would not bite a prostrate man.

Numerous medieval forms of punishment enlisted dogs to degrade the guilty. The oldest example of a derisory punishment can be found among the laws of the Burgundians according to which robbers were forced to kiss a dog's anus in front of the assembled people. In 1008 the archbishop of Milan promulgated a penalty requiring the guilty to carry a dog while walking barefoot through the streets, and in a French law of 1306 a man accused of slaying his lord had to undergo the ordeal of fighting a dog. In his Roland epic, Boiardo recalled such practices by describing how a king ordered his men to turn over alive his most hated foe so that the king could have the captive fight a dog.

During the Renaissance dogs served as symbols of treason and usury and were feared as carriers of the plague. Their bones and teeth were used as amulets with apotropaic powers; along with pigs, dogs most commonly appeared as the familiars of witches, at least in the imagination of inquisitors who occupied themselves with such matters. The worst fate for a Renaissance duelist was to die like a dog, to be "dragged off by one of his arms or legs, with no more respect than would be shown to a dog or a piece of wood" and thrown in the common pit with other dead animals. Such was the death the Friulan avengers wished for their enemies.[11]

Comparing humans with dogs enabled participants and others to explain the passionate fury of vendetta killings by distinguishing kinds of anger. The ancient Greeks first isolated two types of an-

FIGURE 14. Drawing of a dog-headed man, astrological
emblem for the second degree of Aries, "a
quarrelsome and envious man," *right.*

ger: the cold-blooded, calculated anger Odysseus betrayed when
he systematically killed Penelope's suitors, as opposed to the anger
that drove Hector on the battlefield, his *lyssa* a wolfish or doglike
madness symptomatic of rabies. The most likely stimulus of *lyssa*
might be the overwhelming grief that comes from the loss of close
kin, the kind that engulfed Hecuba, who, after she lost all of her
children, began to bark like a dog. According to the Greeks, men
and women in *lyssa* abandoned their humanity and therefore could
no longer be subject to the law, and the disease of rabies retains in
modern times an association with bestial, uncontrollable violence.

Germanic traditions, which were undoubtedly strong in Friuli,
also metamorphosed humans into animals to explain ferocious anger, as can be seen in the sagas about the *berserkirs*, who assumed
the forms of wolves or bears to avenge the dead. Friulan folklore
assisted in imagining such metamorphoses. In a legend that can be
dated from as early as the twelfth century, Attila, the scourge who
destroyed ancient Aquileia, had the face and snout of a dog and the
body of a man. Instead of speaking his orders he barked them.
Indeed the half-dog, half-man became the standard Renaissance
astrological image of a degree of Aries labeled as the "quarrelsome
and envious man," as can be seen in Pietro d'Abano's *Astrolabium
planum* (Figure 14).

Even though they would not have used the same terms as the
Greeks or Germans, Friulans understood the different kinds of

anger when pursuing revenge. Although they most commonly employed the former method of careful planning and efficient execution, as in the murder of Antonio Savorgnan, they were particularly fascinated with the latter form, *lyssa* or going berserk, and they justified even the most cold-blooded killing by arguing that the murderer had been taken over by an uncontrollable rage.

In effect, the dog provided an explanation—to wit, the killers were like rabid dogs, beside themselves in anger, and did not know what they were doing—but the message of the brain-eating dog cannot simply be decoded from a binary distinction between human culture and bestial nature. Neither were humans purely cultural nor dogs exclusively natural. Just like dogs, which were usually tame and obedient, humans usually followed society's rules, but occasionally dogs went rabid and humans berserk. The problem that needed explanation was wildness. Here dogs helped because they provided an observable model for the transformation from domesticity to savagery and not just when they became rabid. There was something in any dog's nature which could go inexplicably wild, something dogs shared with their close relatives the wolves, animals that often preyed on human society. In the two natures of dogs, the servile and the wolfish, humans saw an especially revealing mirror of themselves, of both their need for community and the tendency of some men to tear society apart by murdering others.

In contrast to the ancients, who had such a positive image of the wolf, the mother of Rome, the people of the Middle Ages and Renaissance saw wolves as representing wildness in its most threatening aspect. In describing the earliest settlements of the Venetian lagoon, the *Altine Chronicle* imagined a primordial wilderness occupied by a savage folk who howled like wolves and lived by hunting. Only when they learned the arts of agriculture and civilization did they tame themselves, along with their wilderness habitat.

In Friuli real wolves remained an ever-present threat, recalled by many place names such as Lovària and Lovàries and in numerous accounts of bloody attacks, particularly on children. The howls of wolves could be heard frequently on winter nights when hungry packs descended from the mountains in search of food. Ill protected against these predators, many villagers relied on spike-collared attack dogs which they let loose at night. Dogs best deterred the ravages of wolves precisely because the two species were so similar: a properly equipped and trained mastiff might be the match of a wolf, but he was still vulnerable both to attack and to the temptations of joining the wild pack. In the imagination of contemporaries, the appearance of wolves augured evil events, especially war or tyranny. As Francesco Sacchetti put it in a different context, "more than any other that beast has the desire to kill human nature." [12]

Friulans also believed in wolfmen, but their attitude toward them was contradictory and changing, paralleling the range of attitudes displayed toward the vendetta. Before the advent of inquisitorial procedures in the late sixteenth century, folklore pictured werewolves as benevolent figures who battled devils to save the crops and who served as the hounds of God, tracking down the devil just as good hunting dogs chased foxes. However, under pressure from inquisitors Friulans who were investigated for their alleged magical practices gradually changed their views and began to see werewolves as predators who stole livestock.

In Old German, the word *warg* had the meanings of both *stranger* and *wolf*, an etymologic connection reflected in late medieval statutes that equated the reward for the head of an outlaw with that offered for the head of a wolf. The ominous pronouncement, *caput gerat lupinum*, still in use in England in the thirteenth century, had its origins in a quasi-magical legal formula that transformed a criminal into a werewolf to be hunted down like a dangerous animal, not just because he was outside the law but because he had become, in the words of the law, a wolf.

Friulans also associated wolves with exiles who, as we have seen, became werewolves through a legal metamorphosis. In fact, in reading the Friulan chronicles it is sometimes difficult to determine whether an "attack by wolves" should be understood literally or metaphorically as a reference to a band of outlaws. Faced with roaming bands of outlaws who survived by robbing, Venice frequently added extra bounties and incentives to encourage the killing of these banished wolfmen. Finally, the connection between vendetta and the behavior of wolves becomes most explicit in the term used to describe a formal truce made between feuding parties, the "wolf's peace" (*pace lupina*).

Thus, Friulans connected in several ways the pursuit of revenge with the behavior of dogs, wolves, and wolfmen, connections that envisioned vendetta as a form of wildness. The syllogistic reasoning was simple: avenging men behaved like wolves, wolves were by definition wild, therefore avenging men were wild. Wild animals served as signs of mad impulses found in human nature and as particularly useful receptacles of human vices. Because much modern scholarly work on feuding has emphasized the structural elements of vendetta which make it appear to be a reasonable form of conflict resolution, it might be useful to note the ambivalence that Friulans felt about their own desires for revenge, an ambivalence deriving not only from their mixed legal and ethical traditions but from their very understanding of the nature of humanity and wildness.

References to animal metamorphoses, killings, and wild transformations also recall the vast body of folklore about the armies of the dead. In his largely fictive description of the death in Villach of Gregorio Colloredo, one of Antonio Savorgnan's assassins, Gregorio Amaseo conjured up a diabolic horde rushing to capture the sinner's soul, a reference that imposes a Christian overlay on a deep pagan tradition about phantom armies battling in the sky in clouds and storms:

> [Gregorio Colloredo] was freed from the prison by the anger of the people having been agitated by a terrible cloud within a ferocious storm that struck that town as if the infernal furies with the diabolic hordes raced to abduct that most rotten soul for the eternal torments of the deep abyss; and not satisfied with that, in the following days terrible noises, which turned everything upside down, were heard at night in the cathedral where he [Antonio] was buried, and feeling attacked now here now there, the above mentioned people were so excited in their fury that they pulled the corpse from there and threw him into the Dravo River.[13]

Ottavia Niccoli discusses similar visions seen in storms and clouds near the site of the great battle of Agnadello in which phantom armies composed of the restless souls of dead soldiers transformed themselves into armies of pigs and dogs who rose up in a furious horde that she sees as an expression of beliefs about the wanderings of the dead. Carlo Ginzburg has analyzed a related complex of beliefs about persons who went into battle against evil forces during ecstatic trances or dreams. One of the prime examples of such beliefs comes from the *benandanti* of Friuli, who were set apart at birth by the presence of the caul and who fought as adults to preserve the crops. Ginzburg has found similar beliefs in many areas from Europe to Siberia. All of these groups believed that after a human metamorphosis into an animal, typically a dog or wolf, the changed person fought for good against evil. Ginzburg explains these metamorphoses as symbolizing a temporary death—just as did initiations, rites of passage, and the sentences of exile that transformed men into wolves—and depicts the groups who fought in ecstatic combats as representing the living in a struggle with the dead.

Beliefs about the armies of the dead, which were certainly current in sixteenth-century Friuli, produced numerous homologies to what can be found in descriptions of the assassination of Antonio Savorgnan: the presence of dogs, a combat, and visions of a diabolic horde in a storm. Such homologies enrich the context for understanding beliefs about the dead and the relationship between humans and animals, but they do not explain exactly what happened during the vendetta. After all the assassins of Antonio Savorgnan did not become dogs but brought the animals along to a killing. In the assassination and in the fates of several of the carnival victims, animals were deployed as agents of human retribution. The essential vendetta element seems to be the cooperative relationship between killers and dogs in which the dogs' role is to eat the victim.

The Friulan cases are not isolated examples. A Venetian legend current in the early sixteenth century described the deaths of Doge Pietro Candiano and his son, murdered by a mob in 958. After the people killed them, their bodies were taken to a butcher shop and cut into small pieces, which were thrown to the market dogs. Such a fate continued to be promised to others who violated the trust of the Venetian people, especially to Antonio Grimani who, after his loss of Lepanto in 1499, was the subject of numerous wall posters that threatened to serve him and his sons to dogs. In 1500 the provveditore of Castelmaggiore reported to Venice that some peasants had forcefully boarded a boat on the Po and stolen money from the Milanese ambassador to Spain. The Venetian authorities captured one of the robbers, killed him, and "gave the head to some dogs to eat." Thus, even in cases of summary official justice, the same forms of punishment could be employed as in private acts of revenge, revealing a complex entanglement between public and private notions of justice. Such an interplay can be found in popular lynchings, such as that of Galeazzo Maria Sforza's assassin, who, after he was killed by the crowd, was dragged about the city by children and finally fed to the street swine. And during the wars of religion in France, combatants threatened to and occasionally did feed a victim of the opposite faith to dogs and pigs. Thus, the Friulan examples fit into a broad tradition of feeding an enemy to an animal.[14]

One might begin to look for the meanings conveyed by these acts in the rich religious and literary lore about dogs eating men and women, stories that suggest the possible range of attitudes about the practice. In avenging the death of Patroklas, Achilleus tells the mortally wounded Hektor, in the words of the *Iliad*:

> No more entreating of me, you dog, by knees or parents.
> I wish only that my spirit and fury would drive me to hack
> your meat away and eat it raw for the things that you have
> done to me. So there is no one who can hold the dogs off from
> your head, not if they bring here and set before me ten times
> and twenty times the ransom, and promise more in addition,
> not if Priam son of Dardanos should offer to weigh out your
> bulk in gold; not even so shall the lady your mother who her-
> self bore you lay you on the death-bed and mourn you: no,
> but the dogs and the birds will have you all for their feasting.[15]

In his manic vision, Achilleus identifies himself with the dog, imagining his enemy abandoned to cannibalism and the deserted field of battle.

War was not the only ancient situation that destined a victim to dogs. Jezebel was condemned to be eaten by dogs, "and the carcass of Jezebel shall be as dung upon the face of the field" (2 Kings 9:35–37). For both Greeks and Hebrews the most horrific end conceivable involved turning a corpse over to dogs, whose gluttony made impossible even the most elementary provisions for honorable mourning and burial. The polluting effects of contacts with dogs and pigs permeates the Psalms and can be found in

Christ's commands in the Sermon on the Mount: "give not that which is holy unto the dogs, neither cast ye your pearls before swine, lest they trample them under their feet, and turn again and rend you" (Matthew 7:6). Despite the Christian abandonment of the rigid prohibitions of Leviticus and Hebraic fears of pollution, the medieval penitentials continued to see the eating habits of dogs as especially disgusting. Among the penalties for neglect of the consecrated host was a forty-day penance for those who vomited it up because they had eaten too much beforehand. If they cast it into a fire the penitentials reduced the penance to twenty days, but if they allowed dogs to eat the vomit, the penalty increased to one hundred days.

Renaissance literature continued to associate the hungry dog with fears about dishonorment at death. The most revealing examples from a region near Friuli come from the works of the Paduan dramatist Angelo Beolco, known as Il Ruzante. Working between about 1517 and 1536, Beolco wrote and produced plays that employed peasant characters who commented on contemporary events and mores. The sad-sack character Ruzante, who appears in many of the comedies and was played by Beolco himself, imagined when he felt victimized that he would end up having his starved flesh eaten by dogs and when he felt strong that he could condemn his enemies to the same fate. The image of dogs consuming human flesh appears recurrently in the plays, nearly always as part of an oath or as a vision of perfect revenge.

Similar images can be found elsewhere, especially in Shakespeare. Transforming a man into dog feces denied his very humanity and his chances for proper burial, a result that would have disquieted his survivors and left his soul in torment for eternity. Contemporaries, therefore, understood the presence of a dog feeding on a murdered man as a sign of dehumanization, the most complete form of dishonor.

Many of these examples, from the words of Achilleus to the death of Antonio Savorgnan, emphasize the eating of the head: why is it so often the head rather than the heart, liver, or human tripe? The best clues for an answer might be found in yet another context, that of hunting, from which the forms of revenge killing must have ultimately derived. The division of the bag of a hunt and the servings at a banquet represented and even constructed hierarchies of honor among members of society. The late medieval and Renaissance treatises on hunting, thus, prescribed a rigid code of comportment which divided up the kill according to the social hierarchy: typically, persons of merit or rank received those portions that were large and originated high on the animal's body, cuts from the tenderloin, haunch, thigh, or shoulder. However, the value ascribed to the head was ambiguous inasmuch as, on the one hand, it was not particularly desirable to eat, but, on the other, it was the source of the higher faculties. At medieval royal Irish banquets the head of the prey went to lowly persons such as butchers and stewards. In contrast, in the Veneto and Friuli, the head went to the lord or best hunter; other parts were distributed to lesser men; and the expendable innards of lungs, liver, and entrails were thrown to the hunting dogs. Animals' heads, in fact, had a special significance in feudal homages in the region. In the eleventh century, the doges of Venice received boars' heads to signify feudal dominion over subject towns and decorated the ducal palace with them, probably in imitation of the hunting practice of displaying trophies by hanging parts of the kill in trees. The feeding of a man's head to a dog by Friulans inverted a well-known hunting and feudal practice by giving the most noble part of the kill, the prey's head, to the lowest members of the party, the dog pack. The assassins of Antonio Savorgnan brought down to the lowest possible state the very part that had masterminded so many evils, an act that made his brains no better than the tripes of a boar. Antonio's handsome head literally became offal.

Moreover, the habits of hunters help explain many of the more puzzling events associated with the Cruel Carnival and its aftermath. Several of the members of Antonio Savorgnan's "dog pack" had duties or traits that identified them with hunting. The man known as Ferrarese was Antonio's falconer, the essential expert in the prime aristocratic sport, and the nicknames Vergon (lime-twig) and Smergon (loon), both alluded to the hunting of birds, one of the most popular sports in Friuli, especially in the marshes of the lower plain, in which the Savorgnan had extensive properties. Thus, on Giovedì Grasso Antonio Savorgnan's experts in killing animals served as the experts in killing men. Many of the victims who were systematically dismembered with butcher's knives and fed to the dogs were quite consciously treated as if they were game.

The shared trait of danger links war, revenge, and hunting. An important theme in the hunting literature is of the danger created when boars, bears, and other hunted animals turn on the hunter and attack him. Throughout the Middle Ages hunting represented a necessary exercise for war inasmuch as knights hunted to practice riding and killing and to retain their technical and tactical skills. Following this tradition, Renaissance theorists classified hunting as the "armed peace," a special form of warfare.

Erasmo da Valvasone, a Friulan castellan, wrote a treatise published in 1591 on the history of hunting which makes clear the connection to war by reversing the usual assumptions about historical evolution which supposed that hunting preceded agriculture as a stage of civilization. The first men only killed animals to make sacrifices to the gods, he states, but then after the invention of agriculture goats and boars had to be killed as punishment for destroying crops. Threats to herds and flocks led to the domestication of dogs to serve as guards, and when these animals began to accompany men on their sorties against dangerous wild beasts, the true hunt was born. From the very beginning, according to the Friulan aristocrat Valvasone, the hunt was an aspect of defensive warfare, and over the centuries valiant men continued the practice to facilitate training in the use of arms. By linking the hunt to warfare and by placing the origins of both at an advanced stage in the evolution of civilization, Valvasone tried to remove the taint of primitive wildness from hunting practices and to justify the hunt as a necessary training for aristocratic soldiers.

The similarity between hunting and warfare was so widely accepted that most writers assumed that the eating of meat contributed to the aggressiveness needed in battle. Making an analogous assumption, judges frequently imposed abstinence from meat on violent criminals.

In contrast to the enthusiasm of the nobility, clerical moralists had a strong bias against hunting. True to its urban origins, Christianity evinced a positive horror of the forests and wilds, the domain of pagans and uncivilized brutes, and the place in which the necessary barriers between humans and animals broke down. Early church councils, for example, prohibited bishops, presbyters, and deacons from keeping hunting dogs, and after 826 priests were obliged to refrain from the hunt. John of Salisbury and others wrote harshly about the primitive cruelty of hunters, especially the intolerable exaltation they exhibited when they returned from a successful chase. In a similar vein, an anonymous chronicle of the mid-fourteenth century described the hunting scenes on the tomb of Mastino II Della Scala as "paganisms." Others, such as a Regensburg monk who said hunters had the qualities of dogs and Thomas More who in *Utopia* pointed out that sportsmen act like dogs pursuing rabbits, thought that hunters rejected God's plan for humanity as his most elevated creation.

Apologists for hunting felt obliged to answer these traditional Christian objections to the practice. The Friulan Jacopo di Porcìa argued that the sweet pleasures of hunting, birding, and fishing must be enjoyed to experience the majesty of divine creation. Did not God create the natural world for our use, he asked? Porcìa explained away the objections of Augustine, Jerome, and Ambrose by arguing that they were only against gladiatorial combats with animals. Moreover, he asserted, hunting could serve ethical purposes because it was better than games of dice and cards, which provoked violence, and considerably better for youths than the alternative pleasures of whoring. Erasmo da Valvasone added that inasmuch as the activities of hunters brought them into contact with witches who lived in the wilds and exposed them to the evil eye, they found Christian piety even more important than those who were devoted to more sedentary pursuits.

Criticisms of hunting suggest a fundamental opposition between the practices of hunting and the Catholic notions of morality and ritual, which derived their power from the liturgical celebration of Christ's singular sacrifice. The relationship or polemical opposition between hunting and religious sacrifice recalls the work of Walter Burkert on the rituals of animal sacrifice in ancient Greece. Burkert linked these practices to Paleolithic hunting. Following anthropological theory, he notes that a transition occurred when humans switched their roles from hunted to hunters and took on the deadly attributes of leopards and wolves, created a culture of weapons, employed fire, differentiated sexual roles markedly, and organized cooperative work by family groups and male hunting bands. "From this perspective, then we can understand man's terrifying violence as deriving from the behavior of the predatory animal, whose characteristics he came to acquire in the course of becoming man." Because the practice of hunting as the principal means of obtaining food distinguishes early humans from other primates and because most of human history comprises the Paleolithic Age of hunting, the hunting experience, Burkert argues, can account for many of the most elemental forms of our culture, especially sacred ritual. In ethnographic accounts, hunters report feelings of guilt about killing animals and describe the ceremonial ways in which they reacquired innocence after a kill. The killing of animals, thus, produced a craving for ritual.[16]

One need not follow Burkert far back into prehistory nor need one accept some notion of a hunting archetype to recognize the power of hunting as a model for killing in Renaissance Italy. All the vendetta killers certainly had years of experience as hunters and knew intimately the little rituals associated with the distribution of the kill. They lived in a culture in which hunting was widespread and yet was understood as antithetical to strict Christian morality. Thus, hunting shared with vendetta an ambivalent position as a practice authorized by custom but criticized by the clergy, and for most people hunting produced the most common experience with killing.

As their comments show, the Christian critics recognized that hunters blurred the distinction between human and animal, most obviously in naming themselves after their prey, particularly their most violent prey, with appellations such as Ursus, Lupus, or Smergon, and in identifying with their canine companions in the chase. From the hunt came weapons and the cooperative society of male hunting bands, so analogous to the wolf pack, so similar to an army. To become effective hunters youths had to learn how to suppress inhibitions to killing; and once they had learned how to kill animals, they knew how to kill men. A final similarity proffers a final hypothesis for understanding vendetta. The game killed in the hunt satiated hunger. The desire for revenge was also often described as a hunger. If hunting provided the model for vendetta and hunters ate their prey, then the great temptation of vendetta killing may have been to eat the victim, to follow the logic of the hunt into cannibalism.

Although Friulans would have recognized that "vengeance is an appetite," as Frank Lestringant has put it, they projected their hunger for revenge onto their dogs, who ate the body parts of their victims. Cannibalism, or more properly anthropophagy, was more often heard as a slur or a threat than enacted as part of the practices of revenge. A defamatory sonnet accused Antonio Savorgnan of drinking human blood, and after a street fight in Orzano the victor threatened to stuff a dying man's brains into the mouth of a woman who attempted to intervene; but the accusation and threat seem to have been unrealized metaphors for uncontrollable anger. Even though nearly contemporary cases of revenge cannibalism can be found in Modena, Florence, Naples, Dalmatia, France, and Holland, avengers in war- and vendetta-ravaged Friuli seem to have employed their dogs to act out cannibalistic hallucinations.[17]

Friulans and others understood the passionate hunger for revenge as a kind of wildness. They might accept the necessity of killing others, even see it as a moral obligation to lost kin, but murder was never normal, never without some taint. Even when they planned their revenge carefully and had authorization from the Venetian overlords, as did the assassins of Antonio Savorgnan, they masked their thirst for blood behind the behavior of canine companions. Dogs helped degrade an enemy completely, and rabid dogs provided a model for explaining human behavior when mad blood stirred or *lyssa* took hold.

Behind political calculations, class pride, obligations to friends and relatives, chivalrous tales, solemn oaths, petty disputes about precedence, and punctilious humanistic discussions about honor, all of which fitted out the vendetta, stalked the self's secret shadow, the beast. Unable to admit his guiding influence in their passions, the revengers of Friuli saw him less often as part of themselves than as some alien, hot-blooded animal that they had become. They transfigured self-delusion through symbols and metaphors and even acted out their bestial metaphors by bringing a hungry dog along to eat their victim's entrails or brains. The incorporation of animals into human events facilitated the projection of disturbing human feelings onto them and provided meaning for a certain kind of murder which was feverish in execution yet cold-blooded in anticipation.

In such habits of thought and action the cultural gap between ourselves and our ancestors is wide indeed, a gap that has tempted many modern scholars to discount or ignore the macabre tales of vendetta violence to search for a more rational, commonplace explanation for seemingly irrational behavior. By trying to bridge that gap, however, we may recapture a different kind of reasoning based on a logic of analogies, an alien mental world in which humanity and nature merged with each other, and we may demystify forms of action which repeated the most primitive human experiences.

Friuli still had much to endure. The war dragged on until 1516, provoking further atrocities, and the threat or reality of an imperial invasion reappeared every campaign season. The experience of prolonged warfare changed Friulan society in several subtle but significant ways. Girolamo Savorgnan sought to replace his cousin as a leader; but because of Girolamo's obsession with his own rights and privileges, he never captured the affection of the common people. Learning the lessons of Antonio's *volte-face*, Venetian politicians trusted Girolamo less, eventually reforming the institutions of Udine and the rural villages to break up the solidarity of the Zambarlano faction. The final defeat of the empire badly damaged the prestige and autonomy of the Strumiero castellans, who now had to go into exile or retreat to the safety of their castles.

The travails of repeated invasions and factional strife exhausted a whole generation. After killing four Zambarlano leaders, the brothers, sons, and nephews of the Cruel Carnival victims worked out a relatively pacific *modus vivendi* with their enemies. Although no one forgot what happened in 1511, obligations to avenge a murdered relative were at least postponed. Once the factional coalitions dissolved, the imperative of vendetta became a less vital part of a family's strategy, probably because the need to appear invincible to clients and retainers became less a measure of power. Young toughs still found themselves in trouble, but their acts of bravado failed to excite others and had few political consequences. Artisans and peasants hardly noticed the blood disputes of lords anymore. When the vendetta finally returned in the 1540s under entirely different stimuli, it quickly evolved into an affair among intensely self-conscious gallants who acted out their animosities on the new stage of the Renaissance courts, where men fought with refined courtesy. As a result, in little more than a generation men whose grandfathers and great-uncles had fed their enemies to dogs began to dedicate themselves to a stately pavan of lies given, gauntlets dropped, duels fought.

CHAPTER SIX

Toward the Duel

By the middle of the sixteenth century when the vendetta revived, traditional obligations of revenge competed with new
attitudes toward honor which were made popular by the spread
of courtly manners and the fashion for dueling. Traditional vendetta practices had relied on flexible, implicit rules that encouraged
atrocious ambushes and allowed families to devise their own strategies for maintaining their collective honor. In contrast, the new
ethos relied on explicit rules codified in books of manners and
guides to dueling, publications that portrayed honor as an individual rather than collective trait. Even the most isolated Friulan
castellan came into contact with the new values of aristocratic behavior through the proliferation of books on the subject, most of
which were printed in Venice, the center of Italian publishing, and
through the influence of the many exiled Friulans who found refuge in the north Italian courts. As a result, while old men won-
dered about how to adapt to the changing times, their sons and
nephews self-consciously fashioned themselves as courtiers and
duelists.

Resumption of the Vendetta

The most likely reasons for the revival of the vendetta after more than a generation can be discovered in the declining position of the Savorgnan clan, which sought an outlet for various pressures in pursuing old, half-forgotten grievances against the heirs of the Strumieri. In the first incidents of violence after a twenty-three-year hiatus the vendetta between the Savorgnan and their enemies continued to follow the old patterns: one night in 1545 Ercole Della Rovere was discovered prostrate in the streets of Udine with his throat slit. Although no one saw Ercole's killer, suspicion immediately fell on Tristano Savorgnan, who found a convenient prostitute to provide him with an alibi for the night of the murder. He and his brother Giacomo, grandnephews of Girolamo Savorgnan and members of a minor branch of the clan, were both in their twenties and, in the fashion of the Savorgnan, had begun to gather around them a popular following in Udine. Unfortunately for them, competition for leadership of the traditional Savorgnan clients included the six surviving sons of Girolamo (see Table 7), much the better equipped to succeed. The struggle among the Savorgnan for client supporters weakened their influence in the town, resulting in a loss of the most prized Savorgnan juridical privileges. Their rights in Udine to transport lumber and collect rents on watermills were taken away in 1546 when the independent-minded commune abrogated the clan's jurisdiction over the streams that ran through the city. With this loss, the three hundred-year-old ecologic stranglehold of the Savorgnan over Udine loosened.

Having failed to unify themselves or to recreate a large body of loyal followers, the Savorgnan scattered their energies like shot in little animosities toward others. In 1547 Germanico Savorgnan, a son of Girolamo, killed three Corbelli in an ambush he set for them on the boat route to Venice. A few months after Germanico's banishment, Tristano and a band of *bravi* drew their swords against three Colloredi, a Strassoldo, and a Caporiacco, leaving several of the combatants wounded.

The full fury of the contenders was unleashed in yet another bloody carnival fight in 1549. Girolamo Colloredo and Girolamo Della Torre on the one side and Giovanni and Tristano Savorgnan on the other all went to Padua to participate in the scheduled jousts. The presence of such notorious mutual enemies so worried the rectors of Padua that they required the two groups to swear formal pledges against any trouble. A few days after the pledges, in the labyrinth of blind alleys near the great pilgrimage church of Saint Anthony, a Savorgnan party of eight ran into the Colloredo-Della Torre companions and about twenty of their *bravi*. A desperate fight broke out which left two followers of the Colloredo dead, Giovanni Savorgnan nearly dead, and several others wounded. Tristano barely escaped by finding refuge in a nearby house. In the ensuing investigation, the Council of Ten absolved the Savorgnan from blame and condemned their opponents: Girolamo Colloredo faced perpetual banishment from Venice, Padua, and Friuli; and Girolamo Della Torre was relegated for ten years to Crete, where he had to report on a monthly basis to the local rector. Colloredo could not be released from his banishment under any conditions, and Della Torre might be pardoned only by a unanimous vote of the council.

After the publication of the sentences, Girolamo Della Torre waited in Venice to take passage to Crete. With the intention of seeing him off, several Colloredo and Della Torre relatives journeyed to the lagunar city, choosing a circuitous route to avoid trouble. However, Tristano, whose honor was not satisfied by the sentences of the Council of Ten, had them shadowed and planned an ambush for their arrival in Venice. He hired two spacious Chioggian boats used for transporting fruit: he and his *bravi*, who were heavily armed with harquebuses and swords, hid under reed mats in the bottom of the craft. As the gondola carrying the Della Torre-Colloredo party rowed past the landing at San Marcuola on the Grand Canal, the Chioggian boats pulled along either side. At a signal, Tristano and his men jumped up and let loose a fusillade against the passengers on the gondola. The assailants then boarded the smaller craft and delivered the *coup de grâce* to the survivors. Dead in the attack were old Alvise Della Torre's youngest son, born after his father's murder in 1511 and named in his memory, and the senior Alvise's son-in-law, Giovanni Battista Colloredo. The identities of the victims led contemporaries to remark on the direct link between the events of 1511 in Udine and those of 1549 in Venice. Although the ten immediately arrested other members of the Savorgnan family, Tristano and his men succeeded in escaping to Pinzano, the mountain fortress first granted to Antonio Savorgnan early in the century. Pinzano was so isolated and difficult to approach that the luogotenente complained he could neither surround the refuge nor even determine through his spies if Tristano was still there.

Although the Council of Ten had overlooked Tristano's earlier transgressions, his outrageous ambush in the very heart of Venice could not be ignored. In fact, the ten pronounced the most draconian sentence it had ever emitted against a Friulan criminal, more severe even than the secret condemnation of Antonio Savorgnan in 1511. On August 27, 1549 the council forever banished Tristano from all territories under Venetian jurisdiction, promised to tear down to the foundations his palace in Udine and his other houses and castles, confiscated the lands beneath these buildings so that they would remain forever empty as a perpetual memorial to the crimes (*et Terrenum ipsum si confiscatum super quo nunquem aliquia Fabricari possit ad perpetuam memoriam tanti delicti*), and revoked his and all his descendants' memberships in the Venetian patriciate. If he were ever unlucky enough to be captured, he would be taken to San Marcuola, where the public executioner would read out his sentence and chop off his right hand. He would then be removed to Santa Croce, tied behind a horse, and dragged all the way to San Marco, where he would be beheaded, drawn, and quartered. In the end, only the palace in Udine, the very one from which Antonio Savorgnan had addressed his followers on that fateful carnival morning thirty-eight years before, was torn down. Venetian officials were so thorough in the destruction that they gathered up the remaining rubble and inventoried it to prevent scavenging by Savorgnan partisans. The prohibition against new buildings on the site has remained in force, if only by custom. Today it is used as a municipal parking lot.

Armed with a sword engraved with the boastful motto, MIHI VINDICTAM, Tristano continued to seek revenge from his foes, many of whom were also living abroad under sentences of banishment. The year after the Grand Canal murders, he appeared in Crete and attempted to kill Girolamo Della Torre, still serving his sentence of relegation for his role in the Padua fight. In contrast to Tristano, Girolamo Colloredo wandered to Rome, where after a conversion experience he was admitted into the Society of Jesus.

He wrote letter after letter to his brother Marzio urging him to forget their grievances against the Savorgnan and to accept the mediation offered by Patriarch Giovanni Grimani.

However, Marzio Colloredo showed only contempt for Christian passivity. He became the *de facto* head of the clan and for nearly twenty years devoted himself to avenging the many wrongs visited upon his forefathers. Besides the loss of his father in Tristano's daring Grand Canal ambush, he especially lamented the horrible murder of his maternal grandfather, Alvise Della Torre, who had been thrown to the market dogs in the 1511 slaughter. Marzio soon began to make trouble in Udine. On the feast day of Saint Bernardino in 1551, he and some cousins clashed with a band led by one Marco da Carpi, head of the militia of Portogruaro and partisan of the Savorgnan. Afterward, the luogotenente recommended to the Council of Ten that Marco be removed from the region but also noted that he had been unable to convince the Colloredo to reduce the numbers of their retainers. Each of the Colloredo always had four to eight armed men about him and when traveling expanded the escort to fifteen or twenty. In the opposite camp, the Savorgnan youths shifted their loyalties from the exiled Tristano to Antonio the younger, the grandnephew of the famous Antonio.

Late the following winter Marzio and five others ambushed Antonio in the public streets, killing him and two retainers. News of the attack impelled merchants to close up their shops in anticipation of further street violence, but Luogotenente Francesco Michiel managed to keep the situation under control. In response to these murders the Council of Ten sentenced Marzio, the two Colloredo relatives who accompanied him, and their *bravi* to perpetual exile, confiscated their property, and offered a one thousand-ducat reward for them dead or alive.

Marzio wandered first to Gorizia, then to Milan, and eventually to Florence where he entered the service of Grand Duke Cosimo I. Breaking his ban in 1555, Marzio led a company of armed men back to Udine where they attempted to shoot Antonio Savorgnan's father, Bernardino. They failed to break into the palace room in which he had barricaded himself and had to be content with killing his horses and beating the servants. Another attack on Giacomo Arigone also faltered. In 1559 Marzio was accused of helping some of his relatives murder two men, one a knight of the luogotenente.

During the next two years, Marzio was serving with the Tuscan troops sent to assist Ottavio Farnese in Lombardy and from there renewed his attack on his Savorgnan foes through his son, Ludovico, who fatally wounded Francesco Savorgnan in a nasty street brawl in Udine. In 1561, some Colloredo men and castellan allies ambushed a party of Savorgnan supporters at a crossing of the Tagliamento resulting in a free-for-all among the boulders of the river bank. Only one man survived in the Savorgnan party.

In the most notorious of his attacks, Marzio sent bombs hidden in sealed boxes to Nicolò and Urbano Savorgnan, but the recipients disarmed the devices without injury. There were several subsequent attempts at revenge against the Colloredo for the bombs, culminating in an assault on the steps of the luogotenente's palace, where Federigo Savorgnan hacked down Claudio and Livio Colloredo in broad daylight. After those attacks, the character of vendetta violence began to change.

Marzio himself began to amend his aggressive habits because during his peregrinations he was exposed to a world of courtly refinement, in which men eschewed vendetta and resolved their disputes through duels. Despite his quick temper and fondness for violence, he had considerable success in adapting to his new environment and gradually came to accept the courtly rules of dueling while pursuing his quarrel with the Savorgnan, several of whom were also exiles in other princely courts. We shall return to Marzio Colloredo and the Savorgnan, but first we need to look at the nature of the new manners they learned as courtiers.

THE NEW MANNERS

During the middle decades of the sixteenth century under the thrall of a renewed courtly ethic, many Italian aristocrats changed their behavior, nowhere more notably than in how they pursued vendetta. The Renaissance revival of courtly values shared with earlier medieval versions of the courtly ethic Cicero's *De Officiis* as the principal source of inspiration, but the sixteenth-century movement, which was made popular by Erasmus's *Manners for Children* and Castiglione's *The Book of the Courtier*, both widely available in numerous printed editions, had a far broader and more lasting influence.

As we have seen, traditional representations of revenge relied on a blurring of the boundaries between humans and animals, pigs and dogs in particular. In contrast, courtliness erected rigid barriers between the human and the animal, condemning all animallike behavior in men and women. Giovanni Della Casa's *Galateo* identified the essential mark of boors as eating like pigs; Della Casa described these ill-bred fellows as "those we sometimes see who, totally oblivious like pigs with their snouts in the swill, never raise their faces nor their eyes, let alone their hands, from the food in front of them." As Norbert Elias pointed out, the new manners reinforced an aversion to animallike traits in men and women by encouraging a repulsion to the bodies of animals themselves, especially in the form of meat. During the sixteenth century feelings among the upper classes changed from those of pleasure in seeing and carving up a dead animal at the table to ones of discomfort with anything that reminded diners that eating meat had something to do with killing. Just by adopting refined table manners, such as using a fork and napkin, courteous men and women distanced themselves from their food, creating a layer of manners which, in separating them from direct contact with bodies and with animals, severed the habitual connections of millennia and produced a new sensitivity. In such an atmosphere the habits of revenge which had mixed the human and the bestial by leaving human corpses to be eaten by dogs became especially repulsive.[1]

The psychological as well as social implications of the new manners can hardly be overemphasized. The courtesy books presented good manners as being similar to a fine cloak, and as Erasmus saw it, clothing revealed much more than a superficial exercise of taste, becoming "in a sense the body of the body," the visible sign by which one discovered the character of the wearer's soul. In addition, other outward signs manifest by bearing, gestures, facial expressions, bodily movements, and above all speech revealed an individual's inner qualities. Such a view was, of course, a neo-Platonic commonplace, but the courtesy books of the sixteenth century translated obscure abstractions into practical rules of behavior which subjected the inner person to an outer tyrant, who demanded conformity to a model of behavior which abhorred excess in any expression of feeling.[2]

Thus good manners repressed emotions. The courteous denied or delayed all impulses, never admitted fear, controlled and channeled anger into the duel, and sublimated sexual appetites through elaborate flirtations. The repression of emotions imposed a kind of lie, a socially salutary lie perhaps, but a lie nevertheless. The courteous man or woman lied to others about their feelings and if truly courteous probably lied to themselves. Yet in the deepest irony of all, every word and deed had to appear to be natural, neither artificial nor false, and avoiding falsehood obsessed the theorists of courtesy, so much so that a reputation for dishonesty became the most serious social fault and calling someone a liar the surest step on the path to a duel. A concern for telling the truth necessarily corrected courtesy's requirements of dissimulation, but the conflict between emotional denial and verbal honesty created by the new manners forced the courteous into fitful inconsistencies of behavior which are characteristic of those who try to live in a double bind.

Giovanni Della Casa's *Galateo*, among Friulans probably the most influential guide to refined manners, best illustrates the conflict. Della Casa spent much of his career in Venice and environs, writing *Galateo* between 1552 and 1555 while in retirement near Treviso. *Galateo* charmed so many because Della Casa chose as his narrator an ignorant old man who brought good manners down from the reconditeness of the learned to the level of the simple gentleman who aspired to emulate those in the highest aristocratic circles. *Galateo* not only refashioned conduct but made unmentionable whole realms of human experience: a polite man never alluded to the wrath, gluttony, lust, avarice, or other unseemly desires of others, "in as much as these appetites are not evident in their manners of behaviour or in their speech, but elsewhere." In other words, those things not manifest through the accepted forms of gentle manners and refined speech should not even register themselves in the mind of the gentleman or lady.

Della Casa also condemned a variety of things which had, in his opinion, the attributes of deceit, those things that consist "in appearances without substance and in words without meaning." Dreams in particular should not be openly discussed because they have no basis in reality and are nearly as deceptive as lies that purposefully contradict reality. When repressed, unpleasant emotions would most likely reveal themselves in dreams and slips of the tongue, those little unintended statements Della Casa correctly understood had to be ignored if courtesy were to be upheld.[3]

Although advocating the adoption of good manners, Della Casa seems to have inadvertently uncovered and tried to resolve the very problem politeness created, the forced distancing of self-expression from uncomfortable realities. By denying even the existence of unpleasant emotions, courtesy encouraged an objectionable artificiality of manners which exemplified mendacity. Although he lamented the unfortunate effects of good manners, in particular the proliferation of empty ceremonies, Della Casa resigned himself to a situation that could not be changed and recommended that readers abide by the customs of the time ameliorated by the principles of moderation. Clients of a prince, especially constrained by courteous formalities, had to cultivate the virtue of honest dissimulation, as it was termed, the trait that required silence or at least great discretion in expressing some thoughts. For them to be caught in a lie did not so much mean a loss of personal dignity as a loss of honor in having failed to manage impressions properly.

Among the principal writers on courtesy, including Baldassare Castiglione, Stefano Guazzo, and Giovanni Della Casa, Annibale Romei best defined the relationship between honor and revenge in his dialogue, *On Honor*. He distinguished between, on the one hand, virtue, which is innate, usually hidden, and rewarded by eternal salvation, and on the other honor, which is acquired, always visible, and rewarded by the esteem of society. Virtue comes from the soul. In contrast, honor comes neither from the soul nor the body but from the proceeds of life, such as riches, political offices, influence, friends, beautiful wives, healthy sons, and titles of nobility. Honor exists in the eyes of other men and disappears when their favor is lost. The most likely way to lose the respect of other men is to fail to avenge an injury. One of the interlocutors in Romei's dialogue points out that previous writers (he is referring primarily to the Thomists) had argued against fighting an injust quarrel or offending God when they avenged; but, he counters, those who truly value the honor of the world will never allow their reputation to die away by failing to redress an insult no matter what its cause. An honorable man must prefer death to dishonor, a short honorable life to a long vituperative one. In addition, an honorable man must avoid resorting to the courts of law when he has received an injury because he might be suspected of lacking valor and courage. Above all he must maintain the appearance of the willingness to defend his honor because once it is lost, no matter what the cause, it can never be regained.

By requiring a gentleman to respond to injuries, the principles of honor placed a courtier in an awkward position in that he needed to sustain his own honor and the honor of his house, but he also had to acquiesce in the restraints on his conduct demanded by the court itself. In accepting the patronage of a prince, the courtier joined a voluntary association that subordinated the needs of its constituent members to those of the prince. Private vendettas could injure the authority of the prince; but also through its etiquette the court incorporated its members into a new body that had its own values, separate and distinct from the traditional family values of the aristocracy. In response to the injured gentleman's dilemma, the princely courts developed compensatory measures that tied up revenge in the elaborate knots of the duel. Although the society of the princely courts needed a mechanism such as the duel, princes themselves had to uphold the law, which meant that at best they winked at what was technically illegal. Absurd as the new behavior of the duel appeared, not just to us but to many contemporaries, it had a civilizing effect, to follow Norbert Elias's famous formula. At least in its early phases in Italy, the duel markedly reduced levels of interpersonal violence and even more importantly replaced the collective aspects of vendetta with a highly individualized concept of honor.

Although historically derived from medieval judicial and chivalric combats, the Renaissance duel can be distinguished by the fact that it was a private affair practiced outside of the official institutions for resolving conflicts. Duelists abandoned armor and usually their mounts, employed simple weapons, and chose isolated spots for fighting. The well-mannered accoutrements of the duel evolved in the Italian courts and were exported elsewhere, especially to Spain, France, and England. The technical literature on dueling developed over two centuries from Giovanni da Legnano's work of 1360 to reach its apogee in the middle third of the sixteenth century. Andrea Alciato codified the circumstances that called for a duel in a work that went through six editions between 1544 and 1552, but the best-known authority became Girolamo Muzio's *The Duel*, first printed in Venice in 1550 and republished in five more editions by 1563, thirteen by the end of the century. The Venetian printing industry issued these and similar dueling manuals for the large market of aristocrats from the terraferma.

The rules for the duel created a script for an extended, almost theatrical, performance that channeled the dangerous anger of the participants into a series of formalities which disarmed opponents until they could meet on the dueling ground. More complicated than the actual rules of combat were the regulations that framed the duel, the formulas for insulting, challenging, arranging, and judging. In theory a precise succession of steps preceded a duel. First, one party insulted or accused the other of something contrary to honor. The second party denied the insult or accusation by giving the lie, saying simply, "You lie" or "You lie in the throat." The original accuser then responded with a formal challenge. Because the gentleman challenged had the choice of weapons, it was advantageous to give the lie first, forcing the other to make the challenge. Each of these three stages depended entirely on words rather than deeds, following an assumption that questions of honor had to be made explicit before they actually existed, which of course made dissimulation an effective defense against involvement in a duel.

The whole dueling script hinged on giving the lie. When a gentleman said, "you lie," he meant "you have unmasked me"; that is, the accuser had uncovered a necessary social fiction, and whatever the truth or falseness of the accusation, the fiction had to be reconstituted.

Definitions of lying and methods of giving the lie harbored immense complexities. Giovanni Battista Possevino defined the lie as, "a statement which nullified something said by another, to the disadvantage of the latter's honor, with intent to free the other party from infamy and to force his opponent to offer his proofs." General definitions, however, did not help much in dealing with the ambiguities of daily conversation, a situation that led theorists to classify the kinds of lies. Muzio suggested five types, and the amendments of others produced a list of thirty-two sorts of lies. After struggling over what was a lie and what was not, potential duelists had to follow the polished formalities of the challenge. A gentleman who slipped up at any step in the process showed himself to be an unworthy combatant and gave his opponent an honorable excuse for backing out of the confrontation.[4]

The challenger sent to the challenged a *pegno*, usually a glove but sometimes a ring, belt, or dagger. If the challenged refused to accept the glove, then the bearer must cast it at his feet in the presence of other worthy witnesses. In the legalistic environment of sixteenth-century Italy, challenges were usually accompanied by a document, which was notarized, witnessed by well-known persons, and sometimes printed up for general circulation around the several courts. Muzio recommended that a document of challenge be as brief as possible, specifying the injurious words spoken and giving precise details such as the time, place, and witnesses. However, many of those that have survived are elaborate treatises, whole pamphlets, or even small books, as excessive in detail as a lawyer's brief. Once all of these stages had been properly executed, the challenged gentleman had three options: to accept the challenge, ignore it, or answer it with objections.

Assuming that the disputants got that far, the forms for the actual combat were relatively simple: the challenger met the challenged on a designated field of battle with designated weapons; seconds backed up each combatant; the seconds took precautions against the use of charms or magic; and before a neutral judge each duelist swore an oath affirming the justice of his cause. The fight sustained the theatricality of the duel by restricting violence to a confined space at a designated time and by requiring the presence of an audience qualified to judge the performance.

After the duel another set of intricate rules came into play, completing the frame of controls around a combat that itself could not be controlled. The seconds and a judge determined the number and character of the wounds inflicted on each duelist, whether dead or alive, ranking each injury by a precise scale that evaluated the parts of the body: they appraised the loss of an eye over a tooth, the right eye over the left, a foot over a hand, a wound on the right hand over the left, one on the head over either hand, and a mark on the front of the body over one on the back, but, not surprisingly, a clean thrust through the body counted more than anything else. After cataloguing the wounds, the judge made two different kinds of determinations: who was the superior fighter and who was correct in the quarrel. Actual duels resulted in various combinations of these two decisions; for example, the loser might recant his accusation but not surrender his person, or he could be mortally wounded but still maintain he was correct. There might not be any decision, but according to the rules it was highly doubtful that a reconciliation taking place on the field would be honorable. Although contrary to statutory law, the duel remained legalistic in its forms. Whatever the result, the findings had to be written up, signed by a judge, and certified by a notary.

However, no matter how punctiliously duelists followed them, the rules themselves neither conferred nor preserved honor, which came from how well a gentleman presented himself and how well others accepted his self-presentation. Some men of high repute could break the rules with impunity; others of tarnished name could never follow them rigorously enough. The transaction of honor came when each man recognized the other as a worthy combatant capable of acting out the drama of honor well.

From the very beginning, the dueling fad in Italy provoked controversy, particularly over its ethical value and its relationship to vendetta. Defenders of the practice argued that the duel derived from the principle of self-defense found in natural law, and some went so far as to say that because the Christian injunction to forgive contradicted this natural principle, the duel represented an ethic superior to religion, an ethic that prevented worse evils such as unregulated fighting and assassinations. According to Paris de Puteo, the duel actually executed divine justice because in private battles God usually favored the just, but Puteo recommended moderate punishments inasmuch as God did not always make His will evident. Fausto da Longiano wrote about the "religion of honor," which reserved the duel for true cavaliers. For several of the sixteenth-century writers, Lombard law provided the ultimate justification for the duel. For example, Muzio found twenty-two reasons for private combats in Lombard law and added seven additional ones of his own, but he distinguished these legitimate situations from the vendetta: "the fields of combat," he insisted, "have been established to realize the truth and not to give anyone a means for carrying on a vendetta." Other writers stressed that the purpose of the duel must neither be revenge, which in any case could be obtained without the risk to life of the duel, nor to acquire honor but only to keep or regain it. Indeed, a gentleman who defended himself from an attack by killing his assailant must not accept a challenge from any of the dead man's relatives because pursuing revenge through dueling was dishonorable. On this point, of course, much of the theory of the duel foundered because distinguishing the motives of others was not a very accurate exercise and because aristocratic avengers became particularly attracted to the duel as a means of pursuing their traditional enmities in the guise of the highest fashion.[5]

Opponents of the duel recognized the problems in determining motives and contended that legal proceedings discovered the truth more accurately than duels and provided ample means for redressing injuries. Antonio Massa's book, *Against the Use of the Duel*, published in 1555, argued on ethical grounds that God reserved revenge for himself and enjoined mortals to forgive their enemies. In the climate of the Counter-Reformation, critics identified the duel with vendetta, both of which valued the private punishment of offenses, and as an alternative to these they advocated clemency, which revealed a greatness of spirit through the generous willingness to pardon wrongs.

Perhaps the most effective polemicist against both vendetta and dueling was Fabio Albergati, who lived as a courtier in Urbino and Rome, where he wrote a series of political and moralistic tracts. His *On the Means of Pacifying Private Enmities* of 1583 built its argument on the fundamental principle that "a person must control himself." In it Albergati discussed five ways of redressing a wrong: restitution, the returning to an owner what is properly his; satisfaction, the receipt of whatever is sufficient for the retention of honor by an offended party; punishment, the product of the judgment of a magistrate or prince; vendetta, an injured party doing something to an offender in recompense for what has been suffered; and chastisement, the penalty a superior administers to an inferior. Although not in principle opposed to restitution and satisfaction, both of which recreated balance in a situation of inequality, and supportive of legitimate punishment, Albergati wanted particularly to undermine vendetta and chastisement, both of which created inequalities. Albergati cleverly employed the very arguments of the apologists of vendetta to connect it to the duel and to undermine both practices. Whereas they thought that honor was best sustained when the offended reoffended the offender in conformity with the ancient law of retaliation, Albergati argued that the principal goal of the offended had to be to remove impediments to retaining his honor, which could be achieved best by demonstrating that he was a man of virtue. Although the vendetta might have brought pleasure, it neither ended the dispute, even if the enemy was killed, nor did it preserve honor inasmuch as a murderer was by definition infamous. Vendetta, therefore, failed to achieve the desired results. Following this essentially pragmatic argument, Albergati added that the duel may have been superior to vendetta because the dispute was ended, and the victor retained his honor; but the duel also had crippling problems. Many believe, he stated, that the duel would become a useful expedient when an offender would obstinately reject both restitution and satisfaction. Their argument came from comparing a duel with a judicial proceeding in which the challenger was the accuser, the challenged the accused, and the fight a means of knowing the truth. But in practice, Albergati argued, the duel failed to render real justice and merely fed the vanity of the combatants. Most seriously, it injured the authority of the prince, whose judgments and punishments had to be heeded. In effect, the duel preserved rather than replaced vendetta and had to be rejected for the same reasons.

As even the apologists for the duel recognized, the law had long been hostile to all forms of private combat. In Italy opposition had come from two primary sources: the church, which prohibited it as early as 855, and the city-republics, which rejected the practice because of its association with the lawlessness of the nobles. The Council of Trent in its first session reaffirmed the ecclesiastical hierarchy's old condemnation of private combat, and as the new dueling fad spread, town after town reenacted old injunctions against it. In Milan it became illegal just to respond to an insult by giving the lie.

Venice's Council of Ten passed laws with penalties more stringent than in other cities. A 1541 decree made it illegal to post written challenges and promised ten years banishment just for drawing one up. A generation later Marco Mantova reported that the council's motive in prohibiting duels had been a religious one although the simple need for maintaining law and order might have been sufficient. The universal legal condemnation of dueling presented combatants with both religious and civil penalties for doing what the preservation of their honor seemed to require.

The Friulans caught up in vendettas found the collective burdens of revenge they shared with other members of their families incompatible with the new values of individual honor. By the end of the 1550s, castellans throughout Friuli had read and heard a great deal about dueling, and those exiled to foreign courts were constrained to conform to the new standards if they wished to survive the competition for princely favor. Very quickly, in a matter of a few years, old vendetta practices disappeared in favor of duels.

Revenge by Courtesies

On May Day, the citizens of Udine decorated their houses with boughs and erected the traditional maypole. For the holiday in 1559 they also anticipated watching knights joust in a field of honor marked out for the occasion. Arrangements for the tournament fell to Ugo Candido and Ottavio Zucco, who met to make final plans on the morning of the festival. During their discussions Zucco felt Candido had insulted him in some way and demanded satisfaction. Candido angrily yelled, "You lie." Zucco replied, "I accept the challenge." Several nobles rushed in urging a reconciliation, and as a precaution against a murderous engagement, the luogotenente had the tilting bar taken down. Despite numerous attempts at mediation in the ensuing weeks, the luogotenente failed to pacify the two men and finally ordered them to appear in Venice before the Council of Ten, which, upon reviewing the case, requested the intervention of the ambassador of the duke of Urbino. After a meeting arranged by the ambassador ended with each disputant throwing down his gage, the ten placed both men under house arrest. It was the end of September before the two cooled off enough to submit to a formal peace administered by the luogotenente.[6]

The Candido-Zucco confrontation took a form entirely new for a dispute in Friuli. Demanding satisfaction, giving the lie, throwing down a gage, and accepting a challenge show the first signs that at least some Friulan aristocrats had adopted courtly mores quite different from the traditional ones that promoted vicious ambushes and theatric degradations. The Council of Ten recognized that it was out of its element in these chivalric formalities and called upon a foreign expert to mediate. The ambassador from Urbino represented, of course, the court most responsible for the propagation of the code of aristocratic manners which Candido and Zucco were trying to emulate.

The adoption in Friuli of the new courtly manners, specifically employed to distinguish those endowed with aristocratic virtue from tainted commoners, made final the divorce between the castellans' vendetta and the old factional coalitions that had once bonded upper class disputes with the ambitions of lesser mortals. Clothed in the velvets of good manners, a Savorgnan of the 1560s, for example, would never allow peasant militiamen to do his dirty work for him as had his ancestors half a century before.

Dueling suddenly appeared in Friuli as a by-product of developments in European weaponry and warfare which threatened the status of noble warriors. First, in the midsixteenth century technologic improvements in swordmaking led to the widespread adoption of the needlepoint rapier, which was useless in warfare but extremely deadly in private combat wherein a single well-placed thrust could have fatal consequences. The greater danger of the rapier and the spreading habit of carrying pistols required a code to regulate combat although as critics pointed out, the rules of honor which governed the duel seemed to stimulate rather than inhibit bloodshed. Second, the devastating success of the Swiss pikemen and the use of field artillery during the Italian wars made the infantry triumphant and cavalry largely obsolete, a development that eliminated the rationale for the nobility as the fighting class. The craze for dueling which spread from Italy in the midsixteenth century probably compensated the nobles for the loss of combative purpose which accompanied the military revolution. Thus, Zucco and Candido in their personal transition from a sporting joust to a dismounted duel reflected the general trend of the time.

The influence of exiles quickened the transition among Friulans to the duel as a form of private combat. Marzio Colloredo, who had spent the 1550s avenging the Grand Canal murders, headed up a gathering of Friulan exiles in Florence and Milan while their Savorgnan adversaries found refuge at the Gonzaga court in Mantua. Between 1563 and 1568, the Colloredo and the Savorgnan exchanged a series of manifestos and challenges which reiterated the old quarrels between the two clans and disputed the technicalities of the behavior appropriate to an honorable cavalier. Both sides recomposed the past in light of the explicit rules of courtly honor and the duel, but neither was very consistent in doing so, and nei-

ther admitted any contradiction between seeking revenge and be-
having as courtiers. In contrast to the unanimity of the dueling
apologists, the exiled Friulans envisioned the duel as the potential
fulfillment of vendetta.

They printed most of their charges and countercharges, some as
pamphlets and others as posters for public display. Each document
was addressed to and signed by a specific individual or group, but
the intended readership certainly comprised the larger community
of gentlemen in the courts of northern Italy in which the exiles from
both camps had to maintain their reputations. Urbano Savorgnan
defined the desired readership in his mocking response to a printed
challenge from Camillo Colloredo, "but I do not believe that it was
distributed anywhere except among peasants since no one had heard
of it in the courts or the principal cities." Many of the published
challenges included a list of witnesses from the most distinguished
aristocratic families of northern Italy: signing for the Colloredo
were members of the Doria, Pio, Borromeo, Bentivoglio, Mala-
testa, and Gonzaga families and for the Savorgnan, other members
of the Bentivoglio and Gonzaga. The Colloredo boasted the support of Don Pedro de Mendoza, the Spanish viceroy in Milan, and
the Savorgnan looked to Duke Alfonso II d'Este of Ferrara and
Alfonso Bevilaqua, governor of Modena. The Savorgnan also enjoyed the patronage of the Academy of the Senseless in Bologna, an
obscure chivalric debating society devoted to questions of honor.[7]

As late as 1562 Marzio Colloredo employed shameful methods
that were incompatible with honorable dueling when he sent package bombs to Nicolò and Urbano Savorgnan. Up until this point
Marzio had been quite capable of living in two worlds, fighting
against his old Friulan enemies by whatever treachery he could get
away with but adapting to the rigors of the duel in his disputes in
Milan. In contrast to Marzio's dividedness, the Savorgnan were the
first to assimilate completely the new ethic by suggesting that a
duel might end the old vendetta.

While visiting the imperial court in 1563, Nicolò Savorgnan
widely discussed the situation in Friuli which was almost as troublesome for the empire as for Venice. He was reported to have proposed that to end the enmity between his family and the scions of
the old Strumiero families it would be useful to stage a "contest
of honor." In Milan Marzio heard about Nicolò's words and on

May 10 sent Savorgnan a formal challenge stating that he was prepared to meet Nicolò in a closed dueling ground without armor,
each with a sword, under the sole condition that the result would
produce a permanent peace: "thus, we cavaliers with a risk to a
few can put an end to the deaths of many." In July Nicolò answered the challenge. His *Manifesto of the Illustrious Nicolò Savorgnan
to the Readers* appeared on a large sheet suitable for posting and was
written in an exquisite Tuscan utterly alien to his native Friuli:

> A hard field of battle is truly that where one finds those who,
> deprived of strength and the secure arms of reason, wounded
> by the very pricking of their own conscience, and hunted by
> fear of the Judgment of the World, resort as an extreme
> remedy of their wretchedness to the insane alchemy of false
> appearances. In such a situation I believe that one truly now
> finds Signor Marzio Colloredo.[8]

An accusation of a lie was, thus, foremost in Nicolò's response
to Marzio. Continuing his mocking tone, Nicolò marveled that
Marzio had suddenly become so fierce after years of failing to
avenge the deaths of so many close relatives, but Nicolò would not
accept a contest of honor with Marzio because he had sent package
bombs to Urbano and Tristano. Moreover, Marzio had shown his
ignorance of chivalric form by proposing the type of weapon in
the challenge, a right reserved for the individual challenged. Instead of a duel, Nicolò perhaps facetiously suggested a "contest of
insults." Marzio replied with the rather fanciful allegation that Nicolò had made the bombs himself and sent them to his relatives in
an attempt to besmirch the honor of the Colloredi. The recrimi-
nations escalated until Nicolò retired from the field of invective,
insisting an honorable gentleman could not deal with someone as
lowly as Marzio. However, during this battle of the pamphlets,
violence between the two sides started to dissipate.

From the autumn of 1563 to the following spring, various individuals from the two sides exchanged challenges and responses in
a war of words which mostly kept the printers happy. At one point
Marzio challenged Nicolò again, offering to submit the dispute to
a neutral judge named by the two sides, a tactical shift that attempted to remove Marzio from the opprobrium of the Nicolò's
Manifesto; Nicolò still refused. Apparently Nicolò's attitude em-

barrassed some of his Savorgnan relations because even before Marzio issued his second challenge to Nicolò, Federigo Savorgnan submitted to Marzio a counterchallenge to a duel, saying he supported Nicolò's arguments about the secret bombs but would meet Marzio anyway. Once arrangements for that duel had been set in motion, Camillo and Federico Colloredo proposed to Tristano and Urbano Savorgnan that they also meet on the same field for a final resolution of all the past conflicts among them, but in an exaggerated display of chivalric form, the two Savorgnan refused.

Thus, only the duel between Federigo Savorgnan and Marzio Colloredo remained in place. Given the prohibitions of the Council of Trent, the seconds and judge had to find a secret site for the combat, a search that prolonged the preparations. Arrangements for a fight on the banks of the Po had to be aborted on the day of the duel when soldiers of the duke of Ferrara showed up to arrest the combatants and witnesses. Finally on June 15, 1564, near the isolated village of Arenzano on the Ligurian coast, the duel took place. To prevent any interventions in the fight, the seconds retired to the ship that had brought the two parties to the shore. Only some sailors and local men witnessed the opening of the duel, but their shouts soon brought the seconds back to the beach where they found the two combatants bloodied with several wounds and grappling arm to arm. After separating them, the seconds exhorted them to peace, which the two accepted. Embracing his former enemy, Marzio declared, "the war between us is now over, and in the future I intend to be your good brother."[9]

However, the end did not come so easily. After several weeks of recuperation in Genoa, the two principals could not agree on the major issue of how to make their friendship public, and they departed without resolving their quarrel. Letters and rumors began to circulate presenting conflicting details about the duel. An anonymous pamphlet from the Savorgnan side included the notarized accounts of several eyewitnesses who described Marzio as having fought like a coward. Colloredo finally replied with his own pamphlet, published in Brescia in February 1565.

Marzio's tract went far beyond the immediate issues of the duel to recapitulate the whole history of the vendetta going back to 1511. Opening with a denial that he had anything to do with sending secret bombs, he asserted instead that Nicolò had tried to poison him on three separate occasions. After making this new allegation, Marzio jumped back in time to the atrocities of the Cruel Carnival, emphasizing how the Savorgnan had left the corpses of two of his ancestors in the streets to be eaten by dogs. There followed the long sorry story of the vendetta since that time, complete with details about assaults unknown from other sources. Marzio conceded all the attacks members of the Colloredo had made against the Savorgnan but explained that in each case the Savorgnan had either provoked the fight or deserved to die in retaliation for the murder of a Colloredo. In all he covered some seventeen occasions of conflict between the two families, insisting that his family had never resorted to any of the horrible, dishonorable deeds of the other side, whose crimes included burning corpses, killing old men and priests, and administering poison.

Colloredo's tract is a history, albeit a highly biased one, complete with specific citations of sources and evaluations of conflicting evidence. Although he asserted that he had based his version of the Cruel Carnival on the account with the most prestige, the humanist history of the Venetian wars by Pietro Bembo, he in fact ransacked the Amaseo diary and Colloredo family papers for details that slandered the Savorgnan. To Marzio the complete history outweighed any individual event, such as his recent duel, but he had to rewrite that history to make it conform to the new principles of honor. The character of past deeds became of paramount importance because in little details of behavior and speech one discovered the honor of true gentlemen.

In these waning years of the vendetta, reinterpreting the history of the previous half-century became the dominant weapon, more useful than any sword. In an odd twist, the duel's emphasis on verbal formalities and conformity to a rigid code of honor helped convert violence into a debate about history from which the proof of honor and shame could be truly found.

The duel for a perpetual peace had obviously failed. On August 5, 1565, in answer to the allegations made in Marzio's tract, Tristano Savorgnan challenged him to another duel. By then, however, Marzio had joined Don García de Toledo's expedition to relieve Malta from the Turkish siege. Marzio's brother Camillo presented himself as a substitute duelist, but Tristano refused to accept the substitution, accusing Marzio of having fled to Malta to escape the

Savorgnan. The affair degenerated into a petty squabble although on technical grounds Tristano had a point. Theorists of dueling emphasized that honor must be seen as the attribute of an individual, a trait that could not be transferred even from brother to brother. In the exchange of communications that followed Tristano's challenge, two contrasting notions of honor were clarified, the Colloredo insisting on a more old-fashioned concept that honor based on lineage could be defended by any member of the family and the Savorgnan adopting the more contemporary idea of the individuality of honor.

Once he returned to Italy, Marzio renewed his pamphlet war on the Savorgnan, repeating many of the old allegations and inventing new facts to support them. Although back in 1545 no one had noted such an important clue, in 1566 Marzio reported that on his deathbed Ercole Della Rovere had named Tristano as his murderer, and in discussing Giovanni Battista Colloredo's assassination on the Grand Canal, Marzio raised his father's age by ten years from the last time he had discussed it, apparently to make the assassination of an elderly man appear more dishonorable. Just as critical as the shameful episodes of the past, however, were new issues such as the ability to write correct Tuscan and to employ the proper jargon of a cavalier.

The three principal Savorgnan (Federigo of the duel, Tristano of the Grand Canal murders, and Nicolò the intended victim of the bombs) responded in a joint defense published in Ferrara at the end of April 1566. Besides offering his version of what had happened at the duel, Federigo noted that although Marzio had not personally offended him before the combat, all the Savorgnan considered Marzio an enemy because of his filthy scheme of sending bombs to Urbano and Nicolò. Tristano, who had previously rejected a duel with a substitute because honor was a purely individual trait, now switched tactics and characterized his past actions as a response to the collective shame of the Colloredo. "When I murdered your father on the Grand Canal," he taunted Marzio, "it was because of your threats to murder me. As the blood that gave him life flowed from his veins, your father forgot the inscription on my sword, MIHI VINDICTAM. Now you do not want a test of arms because you do not adhere to the 'rules of knighthood.' "[10]

In Tristano's view, Marzio faced two choices: if he thought the murders of his father, uncle, and others had been sufficiently avenged, he should make peace, but if not, he should fulfill his debt, just as Tristano had done for his side. The most extensive defense of the three came from Nicolò, who carefully went over all of Marzio's published allegations point by point. Showing how Marzio had misquoted the history of Bembo and the chronicle of Candido, Nicolò set out his own historical argument that countered Marzio's alleged errors by relying heavily on the citation of original documents and eyewitness accounts. Several of Marzio's sources for the events of 1511, Nicolò wrote, were madmen who died in the hospital, one was six years old at the time, and another lived outside of Udine during the troubles. In assigning responsibility for the 1511 confrontation, Nicolò reprinted the old letter from Alvise Della Torre to the lords of Spilimbergo which Antonio Savorgnan had used to blame the Strumieri for the breakdown of the peace pact on the morning of Giovedì Grasso. On the basis of that letter, Nicolò refused to accept Savorgnan culpability for any of the notorious deeds of the day. The fact that dogs ate Federico Colloredo's corpse during the carnival riots, Nicolò reasoned, could hardly be blamed on the Savorgnan, who had killed him for legitimate reasons, but must be accepted as the fault of his Colloredo relatives who failed to bury him for three days.

In listing the retaliatory assaults and deaths since 1511, Nicolò agreed with Marzio in most cases about who killed whom—only the murder of Ercole Della Rovere produced a major controversy—but in every case Nicolò had a different view of the circumstances and motive behind the incident. Appended to the three Savorgnan defenses were copies of official documents, usually Venetian ones, which put the Colloredo in a bad light. Those condemning Savorgnan outlaws, of course, were left out.

Marzio took nearly two years to reply to the three Savorgnan. Part of the delay, he asserted, came from the fact that when he went to Malta he had entrusted his files of legal documents proving his accusations against the Savorgnan with someone who betrayed him by turning the files over to his enemies; but also it must not have been an easy matter for Marzio to contradict the apparent historical erudition of the Savorgnan defense. Although he had not been loath to make up evidence in the past, an effective rejoinder would have required research that an exile could pursue only with difficulty.

In his *Response*, Colloredo retraced in tiresome detail much of the same ground he had covered before, adding his own interpretation of the past events, but when confronted with facts inconvenient to his case, he changed his method of argument and recalled the long-standing social distinction of his clan. In answering the allegation that in 1511 the Colloredo had merely been followers of the Della Torre, an assertion that was certainly in part true, Marzio reached back four hundred years into the period of the patriarchs to point out that the Colloredo had been prominent in Friuli for longer than the Della Torre and had always been a mainstay of the castellan faction whereas the Savorgnan had relied on the support of mere commoners. Although irrelevant to the immediate issues, this new argument provided the Colloredo with a more noble lineage than the Savorgnan could claim. Faced with Tristano's taunts about how the Savorgnan had been more valiant than the Colloredo in paying debts of revenge, Marzio composed paeans to all the murders his family had committed during the previous sixty years and reckoned up the deaths. With the precision of a banker he demonstrated how each Colloredo victim had been fully repaid by a specific Savorgnan death. Of course, he had not achieved all this mayhem alone, conceding that his own contribution had been slight, and he could not resist boasting that because his relatives had accomplished so much he felt obliged to drop from his calculations the deeds of those outside his particular branch of the family.

While Marzio was still composing his elaborate response, Troiano Arcano, an in-law of the Colloredo, challenged Federigo Savorgnan to duel. Federigo accepted. After unusually tedious negotiations over the choice of weapons and the field of combat, they met in a secluded spot between Mantua and Cremona on April 14, 1568, for what really became the final duel. The result made all the petty details of the combat irrelevant. Both duelists died. Experts called the decision a draw, and in a Latin epigram Francesco Amulio celebrated the equality of their deaths.

The parity in deaths now made peace likely. The intervention of Venice made it inevitable. A truce signed in 1567 between Sultan

Selim II and Emperor Maximilian II freed the two great empires to attack the republic. As a defensive measure, Venice sought to secure the Friulan border by eliminating the potential for trouble from the feuding families. The Council of Ten authorized the future doge Alvise Mocenigo to negotiate a peace among the Friulans. Mocenigo did not negotiate exactly; he imposed peace by forbidding them to speak ever again about the dispute.

Throughout August 1568 all of the Colloredo, Della Torre, Caporiacco, Strassoldo, Arcano, Dal Torso, Arigoni, and Savorgnan, including even those in exile, signed notarized proxies that authorized the heads of their respective families to act in their name. These heads pledged themselves and all their relatives to the peace, agreeing that if any member of their family broke it, the property of all would be confiscated. Mocenigo, thus, relied on the ancient principle of collective familial responsibility to maintain respect for the agreement. In his final declaration, Mocenigo spoke on the matter of the pamphlet war. He had read the many hate-filled writings that had been exchanged between the two sides and in particular reviewed the Savorgnan response to Marzio Colloredo's last essay, finding the Savorgnan argument quite credible, "but for the greater confirmation and establishment of this holy peace, we wish and we declare that these writings shall not be published any more." He explained why.

> Because, one can truly say that when the writing of such material began, it quickened the passions and the spread of hatreds more than anything else. However, all these noble families, the names of which are too numerous to repeat, must now follow peace and reconciliation. We attest and declare by the authority conceded to us that both sides must desire that everything said or written be nullified, as if nothing had ever been written on this subject. And as a sign of a good and true peace, everyone, one by one, shall embrace the others in a friendly fashion, obliterating all the hatreds and passions of the past, promising in the future with truthfulness of heart in word and deed to use all those gestures of love and benevolence that are usually used among true and faithful friends.[11]

Mocenigo's perspective on the vendetta was too limited for him to assess correctly the provocative effects of print, which had in fact provoked more additional print than violence. The two duels during the five-year period of the pamphlet war revealingly contrast with the numerous atrocities of the previous two decades.

After hearing Mass, the family heads and many others embraced one another and kissed on the mouth. Although neither did sinners become saints nor did hatred change to love through such a ceremony, thus ended the vendetta. It did not really matter whether those who embraced the murderers of their fathers and brothers were sincere in their professions of friendship, but it did matter that they publicly staked their honor and their fortunes on accepting the peace. The whole ceremony was founded on yet another socially useful fiction that ignored inner motivations but demanded conformity in speech and act. This peace worked because for Friulan aristocrats a local reputation for ferocity was by then becoming less essential than their standing as honorable gentlemen in the larger world wherein it was most important to have appearances respected. For many years to come, violence certainly continued to be a way of life in Friuli. But when mad blood stirred, men no longer fed on their enemies like wolves but showed that revenge is a dish best eaten cold.

Conclusion

The vendetta that pitted the Savorgnan against other castellan families, most notably the Della Torre and the Colloredo, began amid the civil wars of the late fourteenth and early fifteenth centuries when the expanding commercial and military power of the Venetian republic defeated the enervated feudal regime of the patriarchs. From the beginning, local rivalries and debts of blood among the Friulan castellans connected to the interests of competing foreign powers and those of other classes in Friulan society. These connections became crucial during periods of crisis provoked by war, especially the Turkish raids of the late fifteenth century and the imperial invasions of the early sixteenth. After the War of the League of Cambrai ended in 1517 the vendetta families in Friuli began to lose their ability to attract others to their private quarrels, the factions faded, and the implications of local controversies for foreign affairs became less vital. Even after the revival of blood vendetta in 1545 the factions were never effectively reconstituted, and the Venetians saw the violence more a criminal matter than a breach of state security. Only when the rapprochement between the emperor and the sultan again made an invasion possible did Venice see the need to bring the contending clans into a lasting

pact of peace, ending for the Savorgnan and Della Torre a vendetta
that had lasted more than ten generations.

Before these sixteenth-century changes, deep structural discon-
tinuities had long branded Friulan history with anarchic vendettas
that survived in the interstices between official institutions of justice. The incompatibility of Venetian and Friulan judicial systems;
the feebleness of parliament and the Venetian luogotenente; the
contradictory operations of government on the village level; the
corruption of decisions made by castellan judges; the incommen-
surability of language and standards of justice at different cultural
levels; and the seeming impossibility of understanding, of consen-
sus, of impartiality, of lawfulness all thrust Friulans into a fear-
provoking labyrinth. Among these windings and turnings Friulans
at all social levels sought security, the most reliable sources of
which were family and clan, community and faction. Family and
clan formed the core of all social groupings that had any consistency or cohesion. Before 1511 the most important of these were
the factions whose character may be best illustrated by the fact that
the two were socially asymmetric; that is the Zambarlano faction
headed by the Savorgnan consisted of a vertical formation that cut
across class lines linking thousands of peasants and artisans to a
castellan clan and in turn to the dominant city of Venice whereas
the Strumiero faction led by the Della Torre created a horizontal
grouping of castellans united in opposition to the Savorgnan, the
peasants, and Venice. One faction incorporated individuals from
various classes and disparate communities, the other represented
most of the members of a single class.

The characteristic tribal feuds of the Mediterranean and Middle
East tend to establish some form of stratification among contenders
who are at least nominal social equals. By revealing differences in
power, these feuds form the basis of local and sometimes regional
politics. In Friuli the struggle of the Savorgnan to rise above other
castellans certainly disrupted the class's social equilibrium, if an
equilibrium ever existed, and the Savorgnan's transitory success
made possible the creation of factional coalitions. Particularly during the time of Antonio Savorgnan when whole villages of peasants
and the artisans of Udine and Spilimbergo joined the Zambarlani
against the aristocratic Strumieri, vendetta represented far more
than feuding among formal social equals. Through it communities

of commoners sought to redress a variety of economic grievances. Only partially masters of their followers and of events, the aristocratic leaders never achieved the "deliberate social engineering" imagined by many modern scholars of feuding. In 1511 artisans and peasants within the Zambarlano faction acted semiautonomously, transforming an aristocratic feud into a vendetta-revolt, following the logic of violence more than the leadership of men. In Friuli vendetta fed on other conflicts, especially those of the countryside against the city, community against community, class against class, and the disaffected against the state. The vendetta provided a model for resolving many social discontents, but it was never the only model, and by the middle of the sixteenth century alternatives had begun to supplant it.

As was the case with many other peripheral regions of Europe in which feuding was common, places such as highland Scotland, Iceland, or Corsica, Friuli found itself enmeshed in the politics of a distant regime which expressed its nominal dominion by trying to alter balances between the contending sides in local and private disputes, actions that favored one group over another, eliminated potential combatants, and established political rewards and punishments. Feuds in these areas were never self-regulating but were instead the point at which local and state politics met and the means for providing justice, which the dominant regime had failed to supply. Vendetta murders were, thus, akin to and a substitute for judicial punishments, murders that conveyed a judgment that the shamed victim was also the guilty party.

If one set up a spectrum of European feuding types, at one end might be medieval England, where royal justice stamped out blood feuds earlier than in any other kingdom, and at the other modern Albania, where governments have hardly touched the endemic tribal feuds in the mountains. Although a feudal and not a tribal society, Friuli in the Renaissance came closer to the Albanian than the English end of the spectrum. After the Venetian conquest in 1420 it fell under the influence of a regime that had succeeded in abolishing the scourge of vendetta among its own patriciate earlier than any other Italian city. In the absence of an efficient policing system, as in England, or the willingness to incorporate provincial nobles into the ruling hierarchy, as in Grand Ducal Tuscany, Venetian magistrates could not hope to inculcate in the Friulans their own habits of restraining violent urges. Although the factions of Zambarlani and Strumieri had become memories by the 1520s and the vendetta between the Savorgnan and their enemies died out after 1568, neither can Venetian policies be given credit for the changes nor did they have any particular success in reducing overall criminal violence in the region after the old vendetta ended. In fact, generally high levels of violence continued and probably increased during the late sixteenth century.

How then did the Cruel Carnival violence of 1511 create the conditions for structural changes, specifically for the demise of the factions and the end of vendetta? The several invasions by Turks and Austrians and the agrarian crisis of the first decade of the sixteenth century pushed Friuli to the brink of a civil war that severely threatened Venice's wobbling dominion already debilitated by other foreign onslaughts. Motivated by serious deprivations and raw fear, the struggling villagers and the poor of Udine accepted the protection offered by Antonio Savorgnan's Zambarlani. At the same time the Venetians placed all their hopes for retaining Friuli in Antonio, whom they sustained with loans, favors, and arms.

The career of Antonio Savorgnan, more than anything else, demonstrates how individual leadership could matter, even in as remote and backward a place as Friuli, bound up as it was by conservative social traditions and an immobile economy. Leadership mattered, not so much because Antonio could control events—he could not—but because the whole social system hinged on him and people like him, the great patrons. Antonio offered villagers and tenants the opportunity to choose a new loyalty, the substance of which was not blood ties or feudal obligation but a patronage system that rested on the double foundations of paternalism and the militia. His paternalism took the form of loans, the repayment of which, it seemed, could be delayed indefinitely. The militia offered men better weapons than would otherwise be available, the solidarity of mutual defense, and a kind of liminal release from the obligations of daily work. Antonio Savorgnan's Zambarlani made social homicide possible by transforming class conflict into vendetta conflict. His service in connecting the Zambarlano villagers to the patriciate of Venice further illustrates how critical were the patrons who served as the intermediaries between intersecting patronage systems, a role the village *decani* performed at a lower social level and on the local stage. Nevertheless, while compensating for the weakness of formal institutions, the highly personal nature of the system created significant hazards.

The Cruel Carnival brought the whole system to the point of fissure because it was so violent and because of the forms that the violence took. Serving as crystals for a murderous crowd, the Savorgnan henchmen co-opted popular grievances for the service of the clan's vendetta, and the fortuitous occasion of the carnival celebration, which allegorized a struggle between the forces of the Fat and Lean, reinforced the vendetta preoccupation with the dismemberment and desecration of the victims' bodies. The horrors of the day remained in the minds of survivors as a poisonous residue that afflicted their judgments for decades, forming a morbid memory against which all future events were measured.

The Cruel Carnival drastically upset the rough balance between the Zambarlani and the Strumieri and made Antonio Savorgnan the unchallenged arbiter of Friulan affairs, a success that made his future missteps all the more a calamity. Antonio acted with the expertise of a brilliant tactician who had honed his skills in many little battles for regional supremacy but seemed to lack the strategic vision his position demanded. When in September of 1511 he thought Fortune had begun to smile on the Austrians and he switched sides, his mistake sealed his own doom, eviscerated his faction, and finally revealed to the Venetians the folly of their reliance on a local lord as the guarantee of their dominion. Antonio's treason inverted the traditional alliances of the Friulan factions, obliging the Venetians to rely on the formerly hostile Strumieri to hunt him down, thus breaking up the established Venetian system of interlocking patronage networks.

Antonio's successor Girolamo Savorgnan, much to his displeasure, never enjoyed the same privileges Antonio had coerced from the Venetians who after 1513 tried to inhibit opportunities for Savorgnan patronage by reforming the communal government of Udine and by allowing the establishment of a peasant parliament, the *contadinanza*. At the same time, the Venetian reforms made marginal the dangerous classes by eliminating the *arengo* of Udine, once the voice of the urban artisans, and by limiting the powers of the peasant assembly. When the vendetta revived in midcentury, none of the major participants could call upon the vast retinue of clients which had empowered Antonio and made the old factions the centerpiece of Friulan life and politics.

Because Antonio's assassination is so amply documented, it serves as the most revealing example of the traditional mores of vendetta killing, which borrowed heavily from the hierarchic values of the hunt. Nourished in innumerable expeditions when lords and their retainers rode out together into the forests in search of game and sport, the hunting ethic with its emphasis on comradeship, cooperation, the acceptance of authority, and the proper forms for killing was easily transferred to the hunting of men. In particular, avengers relied on two practices derived from hunting: the butchering of the victim according to a hierarchy of body parts and the incorporation of dogs into the act of killing. By inverting the normal hierarchic evaluation of body parts, as when Antonio's assassins fed his head to dogs, avengers employed a vocabulary of shame to represent the degradation they hoped to inflict on their enemy.

Dogs became the object of multiple projections through which men imitated the *lyssa* or rabid madness of the dog, thereby transforming themselves into wildmen who lived outside the rules of civilization. Enthralled by the stirrings of mad blood, such men asserted that they were not responsible for their own actions. The hunting ethic provided a psychologically safe and culturally authorized way to express maddening anger, and the connections between hunting and revenge killing help explain the macabre emphasis on the forms of assault and the dismemberment of victims. Thus, the goriest murder became the most socially acceptable murder.

Although functionalist anthropology and structuralism have now allowed us to see how feuding is, in part, a rational and systematic means of resolving conflicts and of maintaining balances in traditional societies, there was in the Renaissance a deep ambivalence about the practice, best expressed in the need to represent revenge murders as somehow the act of madmen. The problem of revenge in the Renaissance was understood less in social than in psychological and cultural terms as a problem created by violent human emotions. The traditional mores of vendetta fighting acknowledged the reality and legitimacy of anger, managing it through carnival and hunting motifs that focused on human and animal bodies. The eclipse of a culture that had accepted the naturalness of the human body, its processes, and its emotions was the necessary prerequisite for delegitimizing revenge, a change that eliminated some of the ambivalence about vendetta but created new problems, the modern problems that come from the repression of emotions.

To think about and represent abstract ideas such as justice and villainy or honor and shame, traditional Friulans had employed analogies, especially analogies with animals, and sometimes acted out the analogies in violent deeds, as if anger had pushed killers across the barrier between the human and the beast. By ceasing to think with animal metaphors, Friulan nobles gave up one major tie that had bound them to the common culture shared by all the classes, urban and rural, literate and ignorant, aristocratic and peasant. For aristocrats the courtly ideology of their class supplanted the once widely accepted mentality of revenge which survived only in a few isolated pockets impervious to outside influences.

As Gabriel Maugain noted long ago, revenge violence began to fade away in much of northern Italy during the last half of the sixteenth century. For him Counter-Reformation piety and the reinvigoration of official justice made the change possible, a view that is undoubtedly correct in some cases but incomplete, especially in explaining the situation in Friuli and other Venetian territories.

In studying the Friulan avengers as individuals, I have found only one member of a vendetta family who had a religious conversion experience and little indication that the administration of justice improved in any marked way. The end of revenge among Friulan aristocrats came with the adoption of refined manners learned during sojourns, often as exiles, in the courts of northern Italy and from reading fashionable books about courtly manners such as Castiglione's *The Book of the Courtier* and Della Casa's *Galateo*, books that also tutored these provincials in the standardized Tuscan that was bringing linguistic unity to the ruling classes of Italy.

In the 1560s as Friulan combatants began to accept duels with their enemies, they abandoned the old vendetta values for a new definition of honor, one that supplemented the collective, hereditary honor of aristocratic birth with individual conformity to an explicit code of behavior. Personal comportment began to change from what might be called the traditional style of defensive duplicity to attempts at conveying trust, a style that betrayed an obsessive concern with the lie. After all, duelists could not fight for motives of revenge but only over allegations of a lie.

The influence of books on courtly manners represents only a part of the effect of the spread of print in a vendetta society. The transformation of revenge narratives from oral legends to published dueling manifestos cooled the enthusiasm for blood as much as anything else. Printed words stirred passions less than spoken words simply because they were communicated at a distance, and print was most often answered with print. In the published versions of the revenge narratives, Friulans went public on a stage very different from the intimate *fogolar* of a castle or the scruffy streets in which they took revenge, a stage on which documentary evidence, the rhetoric of persuasion, and good Tuscan determined the victor in the game of honor. Even after some Friulans began to duel, the accounts of what supposedly happened carried the day better than any deed on the field of honor, especially if the deed was challenged in print. As in theology and science where movable type liberated thought by fixing texts, print drove at least a few Friulan aristocrats out of their provincial isolation into a wider world of relationships in which the private control of anger proved more rewarding than the public display of it.

In accepting a new standard of behavior, Friulan aristocrats formed or reformed their identities through a process that was based less on the imitation of elders in the family and the display of the symbols of clan and faction than on the conscious cultivation of acquired behaviors: the courtesies of speech and comportment, the refinements of dress and manners, a disdain for coarse and rustic ways, the hiding of bodily functions, and the sublimation of dangerous emotions. In the older process youths assimilated themselves to the group through provoking hereditary enemies. In such a culture, aggression helped form and confirm identities for males. The new process shifted the emphasis from aggressive action to the measured response to a provocation, the ability to extricate oneself from a dangerous situation with a cool head and one's honor unblemished. The change was more one of emphasis than of kind, but it foretold a new world that placed great value on

deflecting or channeling interpersonal violence with a view to sta-
bilizing the ruling class. Those who made the transition successfully found themselves in possession of far greater authority than
their forefathers could have ever imagined for they helped create
the modern states with all their enormous coercive powers. Thus,
in the microcosm of Friuli one can trace how the acceptance of an
ideology of civility stimulated an important transformation in human behavior, one that first took place among the patricians in the
successful Italian city-republics centuries earlier and which has yet
to take hold in parts of the globe still plagued with internecine
violence.

What have been missing from this masculine picture, and con-
spicuously missing, are women. The sources reveal their presence
in the conflicts through only a few illusive clues: the mother of
Apollonio Gorghi pleading to save her son's life in the streets of
Udine, the abandoned ladies of the castle at Zoppola assaulted by
peasant rapists, the village women masquerading in looted dresses
as they left Udine, the mutilated corpse of a servant woman found
in a polluted well weeks after the great massacre, the depositions
of female eyewitnesses to the Cruel Carnival. The women were
there, but the exclusively male chroniclers treat them as a mere
backdrop to the grand struggle among men. They were certainly
there in encouraging their men to remember their obligations, in
teaching sons to avenge dead fathers, in shaming husbands into
countering insults. They were certainly there as the sources of rivalry among men, as the audience for what men thought were
brave deeds, as the bonds between rival clans brought together
through marriages. Women managed the estates while the men
fought; they supplied the militias, nursed the wounded, told the
stories around the *fogolar* on winter nights, and adopted the femi-
nine versions of the new manners. By inference from later periods
when criminal records are more complete, one can assume that
Friulan women had a share in the fighting as did Corsican women
in the nineteenth century.

It is revealing that we know so little about women in the Friulan
vendettas. In the eyes of men, vendettas could only be a matter
among men, a belief that created in their relationships with women
an island of repose in which women lived safe from the world of
masculine violence. The exemption of women from violent attack

was in large part a myth, but the myth was necessary for a culture that sustained itself in the anthropophagy of revenge.

The last and perhaps deepest irony of the story told here has been that the wars of the early sixteenth century, which finally destroyed the power of the patriciates in most Italian cities to act independently of a foreign sovereign, also finally helped to bring to the countryside the manners of self-restraint characteristic of the cities. The wars made the pursuit of a career as a soldier and courtier the most likely alternative for many displaced and ambitious men, and in making their careers the courtiers had to conform to the mores of a highly self-conscious and reflexive group. Despite a century and a half of rule, the patricians of Venice had found it impossible to educate, persuade, or force the aristocrats of Friuli to change their violent ways and to act more like the good citizens and businessmen of the maritime republic; but the princely courts of Ferrara, Mantua, and Milan worked the desired miracle in a matter of a few years. The civic values proved to be untransferable to the countryside because they were too closely tied to the experience of citizenship in specific cities, to being a Florentine or a Venetian. A gentleman courtier, on the other hand, did not need to be a Ferrarese, a Mantuan, or a Milanese; he merely had to speak and behave properly, to be an individual of a certain stamp. Although historians of the Renaissance in Italy have long devoted themselves to uncovering how the experience of citizenship related to the development of civility, the civic Renaissance had its limits, especially in ripening a culture that could also nourish the countryside. The final burden of this book has been to uncover the nature of those limits.

Notes

Prologue

1. Unless otherwise indicated the quotes in this Prologue come from Gregorio Amaseo, *Historia della crudel zobia grassa et altri nefarii excessi et horrende calamità intervenute in la città di Udine et Patria del Friuli del 1511*, pp. 509–23 in Leonardo and Gregorio Amaseo and Giovanni Antonio Azio, *Diarii udinesi dall' 1508 al 1541*, ed. Antonio Ceruti (Venice, 1884).

2. Agostino di Colloredo, "Croniche friulane, 1508–18," *Pagine Friulane 2* (1889): 5.

3. Ibid., 6.

Chapter 1: The Friulan Enigma

1. Quote from *The Castle of Fratta*, trans. Lovett F. Edwards (London, 1957), 12.

2. "Dell'imperio venetiano in Italia," Biblioteca Nazionale Marciana, Venice (hereafter, BMV), It. VII, 225 (8512), fol. 8v.

3. Marino Sanuto, *Descrizione della Patria del Friuli (1502–3)*, ed. Leonardo Manin (Venice, 1853), 16.

4. Luigi da Porto, *Lettere storiche dall'anno 1509 al 1528*, ed. Bartolomeo Bressan (Florence, 1857), 178–82.

5. *Relazioni dei rettori veneti in terraferma*, vol. 1 of *La Patria del Friuli (Luogotenenza di Udine)* (Milan, 1973), for Mocenigo, 90; for Morosini, 122; for Erizzo, xliii.

6. Niccolò Machiavelli, *Discourses on the First Decade of Titus Livius*, (book 1, chap. 23) in *Machiavelli: The Chief Works and Others*, trans. Allan Gilbert (Durham, N.C., 1965), 1: 250.

7. Savorgnan's letter is in Marino Sanuto, *I diarii*, ed. Rinaldo Fulin et al., 58 vols. (Venice, 1879–1903), 10: 352–53.

8. Quotation from Girolamo di Porcìa is in his *Descrizione del Fruili con l'utile che cava il serenissimo principe e con le spese che fa* (Udine, 1897), 12.

9. Capretto is quoted in Giuseppe Francescato and Fulvio Salimbeni, *Storia, lingua e società in Friuli* (Udine, 1976), 150.

10. Quotation from Francesco Sanudo cited in Cozzi, *Repubblica di Venezia e stati italiani: Politica e giustizia dal secolo XVI al secolo XVIII* (Turin, 1982), 112 n.

11. Gaetano Cozzi, "La politica del diritto nella Repubblica di Venezia," in idem, ed., *Stato, società e giustizia nella Repubblica Veneta (sec. XV–XVIII)* (Rome, 1980), 1: 95–96.

12. Tommaso Garzoni, *La piazza universale di tutte le professioni* (Venice, 1585), 929–30, cited in Povolo, "Aspetti e problemi dell'amministrazione della giustizia penale nella Repubblica di Venezia, secoli XVI–XVII," in *Stato, società e giustizia nella Repubblica Veneta (sec. XV–XVIII)*, ed. Gaetano Cozzi (Rome, 1980), I:207 n.

13. M. E. Mallett and J. R. Hale, *The Military Organization of a Renaissance State: Venice c. 1400 to 1617* (Cambridge, 1984), 343.

14. Nicolò Monticoli, *Descrittione del sacco MDXI seguito in Udine il giovedì XXVII febbraio*, ed. Gian Giuseppe Liruti (Udine, 1857), 11.

Chapter 2: Approaching Thunder

1. Luigi da Porto, *Lettere storiche dall'anno 1509 al 1528*, ed. Bartolomeo Bressan (Florence, 1857), 276–77.

2. Quoted in Giovanni Forgiarini, "Quattro lettere storiche di Antonio Savorgnan (1457–1512)," *Memorie storico forogiuliesi* 9 (1913): 302.

3. Leonardo and Gregorio Amaseo and Giovanni Antonio Azio, *Diarii udinesi dall'1508 al 1541*, ed. Antonio Ceruti (Venice, 1884), 497.

4. Ibid., 503–4.

5. Cited by Liliana Cargnelutti, "Antonio Savorgnan e l'insurrezione del 1511" in *I Savorgnan e la Patria del Friuli dal XIII al XVIII secolo* (Udine, 1984), 125 n.

6. Marino Sanuto, *I diarii*, ed. Rinaldo Fulin et al., 58 vols. (Venice, 1879–1903), 11: 613–14.

7. Amaseo, *Diarii*, 101.

8. Sanuto, *I diarii*, 8: 446–47.

9. Amaseo, *Diarii*, 101.

10. Ibid., 499.

11. For the council's orders, Archivio di Stato, Venice (hereafter ASV), Consiglio dei Dieci, Misto, reg. 32 (1508–9), fols. 175 (13 July), 179r (27 July).

12. For the quote about Albertino Colloredo, Amaseo, *Diarii*, 500.

13. For quote from the 1513 rent-roll, Archivio di Stato, Udine (hereafter ASU), Archivio Colloredo-Mels, parte 2, busta 3bis, fol. 136v; for the 1530 docu-

ment, Biblioteca Communale "V. Joppi," Udine (hereafter BCU), MS Joppi 592, doc. dated 10 October 1530.

14. ASV, Luogotenenti, Patria del Friuli, filza 132, fol. 239.

15. Quote from Gregorio Amaseo cited in Fabia Savini, "Antonio Savorgnan," *Memorie storico forogiuliesi* 27–29 (1931–33): 275.

Chapter 3: The Tempest of 1511

1. For quotes, Leonardo and Gregorio Amaseo and Giovanni Antonio Azio, *Diarii udinesi dall'1508 al 1541*, ed. Antonio Ceruti (Venice, 1884), 144, 502.

2. ASV, Senato, Terra, reg. 17, fols. 55 and 66v dated 10, 12 October and 11, 12 December 1510.

3. Amaseo, *Diarii*, 504.

4. For Amaseo quote, ibid., 224.

5. For quote, ASV, Lettere di condottieri (Savorgnan), busta 308, published in Giovanni Forgiarini, ed., "Quattro lettere storiche di Antonio Savorgnano (1457–1512)," *Memorie storico forogiuliesi* 9 (1913): 307.

6. ASV, Luogotenenti, Patria del Friuli, busta 133, under title "Extraordinarior. liber primus."

7. For quote from Savorgnan, Fabia Savini, "Antonio Savorgnan," *Memorie storico forogiuliesi* 27–29 (1931–33): 301–2.

8. Ibid., 276.

9. Copies of the letter with insignificant variations can be found in many sources. The text of the possible holograph is published in ibid., 296–97.

10. Ibid., 303.

11. Elias Canetti, *Crowds and Power*, trans. Carol Stewart (New York, 1981), 73–75.

12. Amaseo, *Diarii*, 514.

13. Ibid.

14. For quote, ibid., 515.

15. ASU, Archivio Colloredo-Mels, parte 2, busta 3bis, rotulo dated 1513, fol. 62v.

16. Nicolò Monticoli, *Descrittione del sacco MDXI seguito in Udine il giovedì XXVII febbraio*, ed. Gian Giuseppe Liruti (Udine, 1857), 18–19.

17. ASU, Archivio di Varmo, busta 25, "Artificati relativi alli vantaggi recati alle pubbliche armi contro i tedeschi (anno 1510 e sequenti) dalli consorti di Varmo" and Amaseo, *Diarii*, 499–500.

18. For quote from Bondimier, ASV, Capi del Consiglio dei Dieci, Lettere rettori, Pordenone, busta 189, fols. 335r–36r, dated 3 and 4 March 1511.

19. Amaseo, *Diarii*, 524–25.

20. For first quote, Zaccaria Canecini to the Marquis of Mantua, Archivio di Stato, Mantua (hereafter, ASMn), Archivio Gonzaga, busta 1445, fol. 34, dated 12 April 1511. For second quote, Monticoli, *Descrittione del sacco*, 17.

21. Monticoli, *Descrittione del sacco*, 19–20.

Chapter 4: The Problem of Meaning

1. Statements about a revolution include, "la plebe che sempre desiderano cose novitatis," letter from Andrea Loredan in ASV, Capi del Consiglio dei Dieci, Lettere rettori, Portogruaro, busta 190, fol. 11; "nele revolution de quella Patria," letter from Piero Boldù, ASV, Luogotenenti, Patria del Friuli, busta 134, under title, "Litterarum liber primus"; "revolution di cieli," ASV, Senato, Terra, reg. 18, fol. 166v and "per la Revolution di tempi," reg. 19, fol. 18r.

2. Samuel Leslie Sumberg, *The Nuremberg Schembart Carnival* (New York, 1941), 31.

3. Luigi da Porto, *Lettere storiche dall'anno 1509 al 1528*, ed. Bartolomeo Bressan (Florence, 1857), 279.

4. For quote, Leonardo and Gregorio Amaseo and Giovanni Antonio Azio, *Diarii udinesi dall'1508 al 1541*, ed. Antonio Ceruti (Venice, 1884), 514, 516–20.

5. For quote about Federico Colloredo, ibid., 517. For ordinance of 1490, Antonio Battistella, "Udine nel secolo XVI: L'ordinamento interno della città," *Memorie storico forogiuliese* 18 (1922): 184.

6. For quote about Antonio's anger, Amaseo, *Diarii*, 512.

7. For quote, ibid., 529.

8. For quotes, ibid., 513, 522, 527, and from Porcìa cited in Vincenzo Marchesi, "Friuli al tempo della Lega di Cambrai," *Nuovo Archivio Veneto*, n.s., 6 (1903): 520 n.

9. For quote, Giovanni Battista Cergneu, *Cronaca delle guerre friulane coi germani dal 1507 al 1524*, ed. V. Joppi and V. Marchesi (Udine, 1895), 51.

10. For quote, Amaseo, *Diarii*, 533.

11. For quotes, ibid., 526 and 511, respectively.

12. For quote from Gregorio Amaseo, ibid., 235.

13. For quote from Gregorio Amaseo, ibid., 269.

14. Giovan Candido, *Commentarii de i fatti d'Aquileja* (Venice, 1544), 96v.

Chapter 5: Retaliation

1. For the "for revenge" quote, Agostino di Colloredo, "Chroniche friulane, 1508–1518," *Pagine friulane* 2 (1889): 6.

2. Ibid.

3. Roberto de' Signori di Spilimbergo, *Cronaca de' suoi tempi dal 1499 al 1540*, ed. V. Joppi (Udine, 1884), 23–24.

4. Giovanni Battista di Cergneu, *Cronaca delle guerre friulane coi germani dal 1507 al 1524*, ed. V. Joppi and V. Marchesi (Udine, 1895), 59–60.

5. Emmanuel Le Roy Ladurie, *Carnival in Romans*, trans. Mary Feeney (New York, 1979), 318.

6. For quote, Carlo Ginzburg, *The Cheese and the Worms: The Cosmos of a Sixteenth-Century Miller*, trans. John and Anne C. Tedeschi (Baltimore, 1980), 62.

7. For quotes, Amaseo, *Diarii*, 513 ("famegli et cani de casa"), 508 ("donde li erano eretti come cani ala cazza"), 517 (Giovanni di Leonardo Marangone di Capriglie described as a rabid dog), 524 ("furia di rabiati cani"). For "cani et com-

pagni," ASMn, Archivio Gonzaga, busta 1445, fol. 34, dated 12 April 1511. For Shakespeare quote, *Romeo and Juliet*, 5.1.10–12. For letter closing "vostro cane e schiavo" from Filippo da Pietrasanta to Duke Galeazzo Maria Sforza, dated 20 July 1473, Archivio di Stato, Milan, Archivio Sforzesco, Carteggio interno, cartella 914. I wish to thank Gregory Lubkin for providing me with this last reference. For quote about the Zambarlani, Nicolò Monticoli, *Descrittione del sacco MDXI seguito in Udine il giovedì XXVII febbraio*, ed. Gian Giuseppe Liruti (Udine, 1857), 18.

8. Giovan Candido, *Commentarii de i fatti d'Aquileja* (Venice, 1544), 96.

9. For quote, Ruzante, *La Moscheta*, act 4, scene 3, in Ruzante [Angelo Beolco], *Teatro*, ed., trans. into Italian, and annotated by Ludovico Zorzi (Turin, 1967), 651. I wish to thank Linda Carroll for bringing this passage to my attention.

10. For quote about the laws of Kanùn, Margaret Hasluck, *The Unwritten Law in Albania*, ed. J. H. Hutton (Cambridge, 1954), 73–78.

11. Frederick Robertson Bryson, *The Sixteenth-Century Italian Duel: A Study in Renaissance Social History* (Chicago, 1938), 179 n.

12. Sacchetti quoted in Hannalore Zug Tucci, "La caccia, da bene comune a privilegio," in *Storia d'Italia: Annali*, vol. 6, *Economia naturale, economia monetaria*, ed. Ruggiero Romano and Ugo Tucci (Turin, 1983), 399, 401.

13. Amaseo, *Diarii*, 542.

14. For quote, Sanuto, *I diarii*, 3: 5, 272.

15. Homer, *Iliad*, trans. Richard Lattimore (Chicago, 1951), 22. 345–54.

16. For quote, Walter Burkert, *Homo Necans: The Anthropology of Ancient Greek Sacrificial Ritual and Myth*, trans. Peter Bing (Berkeley, 1983), 17.

17. For quote, Lestringant, "Le cannibale et ses paradoxes: Images du cannibalisme au temps des guerres de religion," *Mentalities* 1 (1983): 7.

Chapter 6: Toward the Duel

1. Quote from Giovanni Della Casa, *Galateo*, trans. with an introduction and notes by Konrad Eisenbichler and Kenneth R. Bartlett (Toronto, 1986), 9.

2. Erasmus is quoted in Norbert Elias, *The History of Manners*, vol. 1 of *The Civilizing Process*, trans. Edmund Jephcott (New York, 1978), 78–79.

3. Della Casa, *Galateo*, 10–11, 19–24.

4. Possevino is quoted and translated in Frederick Robertson Bryson, *The Point of Honor in Sixteenth-Century Italy: An Aspect of the Life of the Gentleman* (New York, 1935), 55.

5. For the Fausto da Longiano quote, Claudio Donati, *L'idea di nobiltà in Italia secoli XIV–XVIII* (Bari, 1988), 97. For "the fields of combat" quote, Girolamo Muzio, *Il duello del Mutio Justinopolitano* (Venice, 1550), 38v.

6. Emilio Candido, *Cronaca udinese dal 1554 al 1564*, ed. Vicenzo Joppi (Udine, 1886), 23–24.

7. The *cartelli* and *manifesti* between the two sides written between 10 May 1563 and 17 February 1568 have been collected together in "Contese cavalleresche tra i Savorgnan e i Coloredo avvenute negli anni 1563–'66–'68," BCU, MS Joppi

116. The quote comes from Marzio Colloredo, *Successo di quanto e passato fra li illu. signori Martio Colloreto, Nicolò, et Federigo Savorgnan* (Brescia, 1565), 66v.

8. Nicolò's initial response titled *Manifesto dell'Illustr. Nicolo Savorgnano a lettori* and dated 12 July 1563 in Ferrara can be found in BCU, MS Joppi 116, fols. 2r–8v and Biblioteca Universitaria, Bologna, MS 1938, opuscolo 1, unpaginated, quote is from the beginning.

9. BCU, MS Joppi 116, quote on fol. 30v.

10. Nicolò, Tristano, and Federigo Savorgnan, *Difesa degli Illustri Signori, Nicolò, Tristano & Federigo Savorgnani, dalle false imputationi date loro & all'honorata sua famiglia, dal Signor Martio Colloreto* (Ferrara, 1566), 3r–18r for Nicolò, 19r–31r for Tristano (27r for quote), 37r–59v for Federigo. Foliation numbers come from the copy in the Biblioteca Nazionale Marciana, Venice.

11. Based on the MS copy in Biblioteca del Seminario Arcivescovile, Udine, Archivio capitolare di Udine, Collezione Bini, Miscellanea, vol. 19. Ernesto Degani published the peace agreement in *I partiti in Friuli nel 1500 e la storia di un famoso duello* (Udine, 1900), 155–71.

A Note on Sources

For a complete discussion of sources, readers should consult the first edition, *Mad Blood Stirring: Vendetta and Factions in Friuli during the Renaissance* (Baltimore: Johns Hopkins University Press, 1993).

This book was based on research undertaken in several archives and libraries, the most important of which include:

Archivio Parrocchiale, Spilimbergo

Archivio di Stato, Mantua (ASMn)

Archivio di Stato, Udine (ASU), especially the collections: Archivio Colloredo-Mels; Archivio Savorgnan; and Archivio Della Torre

Archivio di Stato, Venice (ASV), especially the collections: Capi del Consiglio dei Dieci; Consiglio dei Dieci; Luogotenenti, Patria del Friuli

Biblioteca Civico, Padua

Biblioteca Communale "V. Joppi," Udine (BCU), including the Archivio Civico Utini

Biblioteca Nazionale Marciana, Venice

Biblioteca del Seminario Arcivescovile, Udine

Biblioteca del Museo Civico Correr, Venice

Österreichische Nationalbibliothek, Vienna

There are nine contemporary narrations of the events of the Cruel Carnival in 1511. The most useful is the version found in Leonardo and

Gregorio Amaseo and Giovanni Antonio Azio, *Diarii udinesi dall' 1508 al 1541*, ed. Antonio Ceruti (Venice, 1884), especially the short text by Gregorio Amaseo appended to the diaries, *Historia della crudel zobia grassa et altri nefarii excessi et horrende calamità intervenute in la città di Udine et Patria del Friuli del 1511*. Based primarily on the letters sent to Venetian councils, the entries in Marino Sanuto's *Diaries* comprise the best version of the episode from the Venetian point of view. Sanuto himself never wrote up a separate account, but he did turn his diaries over to Pietro Bembo to be used as a source for his official history of the war period. See Marino Sanuto, *I diarii*, ed. Rinaldo Fulin et al., 58 vols. (Venice, 1879–1903), especially vol. 12, cols. 5–6, 17–19, and passim. Bembo's protégé, Luigi da Porto, recalled various things he had witnessed in Udine in 1511 in his *Lettere storiche dall'anno 1509 al 1528*, ed. Bartolomeo Bressan (Florence, 1857) and carried the emotional burdens of his memories into his famous *novella*, *Giulietta e Romeo*.

Other contemporary accounts include Giovanni Battista di Cergneu, *Cronaca delle guerre friulane coi germani dal 1507 al 1524*, ed. V. Joppi and V. Marchesi, Croniche antiche friulane, no. 1 (Udine, 1895); Giovanni Partenopeo, *La guerra del Friuli contro i tedeschi (1508–1513)*, ed. Dionisio Tassini (Udine, 1916); Antonio Belloni, *De clade Turriana*, in Dionisio Tassini, "La rivolta del Friuli nel 1511 durante la sua guerra contro i tedeschi," *Nuovo archivio veneto*, n.s., 39 (1920): 151–54; Nicolò Monticoli, *Descrittione del sacco MDXI seguito in Udine il giovedì XXVII febbraio*, ed. Gian Giuseppe Liruti (Udine, 1857); and the accounts by Sebastiano Decio and Roberto da Latisana in the Biblioteca Communale, Udine, MS Joppi 66.

Index

Library of Congress Cataloging-in-Publication Data

Muir, Edward, 1946–
  Mad blood stirring : vendetta in Renaissance Italy / Edward Muir. — Reader's ed.
    p.   cm.
  Includes bibliographical references (p.   ) and index.
  ISBN 0-8018-5849-6 (pbk. : alk. paper)
    1. Udine (Italy)—History.   2. Massacres—Italy—Udine.   3. Friuli (Italy)—
History.   4. Vendetta—Italy—Friuli—History—16th century.   5. Savorgnan
family.   6. Delle Torre family.   I. Title.
DG975.U3M85   1998
945'.391—dc21   97-41775
                                                                                CIP